The

GREAT

CHILI

BOOK

D1301809

The
GREAT
CHILI
BOOK

Bill Bridges

Lyons & Burford, Publishers

Copyright © 1981 by Bill Bridges
ALL RIGHTS RESERVED. No part of this book may be reproduced in any
manner without the express written consent of the publisher, except in the
case of brief excerpts in critical reviews and articles. All inquiries should be
addressed to: Lyons & Burford, 31 West 21 Street, New York, NY 10010.

Printed in the United States of America

10 9 8 7 6 5 4 3 2 1

Library of Congress Cataloging-in-Publication Data

Bridges, Bill.
 [Great American chili book]
 The great chili book / Bill Bridges.
  p. cm.
 Originally published: The great American chili book. New York :
Rawson, Wade Publishers, © 1981.
 Includes bibliographical references and index.
 ISBN 1-55821-281-7
 1. Chili con carne. 2. Cookery, American. I. Title.
TX749.B73 1994
641.8′23—dc20   93-33993
                      CIP

Acknowledgments

With very few exceptions, those we told about our determination to write a history of chili were enthusiastic and eager to help. That they remained enthusiastic and helpful over the long haul makes this one of those cases where it is clearly necessary to say, with humble sincerity: Folks, we couldn't have done it without you.

In addition to those mentioned in the text, our thanks to:

Miss Catherine McDowell, Librarian, Daughters of the Republic of Texas Library at the Alamo; Friends of the Library, E. P. Foster Library, Ventura, California; San Antonio Main Public Library; Austin Public Library; Huntington Library; Houston Main Public Library; San Diego Public Library; Tony Hillerman and Linda Lewis, University of New Mexico; Elizabeth Shaw, University of Arizona Press; Elizabeth Tindall, Library of the Missouri Historical Society; Douglas Matthews, Deputy Librarian, The London Library; Reba Collins, Director, Will Rogers Memorial, Claremore, Oklahoma; John Davis, Institute of Texan Cultures, San Antonio; Maj. J. B. Bloxon and M/Sgt. Walter T. Wimberly, Army Culinary Skills Division, Fort Lee, Virginia; Leslie Jones, C–B Ranch, Fort McKavett, Texas; Frances Talbot Fish, Menard County (Texas) Museum; Alexander Fraser, Ann Tobin Rowland, and Blake Rowland; Ann Fowler Kennedy and Tom Nall of Caliente Chili Company; Edmond Bory, Fauchon of Paris; Sally Daigrepont of Shelby Texas Chili; Lenora Cohagan of Wolf Brand Chili; Lyle Van Doozer of Gebhardt's; Dave Swier of Nalley's; John Dyksterhuis and Noah Clemons of Ranch Style Foods; John L. Clark, *Springfield* (Illinois) *State Journal-Register;* Sheridan Crawford, *South Bay* magazine, Redondo Beach, California; Crispin Gill, *The Countryman;* Shiro Yoneyama of UPI's Tokyo Bureau; Bill Tobin, *Anchorage Times,* and his loyal readers, including Dolores Barrett and Dorothy Stouter.

Bill Glasgow, Art Seidenbaum, Sally Holm, Ernie Glaser, Liz Hunt, Joan Buie, Nancy Rees, Lucy and Don Anderson, Dorothy and Chet Oksner, Jakie and Frank McCulloch, Naomi Harrison, Jeanne Croft,

ACKNOWLEDGMENTS

Judy Wimberly, Cha-Ra-Om, Amalia Ruiz Clark, Ed Lusas, Molly Wheeler, Judith Morgan, Sue and Marshall Lumsden, Mary Ellen Hoffmann, Robert Phinney, the late Louise Moon Aldredge, Dana Burks, Patricia and Woodfin Butte, Mary and Jerry Bywaters, Polly and Jim Bransford, Mary Anna Millican Stout, Betty Jane Cooper, Ruth McMurray, Julie Florence, Elaine Bond, Lucille and Bill Cooper, Rachel Dierenfield, Helen Chapman Elmore, Marjorie Cavitt Dixon, Blee Ennis, Mary Arnwine, Jane Haynes, Dr. Elizabeth Hutchison, Arledge and Bill Hodges, Jim Howard, Louise Latham Picard, Vance Muse, Jean Meyer, Louise Samuels, Martha Ann and Clyde Box, Marie and Henry Fox, Myra Struble Edwards, Jane Scholl, George Aurelius, Sylvia Williams, Charley Worley, Si Casady, James E. Moss, Robert Laxalt, Thelma Cone, Lou and Elm Hargis, Rhoda Kruse, Mary Pecsok, Rosalie Reynolds, Col. Wm. W. Watson, Joseph Terrell, Polly Bransford, Frances Dolan Holloran, Hughes Rudd, Barbara McGrath, Bill Foody, Rose Dosti, Nick Chriss, Stanley Marsh 3.

Special thanks to M. F. K. Fisher, Stella Hughes, and Nelle Smith, who prodded the author to get on with it; and to William Weber Johnson, who was an innocent friend until this thing came up.

And, thanks to my mother, whose encouragement, at times when it counted, included the hardheaded kind you can take to the bank.

Special thanks from the Publishers for Marian Leifson's thoughtful editorial advice.

Contents

THE LORE

CHAPTER 1 **Chili Today:** An American Passion   3
Chili by Any Other Name—Is Not the Same . . .
Chiliheads United

CHAPTER 2 **Chili Roots:** Deep in the Heart of Texas   10
The Pemmican Premise . . . An Army Marches on Its
Chili . . . Son of S.O.B. Stew . . . The Moonlighting
Laundresses . . . San Antonio: Remember the Chili
Queens . . . The Canary Island Cumin Connection . . .
The Mysterious Cans of W. G. Tobin . . . The Cowboys
. . . The Irish Stew Theory . . . The Fed-Up Cook
Theory . . . Steppe Father of Chili?

CHAPTER 3 **Chili Confrontation:** A Challenge from the
Midwest   23
Double "L" Illinois Chilli . . . Cincinnati Red

CHAPTER 4 **Chili Chains:** Fiery Fast Food   28
From Shanghai to Houston . . . The Big C in Big D
. . . A Coney Island Is Not in Brooklyn . . . Oklahoma's
Johnny Chiliseed . . . They All Like Ike's . . . A
Tommy's Is a Chiliburger . . . Windy City Chili . . .
St. Louis Slinger . . . Green Bay Super Bowl Chili . . .
The Alaskan Chililine . . . Down East Chili . . . A
Fast Chili Gazetteer

CHAPTER 5 **When Chili Was Cheap:** Food for Hard Times   46
All the Crackers You Can Eat . . . Ptomaine Tommy's
and the Chili Size . . . In the Army It's Still Free

CONTENTS

CHAPTER 6 **Chic Chili:** Where the Elite Eat It 49
Laid Back California Chili . . . Capitol Chili . . . Chili in the Big Apple . . . South of the Border . . . Continental Chili

CHAPTER 7 **Chili Savvy** 60
Taller, Suet, or Drippings . . . Not So Prime Meat . . . Not Older, but Better . . . Chili Grind vs. Hamburger . . . Capsicum & Company . . . Garlic: Loved and Hated . . . Beloved Cumin . . . Wild, Wild Oregano . . . Options and Add-Ons . . . To Bean or Not to Bean . . . The Final Touches

CHAPTER 8 **Tools of the Trade** 75
Chili Blends with the Times . . . Airtights and Bricks

CHAPTER 9 **A Chile Primer** 79
Taking Out the Fire . . . Chile Know-How . . . Red Dust

CHAPTER 10 **Come and Get It** 88
Cooling the Fire

THE PRACTICE: RECIPES

CHAPTER 11 **The Old Ways and the Army Ways** 94

CHAPTER 12 **From Texas** 104

CHAPTER 13 **From the Southwest** 124

CHAPTER 14 **From the Midwest** 134

CHAPTER 15 **From California** 139

CHAPTER 16 **From the East Coast** 160

CONTENTS

CHAPTER 17 **Far Out and Far Off**   167

CHAPTER 18 **The Newfangled Ways**   175

CHAPTER 19 **Saturday Night Specials**   182

APPENDIX A. **Directory of Sources**   191

APPENDIX B. **Directory of Organizations and Publications**   195

GLOSSARY   196

BIBLIOGRAPHY   203

INDEX   211

To Anne Elizabeth and Elizabeth Ann

Apologia

Chili is largely a state of mind; consequently predesignated quantities are not as important as your own instincts in estimating how many a recipe will serve. Since most of the recipes included in this book are personal, some contributors have chosen to include quantities, and others, who work by assessing the crowd, have left it to you. All large-quantity recipes, however, indicate how many will be served.

PART I
THE LORE

CHAPTER 1

Chili Today: An American Passion

Texans have been eating chili for well over one hundred years; some say since as far back as the eighteenth century. But it was not until 1977 that chili gained official status as the State Dish of Texas. Not exactly a stew, not exactly a soup, chili is a simple, robust, all-American food, traditionally served in a heavy chinaware bowl and eaten with a spoon. A proper chili parlor—or chili host—would provide crackers, chopped onion, and a hot condiment on the side, and would ask before adding beans to each serving.

Chili lovers know there is controversy enough in even this short statement to keep a passionate debate going for hours, as to the origins, ingredients, preparation, and serving of the "simple" dish of chili.

In fact, the nourishing cowboy chili once ladled up from a steaming campfire kettle has taken on complexities that would awe Escoffier, and make an old-time chuckwagon cook swallow his chewing tobacco in disbelief.

Generations of chili cooks, convinced theirs is the One-and-Only recipe, have escalated chili-making to cult proportions. Chili is now served in silver chafing dishes at hunt breakfasts, inaugural ball buffets, and smart supper clubs.

Early in this century chili's popularity spread outside of Texas, especially in the Midwest. During the Great Depression the dish was widely available at lunch counters because it was cheap and substantial, and usually came with unlimited crackers and ketchup. The rationing of meat, fats, and certain spices during World War II forced it off the menu in many places, and chili went into a decline. Its

3

rebirth in the 1960s may have been prompted by President Lyndon Johnson's passion for Pedernales River Chili (page 110), which was often served at the White House and always stocked on Air Force One. At any rate, the renewed interest sparked the chili cook-offs which today are nationwide among competitive chili lovers, each claiming to have the One-and-Only recipe.

In 1962, chili expert and fourth generation Texan Frank X. Tolbert wrote "That Bowl of Fire Called Chili" for the *Saturday Evening Post.* The article generated more than 30,000 pieces of mail and prompted Tolbert to write a book, *A Bowl of Red,* in 1966. "The emphasis in this book," Tolbert wrote, "will be on the world-famous, seldom-found-today, original Texas-style bowl of red" which didn't "contain any vegetable except chile peppers, the burning capsicums, and a few other spices derived from the plant kingdom—no tomatoes or chopped onion."

Chili by Any Other Name—Is Not the Same

The confusion about chili and chile con carne has persisted for over a century, despite the continuing efforts of chili enthusiasts to set the record straight. To add the Spanish words *con carne*—with meat—to chili is redundant. Chili *is* meat, usually beef, flavored with ground red chile (the fruit of the capsicum), plus garlic, cumin, oregano, and sometimes other spices. Chile con carne, on the other hand, is green or red chile stewed with enough meat to flavor it. It can be delicious, but is another dish entirely.

Whatever they choose to call it—chili, chilli, chile, or chili con carne—ever growing numbers of Americans are eating it. Although diehard chili lovers profess to scorn canned chili, it is one of the top-selling canned foods in the country. Every major American meat packer cans it, and chili is marketed under almost every American food brand label.

Some chili brands are found only regionally; some are widely distributed. Gebhardt's, now owned by Beatrice Foods, is the brand most likely to be found on market shelves around the world (page 120), even in countries like West Germany, where it is called "Texas Gulasch," because there is no German word for chili. (In fact, goulash is a lot closer relative of chili than some Texans may want to admit.) When William Gebhardt began canning his chili in San Antonio in 1911, he first tried labeling it "carne con chili" for the sake of accuracy, but it never caught on. Wolf Brand, of Corsicana, Texas, now owned by the Quaker Oats Company, is marketed in a three-state area, but is second only to Hormel as the largest selling canned chili in the world. Another Texas chili popular in that market area, and unavailable elsewhere, is Ireland's Iron Kettle Brand chili, made by Ranch Style, Incorporated, of Fort Worth. This firm also packs the very popular chili-flavored Ranch Style beans, which have a wider market in the West.

The renewed fervor for chili in the 1960s marked the introduction of "chili mix" (powdered chili ingredients to be added to meat and optional beans) to the chili world. These mixes have a more customized taste—from hot to hottest—than the familiar chili powders found on the spice shelves, which are blended to appeal to a wide market. Chili mixes are conveniently packaged in metal foil envelopes, brown paper, or clear plastic bags; they're canned in paste form, and are also sold as cellophane-wrapped "bricks." More recently, liquid chili mixes in cans and glass containers have become available.

The late newspaperman Gordon "Wick" Fowler is credited with one of the first (and most famous) mixes. Fowler's long experience as a chili cook and his reporter's curiosity led him to sources of supply for chili ingredients unknown to others. He made up packets of these special ingredients to take on assignment to Los Angeles, to Mexico City, or to Vietnam. Matt Weinstock, a popular Los Angeles newspaper columnist of the day, reported that "Wick Fowler's chili (page 109) brought tears to the eyes and perspiration to the brow, but it was so great that the memory lingers on."

The ever-generous Fowler gave away his flavoring packets to friends and chili enthusiasts fortunate enough to be around while he still had them. Before long, however, the demand got so great that it was either go into the chili mix business or go broke, since he had recently retired.

Fowler went into business. He founded the original Caliente Chili Company on Red River Street in Austin, and began packaging his 2-Alarm chili mix in quantity. He still gave a lot of his chili mix away, but he started selling a lot, too, to Texas supermarket chains and by mail order.

There is the now-famous story about the hot letter an early mail order customer wrote Fowler about the seven weevils that had turned up in the packet of masa flour, included as a "tightener" in his 2-Alarm mix. Fowler wrote back apologizing for the presence of only seven weevils, since, he said, there should have been nineteen. The missing twelve would be on their way in the next mail, Fowler promised.

At Caliente these days, they say the letter writer is still a regular customer, along with others all over the world. Additionally, Wick's mix is handled by stores as dissimilar as the elegant Henri Bendel's and Zabar's in New York and the Alpha Beta markets in California, as well as other more and less conventional markets nationwide.

Chiliheads United

Because chili-making has become such an impassioned issue, support groups have mushroomed to champion opposing chili convictions. There are three organizations with growing worldwide memberships that gather periodically to perpetuate chili lore and to fan the flames of the One-and-Only arguments. The earliest of these is the Chili Appreciation Society International (CASI), founded in Dallas in 1939 by magazine publisher George Haddaway. It has been variously described as "a group of hungry newspapermen" and "a bunch of millionaires who used to gather once a month to taste chili and argue about how to bust up the crackers they used in it." CASI's chapters are called pods, perhaps in homage to an idea expressed by Joe Cooper in his book *With or Without Beans*. Cooper envisioned a great fraternity of chili lovers—Fellows of the Red Squeezin's of the Chili Pod (FORSCP). He thought chili lovers should be called chilicrats, but CASI members like to be known as chiliheads.

Chief CASI rival is the International Chili Society (ICS), founded in California early in 1975 by a splinter group headed by ex-Texans C. V. Wood, Jr., and Carroll Shelby. Both CASI and ICS hold "world championship" chili cook-offs each fall. The third organization, the International Connoisseurs of Green & Red Chile (ICG&RC), was founded in 1973 in Mesilla, New Mexico, and is now headquartered in nearby Las Cruces, also home of the highly supportive New Mexico State University. The ICG&RC is more interested in chile—the capsicum—than chili (which they insist should be spelled with an "e" in the New Mexican manner).

The first CASI cook-off, held in October 1967 in the ghost mining town of Terlingua, Texas, ignited the spark of interest which would later attract hundreds and then thousands of people to chili cook-offs. By 1978, John M. Crewdson, writing for the *New York Times*, noted that the annual Terlingua fracas had divided into two groups— the "revelers" and a "smaller group of chili cognoscenti who sound like a bunch of wine snobs with their talk of 'nice afterbite,' or 'subtle texture.'" Such talk, he said, could "drive the non-initiated to distraction with debates on the merits of hand-cubed or coarse-ground meat."

The ICS cook-off, a charity benefit, recently held at the Paramount Ranch, traditionally has been held near Rosamond, California. Because of its proximity to Hollywood, the ICS affair attracts movie and TV personalities. These in turn attract thousands of spectators, who cover the desert with campers, motor homes, dune buggies, and motorcycles. In 1979, the thirteenth annual ICS cook-off attracted more than 30,000 people who watched thirty state or regional champs attempt to prove that their chili was the One-and-Only.

One of the ICS founders, C. V. Wood, Jr., is the man who bought and moved the London Bridge from its historic location on the Thames River to the Arizona desert. Wood is an owner of the Rangoon Racquet Club in Beverly Hills, which, of course, serves chili. Wood is a man who obviously does not do things in a small way; his own recipe for chili (page 140) is one of the most complex in the history of chili-making.

Another ICS founder, Carroll Shelby, is an ex-Grand Prix racing driver (co-winner of the Le Mans 24-hour, 1959), who has made chili (page 139) for drivers and pit crews all over the world. He owns Shelby Texas Chili Company, which packages "Carroll Shelby's Original Texas Brand Chili Preparation," distributed principally on the West Coast.

In the early 1950s, chili was much on the mind of a Dallas newspaper-and-public-relations man named Joe Cooper. To Cooper, Texas encompassed most of the known chili world of that time. So he set out to write a book containing all the chili history and lore he knew and could collect from other chiliheads, mostly Texans. The book, titled *With or Without Beans,* was published in 1952. Although it is now long out of print, *Beans* is recognized as the first classic on the subject of chili. The few remaining copies of its single, small edition are eagerly sought by chili fans.

7

If Cooper could visit one of today's big chili cook-offs, he would see proof that his predicted decline of the chili arts never happened, due in some part to him and to *With or Without Beans*.

In Texas, there is a cook-off nearly every weekend, and there are as many cook-offs as there are types of chiliheads. There are cook-offs for servicemen, for the handicapped, and for women only. There is a Chilympiad and a Czhilispiel. On Easter weekend in 1980, near Alpine, Texas, there was a "Cathedral Mountain Chili Cook-off and Easter Egg Hunt with Sunrise Services," the latter conducted by self-styled "Oeste" Texan Sam Pendergrast. The official Nevada State championship cook-off is held, naturally, in a Las Vegas casino. Cook-off teams include competitors from Guadalajara and Anchorage, from West Germany and Hawaii. A Texas-based Japanese chili team wears full samurai regalia and stirs its chili with an ancient Japanese sword. A Kentucky team wears buckskins and coonskin caps. Competitors (and presumably spectators) at a California cook-off held at a nudist resort near San Bernardino wear nothing at all. Sam Lewis, of San Angelo, Texas, the inventor (in 1977) of the jalapeño lollipop, claims to have the world's largest chili cooking team, called the Cross-Eyed Mule, with over 1,700 members. He claims that 1,668 are honorary, including three from the USSR. Competitors travel hundreds of miles to shoot it out gastronomically with their peers, cooking with iron pots and portable stoves.

A chili media has sprouted in recent years to keep chiliheads informed of the latest issues. A monthly tabloid called the *Goat Gap Gazette (GGG)* is the bible of the chili world. It was founded by John Raven (known as Bad McFad to chiliheads) in 1974. The following year he sold it to a friend, Hal John Wimberly, for 20 dollars. From its mimeographed beginnings, and subscription list of twenty, the *GGG*, published in Houston, has become indispensable to its readers around the world.

Bob "Yeller Dog" Marsh originated the Sunday radio "Chilicast" on San Antonio station KBUC (there is also a radio Chili Hotline on Houston's KILT). Marsh is the owner of Yeller Dog's, a "chili saloon" in the San Antonio suburb of Leon Springs, and markets his own "Hoot 'n Holler" chili mix (page 191).

Saying that the passion for chili is worldwide no longer suffices. On the second day of the 1975 Apollo-Soyuz linkup, the gnawing hunger for chili, known to its victims as chili pangs, occurred in space. Apollo astronaut Tom Stafford got that familiar feeling. His remark to the Russian cosmonauts, "Hey, wouldn't a hot bowl of chili go great right now?" was recorded for posterity by the memory banks at the Houston Space Flight Center.

Texas, New Mexico, and sometimes Arizona, as well as cities such as San Antonio, Springfield (Illinois), and Cincinnati, all have claimed chili for their own. It also has been claimed that chili was invented by the army, the Texas Rangers, Confederate officers, American Indians, a Spanish nun, a Chinese chuckwagon cook, an Irish chuckwagon cook, Canary Islanders, Czechs, Greeks, Magyars, and the mountain people of the Caucasus. Mexicans, on the other hand, heartily disclaim any connection to chili, although for years people who don't know any better have persisted in placing chili's roots in Mexico. But the chile capsicum, which the Spanish brought home to Europe from Mexico, was adopted by the whole world.

Despite its universal fame, those who have eaten chili elsewhere say that the closer one gets to Texas, the hotter the chili. As Texas songwriter Ruby Allmond puts it:

Ah, ha, Texas Red
Makes the heat devils dance in the brassy sky
The buzzards hover and circle and fly
They know pretty soon everybody's gonna die
From eatin' Texas Red
Try a bowl of Texas Red.

"Texas Red"
© Ruby Allmond, 1977
Used by permission.

CHAPTER 2

Chili Roots:
Deep in the Heart of
Texas

There are almost as many theories about how chili originated as there are One-and-Only chili recipes. Some accounts are highly exaggerated, some are tongue-in-cheek, and some are true to the tradition of the classic American tall story. The only thing on which all knowledgeable disputants agree is that chili as we know it today is as American as apple pie.

In a *New York Times* article, the food-writing team of Waverly Root and Louis deRochement wrote, "It might be described as native foreign. It is native, for it does not exist elsewhere; it was born on this soil. But it is foreign in that its inspiration came from an alien cuisine." Food critic Craig Claiborne wrote, "One knows that chili originated in the Southwest [and] was of Mexican inspiration."

Everett Lee DeGolyer, known simply as E. DeGolyer, was the first renaissance man of chili (page 107) and one of the early scholars of chili lore. Widely quoted in chili circles, he studied chili just as intently as he did literature, the arts, or the petroleum business (the last having made him a millionaire, allowing him to fruitfully pursue the former). DeGolyer was one of the earliest to insist that chili, as Americans know it and cook it, is not of Mexican origin, a statement he documented through research.

The Pemmican Premise

DeGolyer believed that chili had its origins as the "pemmican of the Southwest," made of jerky, fat, and native chiles, pounded together

10

to form a highly concentrated and nutritious nonperishable trail ration. He found an early mention of pemmican chili in *Mexican Gold Trail*, the journal of George W. B. Evans, who took the dangerous Chihuahua trail to the California gold fields in the mid-1800s. "Beef is prepared for the long journey by pounding it together with lard and pepper," Evans wrote. "So mix these articles that no fear need be apprehended of its preservation in all kinds of weather, and salt and pepper and lard become useless, as these ingredients are already part of every meal you make with this mixture. A small pinch of this . . . thrown into a pan or kettle of boiling water with a little flour or corn meal for thickening, will satisfy the wants of six men at any time; and it is a dish much relished by all."

Evans had been introduced to the dish that Coronado's historian Casteñeda had described almost 300 years before, when the Spaniards found the Plains Indians cooking it:

> They dry their meat in the sun, cutting it into thin slices, and when it is dry, they grind it like flour for storage and make mash to eat. They cook it in a pot, which they always manage to have with them. When they put a handful into the pot, the mash soon fills it, since it swells to great size.

It seems obvious that chili would originate where there was an abundant supply of its two prime ingredients, meat and chile. The meat—buffalo, venison, and, later, beef—was available in staggering quantity on the plains of southwest Texas. So was the chile, in the form of the tiny, fiery hot chilipiquín, which still grows wild in that area, and as far east as Louisiana. On the plains, in fact, little else was available in such abundance (except, perhaps, buffalo chips).

Since meat, the staple food in the plains country, turned up in some form with monotonous regularity at almost every meal, it was inevitable it would be combined with the local wild-growing chile. Pemmican chili, one of the first chilis of which there is a written record, is about as basic as chili can get. But jerky doesn't have to be made into pemmican before it can be made into chili. It is only necessary to cut it into small bite-size or smaller pieces, reconstitute it with water, and add the chile. Since fat turns rancid in drying and must be scrupulously removed from meat before it is jerked, it should be re-added, as it is to pemmican when that is made. Instead

11

of cutting jerky into pieces for chili, it can be pounded, northern Mexican style, into the stringy fluff called *machaca*, and then cooked with fat, water, and chile to make Sonora-style chili (pages 94–95 and 128).

In wagon trains passing across the sparse wilderness of west Texas, food was eaten on the move. Enough was usually cooked at evening meals to last until the next evening. Jerky and pemmican were the prime fare of these on-the-trail meals, and if the early plains travelers ate it unadorned before they got to New Mexico, they were introduced to chili embellishments once they had arrived. Travelers going east are certain to have carried the "makings" for jerky or pemmican chili—or both—with them on the trail, just as the forty-niners carried them west from Chihuahua, and the mountain men carried them from their Taos rendezvous all over the West and Southwest.

An Army Marches on Its Chili

One theory about the origin of chili has it originating as a portable field ration. Gwynne S. Curtis, Jr., a retired air force colonel, said, "The chili my family prepared when I was a kid in Dallas came in the form of a dehydrated brick from Boedecker's grocery store in Oak Cliff. It seemed to me that there was something odd about this brick chili—it was so different from the usual kind—and I asked my constant companion and grandfather, Victory Birdseye Curtis, about it. He told me that in the early days of Texas there were all kinds of military and quasi-military actions involving the Texas Rangers, the U.S. Cavalry, the Mexicans, and marauding Indians.

"In those days of impossible food logistics to support a large or small expedition, some very practical Tex-Mex techniques were employed, and dehydrated brick chili, sometimes made with frijoles, was carried in saddle bags."

So, according to Victory Birdseye Curtis, chili in brick form came about through military necessity. It provided a light, easily carried, long-lasting, and nutritious ration; one that, above all, tasted good day after day.

Army food on the American frontier was truly bad, particularly for troops in the field. In 1890 some units were still being issued Civil War hardtack dated 1863. It is no wonder that men spent their meager pay to buy outrageously priced canned beef and other goods at the post traders' stores. Few army cooks had any talent for preparing food, and most of it was boiled. After years of listening to complaints, the army finally began training men selected to be cooks. But by that time, chili was firmly established on the army menu. So chili owes its enlistment as army chow to the rank and file, not to the quartermaster.

Sam Arnold wrote in *Fryingpans West*, "In military inventories of the Indian War period," the listing of red pepper and red chile was commonplace, "a sure indication that somebody had learned to add a little western savvy to the pot." By 1909 the army was well along in upgrading the capabilities of its cooks (pages 99 to 103).

Son of S.O.B. Stew

There is no doubt that the chili found today at American bases all over the world goes far back into military history. There is just as little doubt that soldiers on the western frontier in the nineteenth century were ripe for rib-sticking food of any kind. But did these hungry troops originate what would become America's national dish? Almost, say the boosters of the *lavandera* theory of original chili.

Mel Marshall, of Phillips, Texas, a writer, sportsman, and western history scholar, and a chili cook to be trusted, claims, "Chili originated on the Rio Grande. It was created by the *lavanderas*, or washerwomen, who'd come north with the Mexican armies in the 1830–1840 period, and stayed when these [armies] retreated to serve the Texas militiamen who kept border-watch. The Comanches had driven away most of the Mexican *rancheros*, but there were a few scrawny half-wild cattle, and the little border deer, weighing only sixty to seventy pounds field-dressed, and stray goats wandering along the riverbanks.

"The meat from these was tough and stringy and needed long cooking, and the *lavanderas* had little to use for seasoning except the native wild marjoram and red chile. From these scant ingredients the *lavanderas* created son-of-a-bitch stew, and the dish known today as chili is a lineal descendant of these stews. The stew itself was commonly cooked in border deer camps when I hunted that area in the 1920s."

Son-of-a-bitch stew, sometimes politely called S.O.B. or Son-of-a-gun, is a much-loved dish among cowboys. It is made from the "innards," including the marrow-gut, of a fresh-killed calf or steer.

13

The Moonlighting Laundresses

The *lavandera* connection with soldiers and chili may have been established even before the troops got to the Rio Grande. In *With or Without Beans*, Joe Cooper tells of "a non-documented incident of 1835, when the Republic of Texas was mobilizing an army in San Antonio . . . and . . . officers [contracted] with a Mexican woman to feed the embryo army. With facilities for mass feeding non-existent, she made huge pots of meat stewed with red pepper (chili?) together with stacks of tortillas which were served on makeshift tables on a village plaza."

According to Cooper, "Some suggest this incident, if it actually happened, was the origin of San Antonio's chili queens." A woman with a lot of huge pots on hand certainly suggests someone in the *lavandera* line. This suggestion, that the famed chili queens of San Antonio's plazas sprang from this Texas GI chow line, is contested in the WPA-funded Federal Writers Project *Texas, a Guide to the Lone Star State*, which claims that the chili queen stands date from 1813. It is documented fact, however, that chili-making *lavanderas* did make connections with American soldiers during the War with Mexico in 1846 and 1847.

The mere title of S. Compton Smith's 1857 book, *Chile Con Carne; or, The Camp and the Field*, indicates that the American army of the day was more than just acquainted with chili. An acting surgeon with General Zachary Taylor, Dr. Smith wrote often of chile con carne, which he defined as "a popular Mexican dish—literally red pepper and meat." The Americans found this chili everywhere: the local *rancheros* would appear at American camps with "their stock-in-trade, consisting usually of *carne seco* and *carne fresco, leche de cabro, chile con carne, tamales, frijoles, tortillas, pan de maiz,* and other eatables." On the trail, the American soldiers once surprised a group of Mexican lancers, who, according to Smith, "seated around their fires, were in the act of taking their suppers. Our unexpected arrival somewhat interrupted their arrangements—so much so, that they immediately took to the cover of the chaparral without so much as untethering their horses, which, of course, fell into our hands.

"But what was most interesting to our hungry fellows, of all the camp equipage they left behind," Smith wrote, "were their steaming pots of *chile con carne*, which, in their hurry to vamoose, they had left upon the embers. . . . As our men were greedily feasting upon

14

their *chile con carne*, we were much amused by a sudden assault upon them of a party of women." According to Smith, the women each rescued a pot "of the savory mess" and disappeared into the chaparral.

"These Mexican troops seldom move without a crowd of women accompanying them," said Dr. Smith. The reasons were obvious: the women could not only cook the chili, but they were also capable of snatching it from the jaws of defeat.

During the frontier period, American military regulations allowed three groups of females to reside at western posts: laundresses *(lavanderas)*, servants and wives and daughters of officers. As they always have, the laundresses did more than wash socks for the troops. Many of them made extra money by making and selling food to the always hungry soldiers. With Taylor's army along the Rio Grande, the *lavanderas* no doubt used the soldiers' individual rations, spicing the pot with the game, chile, and wild marjoram that are still to be found in that area. At least one officer's wife wrote home that the post laundresses were making "fortunes" in this seller's market, and refusing to do what the army tolerated them to do—laundry. When a general took note of this situation in 1876, the days of the laundresses—at least officially—were numbered. In 1878, they were officially banned from army posts.

San Antonio: Remember the Chili Queens

San Antonio, Texas, has been the hub of military (and possibly chili) activity since its founding in 1691. The military activity is easy to document. Not so the arrival (or the origination) of chili. Many people have tried to establish the date and there is considerable variance in their findings.

The Plaza de Armas, later called Military Plaza, was one of the first chili hot-spots in the presidio of San Antonio de Bejar. Over the years, the Plaza was used by the soldiers of seven wars and scores of military actions, Indian skirmishes, and border scrapes that involved volunteer militia, posses, the Texas Rangers, and more. Between wars, parades, and other military and political formations, San Antonio's Military Plaza—like Spanish plazas the world over—was used as a market in the daytime and for recreation and people-watching at night.

The famous nighttime chili queen stands of San Antonio were a natural outgrowth of this tradition, but the beginning of the chili queen tradition is hard to pin down. The first food vendors on the Plaza operated from ground level: they squatted, Indian fashion, and dished their wares out of earthen pots or *ollas*. The burning question is: did those *ollas* contain chili? And if not, just when did chili become—as gumbo is to New Orleans and clam chowder is to Boston— San Antonio's dish? For chili is, without a doubt, San Antonio's dish.

In *San Antonio, The Flavor of Its Past,* historian Donald E. Everett claims that "what the early chili queens served was not the dish relished by today's connoisseurs." Everett says that the earlier stands were selling something more like *mole poblano* (meat in a rich and complex chile sauce, which includes chocolate).

Frank Bushick, in his book *Glamorous Days,* claims San Antonio chili goes back to the early 1700s. He intimates that it was the high esteem in which the chili queens and their Plaza stands were held that resulted in swift punishment, back in Civil War days, for those who did not show them the proper respect: "Bob Augustus was a DeWitt county cowboy who stepped off into space at San Antonio during the Civil War. He had come to town to enlist in a company being made up for the Confederate army, but got too much tarantula juice under his belt [and] cavorting around on his cow pony, he overturned a lot of chile con carne stands on the Plaza. While waiting at the old Bat Cave city prison to be tried . . . the Vigilantes took him and hanged him to a cottonwood tree."

Besides upsetting these hallowed city landmarks, Augustus was also suspected of horse stealing, which may have had some bearing on the quick disposition of his case.

The Canary Island Cumin Connection

Chili connoisseur and historian Charles Ramsdell, author of *San Antonio,* states flatly: "The one thing that comes from San Antonio, Texas, and nowhere else—is chili con carne." This neatly fits in with a theory of H. Allen Smith and John Cone that chili was created by some Canary Islanders, who were among the first settlers of the village which grew up around the presidio of San Antonio. The original fifteen families of Canary Islanders arrived in March 1731, after a months-long march overland from the port of Vera Cruz, where they had landed in the New World. Smith proclaimed cumin the spice

16

that gives chili its chief identifying flavor, insisting that "cumin is as essential to chili as meat is to hamburger." Smith contended that the transplanted Canary Islanders brought cumin with them and added it to the San Antonio mealtime mainstay of *carne en chile colorado* (page 129), and—chili was born.

The Mysterious Cans of W. G. Tobin

Oddly overlooked by San Antonians (and others) in the search for chili's beginnings is William Gerard Tobin. This distinguished citizen of the chili city individually embodies many of the theories and claims advanced about the origins of this dish. Tobin, who arrived in San Antonio from South Carolina in 1853, was involved in every military and paramilitary connection to chili claimed by those who theorize along these lines. In loose order, he was marshal of San Antonio, a captain of Texas Rangers, a commander of border and Indian fighters (under Robert E. Lee), a brigadier general of the Texas militia (appointed by Sam Houston), and a captain in the Confederate army.

Tobin was already famous in San Antonio for his chili in the 1870s. By 1879, he had patented a recipe for his chile sauce, and possibly his chili. He also had a close connection with the Canary Island cumin-bearing settlers of San Antonio; he married into the Curbelo and Delgado families, two of the original Canary Islander group. But what makes Captain Tobin a major figure in chili history is the fact that not only was he a celebrated chili cook among his contemporaries in San Antonio, but also he was very probably the world's first canner of chili. Why he goes unacknowledged in the chili world, particularly in the town that claims to be the capital of that world, is a mystery.

Tobin was also proprietor of the Vance House, a hostelry on the site of today's Gunter Hotel, which was used as a military headquarters before Fort Sam Houston was established. There his chili became famous, especially among the American army officers. In 1884, the *San Antonio Express* ran a story about the chartering of the Tobin Canning Company of San Antonio that included the following:

> . . . to be introduced here is the chili-con-carne canning factory now in the course of construction near San Pedro Springs. The

head of the company is Capt. Wm. Tobin. The manufacture of chili-con-carne here is one which will probably become a very extensive and lucrative industry. Heretofore, the chili, although the patent and process is a San Antonio invention, was made in the north and imported here.

Unfortunately, Captain Tobin died suddenly just two weeks after this announcement and the factory on San Pedro creek apparently never got into operation. Just where the captain canned his chili in the years *preceding* 1884 is a mystery, which vague reports only intensify. However, a few years ago, some beautifully printed old-fashioned labels turned up in a dilapidated ranch building at the headwaters of the San Saba River, west of Fort McKavett. The labels read:

W. G. TOBIN'S
CHILI-CON-CARNE
Prepared at the RANGE CANNING CO.
Fort McKavett, Texas

The ranch where the labels were discovered was founded in 1876 by Colonel William L. Black. According to one source, Colonel Black and Captain Tobin got together because of their common interest in goat meat, which Colonel Black canned commercially.

Alexander Black, the colonel's son, who was born in 1896, and now lives in Palo Alto, California, remembers playing around the cannery as a child, although he was not allowed inside because of the dangerous belt-driven machinery. He states flatly that no chili was ever canned there. But stories in the *Menard* (Texas) *News,* the *San Angelo* (Texas) *Standard-Times,* and elsewhere say that Black went into the canned goat chili business when sales of his plain canned mutton lagged. This might well have been before Alexander was born, according to an account by Colonel Black published in *Sheep and Goat Raiser.* And there are those framed labels of W. G. Tobin's "chili-con-carne" hanging on the walls of Tobin's descendants in San Antonio.

If the facts of the story are ever unraveled, Captain William Gerard Tobin may belatedly get his due from the chili world, and be celebrated as the first canner of chili and one of San Antonio's most illustrious chili cooks.

The Cowboys

Robert E. Stuart of Dallas has been researching chili since 1931 and is convinced that "what we know as chili originated on the cattle trails and was popularized in San Antonio hurdy-gurdys." His findings shed light on how some of the other spices found their way into the chili prepared by chuckwagon cooks on the range and on the great trail drives north out of Texas in the late 1800s. Stuart says that "black pepper was worth its weight in gold after the Civil War, when paper money was worthless and barter was the method of commerce. The indigenous wild-growing chile, along with wild onion, garlic, cumin, and paprika peppers, were traded as money."

On a typical trail drive of those days, the herds were formed north of San Antonio and basic provisions were loaded in a train of wagons. These provisions included salt, salt pork, flour, dried beans, bacon sides, cornmeal, sugar, and coffee. For spices, the more self-sufficient chuckwagon cooks (Stuart calls them *campuks*) used indigenous plants and some even planted "spice groves" along the way, which they harvested on the way up or back, depending on the season.

The location of the groves became top secret information. Some of the more observant chuckwagon cooks may have picked up this helpful habit from the Plains Indians, who were known to plant maize along their trails during seasonal migrations. The basic menu for the trail drive, says Stuart, included "spitted beef (now bar-b-que), and deviled beef with chiles (now called chili)."

"When the campuk butchered beef he threw the trimmings in a special large iron fire pot well blackened with soot. When crammed full of bits of meat, fat, gristle . . . everything except the hide," it hung over the four-foot low end of the cookfire to slowly simmer down for at least three days. As the fat and meat simmered, the mixture was stirred with a wooden "chilistick," so called because it absorbed the finished deviled-beef-with-chiles taste and odor and couldn't be used to stir any other foods.

While the chili cooked, Stuart says, the campuks threw in handfuls of spices according to their own "tastin' " (*recipe* was a dude's word). Beans might have been added if the mixture turned out too light or the meat was extra tough and stringy. Some, according to Stuart, used brown rice for a change from the daily frijoles, as in the 1896 army recipe (page 99) for chili. Maybe this is where the army got the idea—or vice versa.

19

San Antonians are sure to say that cowboys and their cooks—like the soldiers—learned about chili in San Antonio and took the knowledge with them on the cattle drives. Stuart's findings show just the opposite. He insists the cowboys took their fondness for chili into town with them, and it was the chili queens who learned how to turn their *carne en chile colorado* into American chuckwagon "deviled beef" in order to cater to cowboy tastes.

The Irish Stew Theory

Something that happened in the east Texas town of Corsicana many years ago illustrates another version of how chili originated. In an informal paper he titled *Chili in General, Wolf Brand in Particular*, Doyle L. West, one of the early owners of Wolf Brand, a pioneer canned chili, claims, "Chili as we now know it originated among the cowboys whose cooks had been preparing for them the time honored 'Irish Stew' (which probably isn't Irish either). Somewhere or other the cook ran out of his black pepper and in searching for a substitute was, of course, offered red pepper by the Mexicans or perhaps Indians of the territory. The pepper native to the country, prior to the development of our domesticated milder types of pepper, was extremely hot. And it is probable that this cook used about the same quantity of this red pepper as he had been using black pepper in his Irish stew. The cowhands, of course, exclaimed about this additional heat in their food, and were given the explanation by their cook that that was the chili, which was the generic term applied to all of the red peppers by the Mexicans and Indians. As time wore on, the dish itself became known as chili."

The Fed-Up Cook Theory

Woody Barron, long time managing editor of the *Tribune-Herald* in Waco, Texas, holds to the same theory, but with a slightly different approach. It takes into account the legendary bad temper of chuckwagon cooks, whose everyday dispositions have been described as "about like that of a teased rattlesnake." According to Barron, chili was born when a chuckwagon cook got fed up with his clientele's complaints about the tough beef he was serving. "So, to cure the gripes," theorizes Barron, "he chopped up the beef into small pieces, tossed them into a pot with a handful of chili peppers, for revenge, and boiled the concoction until the beef was tender." The griping stopped. Chili lovers will draw their own conclusions here, which is pretty much what Barron did about this whole story. But he insists that chili is a Texas dish and his own version (page 111) is "hot enough to cure a six-week hangover."

Steppe Father of Chili?

Doyle West is right of course about stew not being exclusively Irish. People have been making stews since they first started fooling around with fire. It is ingredients and methods that set stews apart— or relate them.

With this last in mind, chili history buffs will find food for thought in writer Joseph Wechsberg's thoughts about *gulyás*—or goulash— in *The Cooking of Vienna's Empire*, one of the Time-Life Books "Foods of the World" series.

Gulyás, says Wechsberg, "was invented for the same reason as other stews, ragouts, hashes, and thick soups: it was nourishing and inexpensive and it had a good taste. But most important to men who had to wander far from home, it could be prepared from previously dried ingredients that could be transported easily—a kind of ancient survival ration.

"Before setting out with their herds, the Magyar shepherds cut meat into cubes and cooked it with onion in a *bogrács*, a heavy iron kettle hung over an open fire out on the *pusztá* (prairie). They stewed the meat slowly until the liquid was gone, dried the remnants in the sun and put them into a bag made from a sheep's stomach. . . . When they were hungry they took a piece of the dried food, added water, and reheated it in their kettle."

In the sixteenth century, after the capsicum reached Europe and the iron kettle reached America, the relationship between goulash and chili got even closer. Paprika, now the national spice of Hungary, became the classic ingredient in goulash; and the iron kettle became the classic chili cookware of the prairie.

The remarkable similarity between condensed dried *gulyás* on the one hand, and pemmican and brick chili on the other, may be due to the common central Asian ancestor some claim for the Magyars and the American Indians.

Chili lovers will recognize the edge in Wechsberg's words when he complains that the worldwide popularity of his beloved *gulyás* produced "silly imitations and wilful distortions" of the true dish. There is even a Czech goulash, he says, made with sauerkraut.

In Texas, these words cut close to the bone. Out on the Texas *pusztá*, where the Czechs settled in 1850, it's chili with sauerkraut that simmers in the old iron *bogrács* (page 169).

CHAPTER 3

Chili Confrontation: A Challenge from the Midwest

In 1967, midwesterner H. Allen Smith wrote an article about chili, "Nobody Knows More About Chili Than I Do," in *Holiday* magazine, which finally brought the controversy with Texas to national attention. By expressing the pent-up frustration of ignored, and even scorned, non-Texan chili cooks, Smith became the leader and champion of this faction.

Only weeks after Smith's article appeared, challenges already had been issued and accepted. The chili cooking contest that would spawn today's frenzied cook-off scene was arranged between Smith and the reigning Texas expert, Wick Fowler, who, as noted, had more or less stumbled into chili missionary work through the encouragement of Texas friends. The great cook-off was held in Terlingua, Texas, in October 1967—and was declared a draw. In light of earlier visits by Yankees to Texas chili country, the decision displayed marked restraint by the Texans.

Nevertheless, Smith's boisterous allegations regarding his treatment at the hands of the Texans were shortly afterward put to use. His account of the affair, *The Great Chili Confrontation*, became the first major book about chili to use the word in its title. Along with Cooper's *With or Without Beans* and Tolbert's *A Bowl of Red*, *The Great Chili Confrontation* is considered the third classic on the subject. Like *Beans*, *Confrontation* is also out of print and much sought after by chili aficionados.

No two chili recipes so well represent the two major opposing bodies as do Fowler's and Smith's (pages 109 and 134). Of course,

Smith included beans in his chili, and both recipes called for tomato, but these are yet other controversies. Whatever the ingredients and methods, chili must inevitably end up either thick or thin. The faction Smith championed is revealed by the nickname "Soupy" bestowed upon him by Frank Tolbert. Smith retaliated by describing Wick Fowler's culinary style as "early truck stop."

Double "L" Illinois Chilli

When the *Illinois State Journal* proclaimed Springfield as the "chilli capital of the world," it drew guffaws from Texas, mostly because the use of two "l's" in the word indicated midwesterners couldn't even spell chili. Nevertheless, midwesterners continue to insist that the One-and Only chili can be found there, and nowhere else.

Nobody knows for sure how chili got to the Midwest. Some say that San Antonio boosters included a replica of a chili queen stand in their 1893 Chicago World's Fair exhibit and fairgoers mobbed it to taste chili for the first time. A more meaty account is that one of the chili cooks at the 1904 St. Louis Fair allegedly sold a One-and-Only chili recipe to Charles O. Taylor of Carlinville, Illinois, for 30 dollars. (In Texas, selling One-and-Only chili recipes is pretty much on a par with selling shares in the Brooklyn Bridge in New York.) Taylor claimed the chili soothed his ulcers and he figured he could get well with chili in Illinois in more ways than one.

Taylor opened a chili parlor on Main Street in Carlinville between a saloon and a livery stable. Chili not only did well for the Taylor family, it became an important part of the economy of that entire area of Illinois, particularly Springfield.

Today, Taylor's chili parlor is run by a grandson, Ed Taylor. The business moved from Main Street to South West Street in 1919; otherwise, the family ownership and the chili are the same as they were when Charles Taylor started his chili pot bubbling in 1904. Two of Taylor's great-grandsons, Ed's sons Tom and Ed, Jr., are learning the business and the family's still-secret recipe for chili, about which Ed Taylor will say only that it has no tomatoes. Like most midwestern chili, Taylor's has beans, but Ed stresses that they are added at the time of serving—the chili is cooked without beans.

Ed Taylor makes a change or two in the story of how his grandfather came by his chili recipe. He says the recipe changed hands when his grandfather bailed a Spanish-speaking chili cook out of jail. But he agrees that St. Louis Fair chili did cure his grandfather's ulcer, by stimulating his digestion, just as the *Encyclopedia Britannica* says the capsicum will do. One interesting sidelight on the chili recipe Charles Taylor acquired may offer still another lead in solving the mystery of Captain Tobin's chili: Ed Taylor says the original recipe called for goat meat. "It's a little scarce in these parts," he says, smiling, "so we've always used beef."

Despite abuse from Texas, chili is still spelled with two "l's" in Illinois. The unique spelling began in 1909 when J. A. Bockelmann, an ex-typewriter salesman, co-founded the famous Dew Chilli Parlors. Sixty years later, Bockelmann decided to "straighten 'em out on the double L in Chilli." He wrote the *State Journal-Register* that when he opened his business on South 11th Street he naturally needed a name—and a sign. "I noticed a sparkling dew on the grass," he said, and so "wanting a short name (plus a catchy one)," decided on "The Dew Chilli Parlor and Lunchroom." The sign painter, James Sheehan, rebelled about the spelling, but Bockelmann said he had checked Webster's Dictionary. "Turning to the C's I soon discovered the word CHILLI, also spelled chile or chili. But! the big black word was first—so I said that is it. Man oh man! did that upset the sign painters around town."

Spelling it with two "l's" has upset a lot of other people—including Texans—down through the years, but Bockelmann knew the value of keeping the town talking about his "chilli." Although there are some who don't, most of Springfield's chili businesses have hung on to Bockelmann's spelling.

The justification for Springfield calling itself the "Chilli Capital of the World" is amply evident in the *State Journal-Register's* special chili section. With over thirty chili (or chilli) joints advertising in the section (including the local Knights of Columbus Club Cafe), and statistics indicating that over 4 million cans of chili were coming off Springfield cannery lines each year, the city of Springfield would seem to have more chili action than many states. Springfield also has Joe DeFrates, whose chili has won at both the Terlingua, Texas, and Tropico, California, World Championship cook-offs.

Until he decided to take it easy, and cook chili for charity (he mostly judges cook-offs nowadays), DeFrates headed the Springfield company which produced Chilli Man Chilli and Chilli Mix. The firm is now operated by Canteen Corporation, a subsidiary of Trans World Airlines, in Litchfield, Illinois.

DeFrates says his father, Walt "Port" (for Portuguese) DeFrates, brought his love for chili back to Springfield from Texas around 1914. Port DeFrates worked for a time as a bartender in the old Heidelberg Room of the Hotel Adolphus in Dallas. He became addicted to the chili served in a little chili parlor in the Adolphus arcade. When he went home to Springfield, he opened his own place, which he called the Heidelberg, where he used to dish up the chili he made to his friends. Eventually, the DeFrates family saw the light and went into the chili canning business. Since Bockelmann had already established the double "l" spelling for chili in Springfield, the DeFrates family used it when they came up with their own Chilli Man brand name.

Walt's brother, Ray, also got into the chili business, with Ray's Brand Products. Ray's daughter now heads the firm in Springfield.

Cincinnati Red

Cincinnati chili lovers believe that chili originated in their city, or at least the "secret" of chili arrived in Cincinnati first—possibly from somewhere in the eastern Mediterranean area—and later filtered down to the yahoos in Texas. Even Texans have to admit that DeWitt Clinton Pendery, one of the leading contenders for the title of the originator of chili powder, came from Cincinnati first and Fort Worth second. Pendery began blending powdered chile, oregano, cumin, and garlic into chili powder in 1890, as part of his Fort Worth business, the Mexican Chilley Supply Company, and called the powder Chilomaline. True again to his Cincinnati heritage, Pendery was one of the earliest advocates in Texas for chili-topped pasta, the dish known as chili-mac, which Cincinnatians insist reaches its peak of perfection in their hometown. All over the Midwest, chili-mac is a winter supper institution.

Cincinnati's dominance in the chili-and-pasta world is credited to two local food chains, the Empress and the Skyline. Both are usually mentioned together, and are historically—although involuntarily—related. The Skyline chain was founded by an ex-cook from the Empress, who is said to have taken his chili recipe with him. The matter is disputed by the two families involved—one Bulgarian and the other Greek. The Kiradjieffs were the first in the field, and began serving chili in the Empress shortly after it was opened in 1922. The Lambrinides own and operate the Skyline chain, which came along in the 1940s. Whoever created the recipe or brought it to the state of perfection Cincinnatians claim it has, was inspired to add old-country spices to the American dish. Cincinnati chili could contain one or more of the following: cinnamon, allspice, clove, nutmeg, ginger, mace, coriander, cardamom, turmeric, mustard. Any attempt at recreating the original (or originals) must include one or more of these spices in just the right proportions (page 135).

Empress and Skyline chili is available straight, but faithful customers come for the famous combinations: Two Way, Three Way, Four Way, and—the ultimate—Five Way. So widespread have these terms become that calling for them by name almost anywhere in the Midwest will provide a version of the original—pale by comparison, Cincinnatians insist—but nevertheless with all the essentials in place and in approximately the proper order.

Two Way is spaghetti with a chili topping. Three Way adds a layer of grated Cheddar cheese. Four Way comes with an additional layer of chopped onions, and Five Way—bean lovers rejoice—starts the whole operation with a base of beans. Some enthusiasts pile on an additional layer of crumbled oyster crackers.

Despite what Texans like to say to the contrary, chili-mac, or spaghetti red (as it is sometimes called in the Southwest), has been just as welcome there as in the Midwest. Like beans, spaghetti is a naturally compatible partner to chili. Chili-mac is one of the classic, ever-popular American hard times foods which remain popular in good times, too. Ike's in Tulsa, along with countless other chili joints in Texas and the Southwest, have offered spaghetti as an alternate to beans with its chili for decades.

CHAPTER 4

Chili Chains:
Fiery Fast Food

In his history of Wolf Brand chili, Doyle West tells how a ranch cook outside of Corsicana used to haul his chili into town in a wagon, park in front of the saloon, and sell it by the bowl from the tailgate. This is how Wolf Brand chili got its start.

In the same way—taking their chili to town—other chuckwagon cooks spread the popularity of chili up along the cattle trails from Texas to Montana. It would have been entirely in character for a chuckwagon cook, his belly full of cattle drives and making five dozen biscuits in the freezing dark before every dawn, to draw his pay and put it down on a snug little eatery in some town along the trail.

It is said that the great majority of chuckwagon cooks are made out of "mad, old wore-out" cowboys, too crippled-up to ride with the herd anymore. The exceptions are born to the work, like Richard Bolt, whose daddy, a range cook, taught his son the fine points of the trade. How well the son learned may be drawn from the fact that, in his lifetime, Bolt worked for the Moon, Matador, 6666, JY, Triangle, Waggoners, T. J. Richards I, and Pitchfork ranches. From owner to range boss to cowhand, nobody ever sent Bolt's chili back to the cookfire (page 117).

From Shanghai to Houston

Diehard Texas straight chili types see the mating of their revered dish with pasta as a damned Yankee plot to blacken (or whiten) chili's pure name. They must be unaware of the similar heresy taking place in their own midst—in Dallas, of all places, that citadel of conservative chili tradition. This time, the guilty ingredient is rice. Ray Shockley, at Wolf Brand Chili, has a letter from Texas legislator T. H. McDonald, of Mesquite, which says in part, "What is better than a bowl of rice covered with your chili? It can't be beat." On the other hand, Martin Waldron, in a story for the *New York Times* News Service, bitterly attacks the chili and rice habits of Trenton, New Jersey, where he works. Waldron obviously has never visited Shanghai Jimmy's in Dallas, where chili and rice is king.

Jimmy, who moves around a lot, at last report was operating his chili rice emporium on the premises of an ex-taco stand on Lemmon Avenue. This is just the latest stop in twenty-five years of restless moves around the Dallas area. But the chili rice stays the same.

Jimmy was born restless and a loner, christened Jimmy James, in Jackson, Minnesota. After enlisting in the army in 1919, at old Fort Logan, outside Denver, Jimmy was sent to the Far East and in 1920 he joined the 15th Infantry in Tientsin, north China. Jimmy didn't cook while he was in the 15th Infantry because he knew that with his maverick temperament (which is about perfect for a chili cook), he would be in trouble if he tried to cook the army way. It wasn't until he got out of the army in 1925 that Jimmy got around to cooking chili at a little restaurant he opened in Shanghai and called the Broadway Lunch, after the street on which it was located. He later expanded into a chain, called "Shanghai Jimmy's."

Jimmy remembers the Shanghai of those days as "the most cosmopolitan city in the world—there were over fifty nationalities represented there. Nobody there had chili, though, until I cooked it. They loved my chili. The British and Indians were accustomed to curry and some of the Chinese loved hot food, and they took to chili right off. I got a lot of my spices—like cumin—at Indian condiment shops." Jimmy remembers well the inspired customer request in 1933 that changed forever his method of serving chili.

"Back then I served my chili with beans, the little red kind like you get in Louisiana," Jimmy said. "Well, one afternoon, a customer came in and said, 'You know, I love your chili, but beans do something to me. Can I have it with something else?' Well, our lunch special that day was meat loaf and mashed potatoes, so I said, 'How about mashed potatoes?' and he said okay, but when I checked, the mashed potatoes were all gone. We always had rice because we served two

29

kinds of curry all day long, so I said, 'How about rice and chili?' and he said okay. So I fixed up the chili for him with rice and he started eating it, and in a while he looked up and said, 'You know, this is *good.*'

"Then a friend of mine came in for lunch, and he said to the chili-and-rice fellow, 'What's that you're eating?' and the fellow said, 'Rice with chili.' My friend said, 'That looks good to me,' and he had some. When he said, 'Boy, is this good,' *I* tried it, and it *was* good, and I put it on the menu and in a month it was outselling chili with beans. Finally, we sold almost no chili and beans, it was all chili and rice, and that's the way I've been making it ever since."

"When it comes to chili," Jimmy says, "I make the real article, out of lean beef—what they called peeled round—trimmed, no skin, no gristle, no fat. A man in here the other day saw me preparing my chili meat and he said, 'This is gourmet chili.' In his opinion— his daughter is married to that Murchison son, you know, so he is right up there in that category—I have the best chili in Dallas. He says the Brook Hollow Country Club here has second best, and the Dallas Petroleum Club's chili comes in third. His own son-in-law has something to do with chili and the Dallas Cowboys, and this man rates that Cowboy chili *fifth.*"

Jimmy starts off his famous concoction with a fairly mild (for Texas) chili, and lets his customers arrive at the degree of hotness they prefer by using one of his *salsas.* There is a dry one and a wet one made with cider vinegar.

"If they want to really burn up," he says, "I have a straight red pepper here that they can use to make it as hot as they like."

The Shanghai Jimmy menu follows the Cincinnati system of numbering the various levels of complexity offered, all based on the famous chili and rice combination, which is called the Number One. The mixtures build—with added ingredients and quantities—up to Number Eleven, which is the Special Chili Rice, a sixteen-ounce tub of "beautiful rice with two dips of chili, chopped celery, sharp grated cheese, sweet relish, finely chopped onion, and a package of oyster crackers . . . mix real well for that special taste." As might be expected, Jimmy clams up when pressed to reveal more about what makes his chili rice so deliciously good.

Tom Erwin, of Houston, and previously Dallas, has been following Jimmy around Dallas ever since he opened on Greenville Avenue in

1953. Erwin thinks that he has Jimmy's chili rice secret unraveled enough to save him a fortune in airplane fare between wherever he is at the moment and Dallas (page 121).

The Big C in Big D

Frank Tolbert's Texas Chili Parlor and Museum of Chili Culture, on Main Street in downtown Dallas, opened in 1976 with the proprietor smelling loudly of the garlic he had personally chopped for the seventy-five pounds of chili prepared for the grand opening. The place gained instant acceptance, not only with Dallas chili lovers, but with itinerants of the chili world, who would no more think of passing through Big D without a visit to Tolbert's than they would of allowing their home freezers to run out of chili. Now there is a second Tolbert's on Cedar Springs, officially called Tolbert's Chili Parlor and Saloon.

Cafeterias can be good sources of inexpensive chili, and the popular Highland Park Cafeteria in Dallas is a good example. Described by restaurant reviewers and food critics as one of the best moderately priced places to eat in Dallas, it is also said to be a favorite of famed pianist Van Cliburn. The line stretching from the front doors down Cole Avenue is said to get so long that veteran customers bring lawn chairs to ease the waiting.

Highland Park's president, Edmund Yates, says that as far as he knows, chili has been served since the place opened in 1925. "About the only point I can make about [our] chili is that we use toasted cumin seed in the recipe. We find, like most good chili cooks, that this adds a definite flavor."

Dallas also had Lang's, an enduring chili legend. Actually there were two Lang's, each run by one of the Lang brothers, Henry and George. The cooks at each made a chili that was just a little different from the other—nothing new in the world of stubborn One-and-Only chili cooks. According to Frank Tolbert, the main difference is that one chili was made with cubed meat, and the other with ground.

In the cubed meat recipe, attributed to a Lang's cook named Will Clark, whole cumin seed is parched in the oven and then crushed. Clark used no water in his chili, only the liquid exuded from the braising meat. He poured off this liquid as it accumulated and then returned it to the pot as needed during the slow cooking.

In the 1950s, Dallas newspaperman B. C. Jefferson recalled to

Joe Cooper that when a customer gave his order, the waiter yelled back to the cook to dish up "one straight," or "one medium," which meant with beans. "In a bowl" meant a larger helping, which cost 25 cents instead of 15 cents.

Texas author Sam Huddleston wrote that there probably was no place in the Western Hemisphere with better chili than Lang's. "You didn't eat Lang's chili," he said, "you experienced it." Huddleston composed his own chili recipe (page 114) based not so much on Lang's chili of record, but Lang's chili of cherished memory. As Huddleston put it, "I know of only three men in the world who know how to make a decent bowl of red: H. Allen Smith and Wick Fowler. The third gentleman I have reference to is me. When you're a genius, it is hard to be modest."

Shortly after the end of World War II and food rationing, which caused the demise of many beloved chili emporiums, a returning veteran, Major Robert Sprinkle Pool, opened a chili parlor on Commerce Street in Dallas, just across from the original Neiman-Marcus. Pool's chili filled the vacuum that had been left by the departure of Lang's, and his emporium became a gathering place for notable professional Texans of the time—not the least of whom was Pool himself. It was at Pool's, over bowls of his special chili, that visiting journalists were advised on Texas attitudes, and the disaster of the Alamo and the victory at San Jacinto were rehashed again and again.

Pool's preoccupation with Texas eventually led to the closing of his chili parlor. First he took off on what he described as a circumnavigation of Texas with author Mary Lasswell, to research the book *I'll Take Texas*. Later, he moved to Austin to continue his serious study of Texas history.

The first "new generation" chili place to open in Dallas (in 1957) was Larry Lavine's Chili's Restaurant, housed in an ex-stagecoach depot on Greenville Avenue. Lavine serves beans in his chili, but also offers it straight—at the same price. Now, there is another Chili's in Dallas; and there are two in Houston, one in Denver, and one in Cupertino (near San Jose) in California. Other chili parlors in the new style include the Texas Chili Parlor in Austin, Texas, and the Chili Factory in Santa Barbara, California.

El Paso is far more oriented to Mexican and New Mexican style *carne en chile colorado o verde* than it is to true chili, although excellent chili may be had there at the long-established business lunchtime haunt, Sol's, in the downtown financial district, or at Smitty's, out near the airport. Smitty's is so famous for its barbecue that people just don't get around to trying the chili. They should.

A Coney Island Is Not in Brooklyn

In 1926, when Tom and James Papadakis opened the original James Coney Island (James won the coin toss) on Walker Street in Houston, a hot dog was a nickel.

Now, at the six Jameses around Houston, the price is 40 cents, but the quality is still a closely supervised family affair. The two sons of Tom and Helen Papadakis run the business, but Helen can still tell just by looking if the chili is up to James standards. Since the same man has been cooking it for almost forty years, it almost always is. James chili, as might be expected, is made by a family-held One-and-Only recipe. Many Houston chili lovers claim that James chili— the special variety made for selling by the bowl and in pints and quarts and in pound-size frozen bricks to go—is the best not only in Houston but in the world.

The Papadakises say a man once had some James chili analyzed by a chemist in an unsuccessful attempt to learn its secrets, even though the ingredients of James Brick Chili are right on the label for everyone to see, in order of the volume of their use as the government directs: "beef, beef fat, tomato, cracker meal, spices and salt."

Oklahoma's Johnny Chiliseed

Baxter Poff might be called the Johnny Appleseed of chili joints— or better yet, Johnny Chiliseed, for he founded chili establishments in Texas, Oklahoma, Kansas, and Colorado. It is the Oklahoma City Baxter's on N.W. Second Street, however, that lives on in the memories of chili connoisseurs.

It was Baxter's brother, Henry, who cooked the chili at the Oklahoma City parlor, and it is Henry, now retired in Fulton, Kentucky, who supplies the record of the Poff chili odyssey.

Today, Henry Poff is content with the knowledge that Baxter's lives in the hearts of thousands of chili lovers. "I had every Oklahoma governor from 1917 to 1956," he remembers. "They would come in and sit at the table with a working man. Will Rogers and Wiley

Post ate my chili. And for the newsboys, we had what we called a bowl and a dash, a bowl of beans or vegetable soup with a dash of chili. It was just five cents." Three generations of many families in Oklahoma City have been Baxter's fans.

Age has forced Henry Poff to give up his chili supply business, but he has generously shared not only the original Baxter's chili recipe (page 124) but the formula for Baxter's Chili Mix (page 124).

They All Like Ike's

It has been reported that Dallas chili sage E. DeGolyer preferred the chili at Ike's in Tulsa to any then available in Texas. Ike Johnson came to Oklahoma from Virginia, by way of Texas, where he presumably learned to make chili. Like DeGolyer, Ike was an oil man first and a superior chili-maker second. When he started making his chili in Tulsa during its boom town days, Ike found himself feeding every hungry oilman in town for free. In self-defense, he opened a joint near the Frisco depot. Having to pay for Ike Johnson's chili didn't discourage anyone in Tulsa. They lined up for the privilege, and Ike's was off to more than seventy years of chili-making history.

Johnson soon moved some relatives up from the family place in Honey Grove, Texas, and showed them how to make chili by his One-and-Only recipe. He went back to the oil business, where he did well for the rest of his life. His lasting fame, however, comes from the chili that is now served at the chain of Ike's Chili Parlors in Tulsa. Will Rogers is on record as favoring Ike's chili, and was a frequent customer. In fact, Rogers had a bowl of Ike's chili the night before he left to join Wiley Post on their ill-fated flight to Alaska. The ever-gentle Rogers would never have hurt a chili cook's feelings by saying he preferred another's chili, so he was inclined to say that he favored whatever chili he was eating at the time. According to Dr. Reba Collins, director of the Will Rogers Memorial in Claremore, Oklahoma, Rogers ended up having more "favorite" chili joints than George Washington had beds.

In the old tradition of classic chili joints, Ike's provides its customers with additional chili powder, green peppers, and vinegar, and bowls of small, dry, red chilipiquíns (called petine peppers at Ike's). Tough-mouthed customers can crush these according to taste over their individual bowls of chili. One of the traditional pastimes of both old-timers and Ike's staff is watching the dudes come in and mistake the bowls of chilipiquíns for redskin peanuts, then pop a handful into their mouths.

In 1959, the Ike's that had been located on West Third Street for over thirty years was replaced by a Piccadilly cafeteria. This was not the total loss to the chili world that it may have seemed at the time, since the two Piccadilly's now operating in Tulsa serve chili, usually on Wednesday nights. Johnson's fans will be happy to know there are three Ike's still operating in Tulsa.

A Tommy's Is a Chiliburger

At Tommy's, the Los Angeles all-night drive-in at Beverly and Rampart that has grown into a chain, chiliburgers are not on the menu. A Tommy's *is* a chiliburger—a unique meld of beef-chili-tomato-mustard-onion-and-pickle flavors. Those who have tried to re-create a Tommy's at home discover that the big secret of its flavor is the marvelously thick red-ripe tomato slice, laid next to the meat patty before the final dip of chili. The luscious ripeness, size, and thickness of the tomato slice at Tommy's seldom vary, in season and out, high prices or low. A Tommy's is added evidence that Wick Fowler was right in his stubborn insistence that tomato brings out the flavor of chili.

Californians travel the state to get to Tommy's. Through the day and night Cadillacs, Jaguars, and BMW's, as well as low-riding Chevvies and vans, back up in a parking lot occupied by a tiny hut just big enough to house a three-person team of cook, helper, and cashier, and the raw materials. The inside space is so small that soft drink coolers are outside; customers serve themselves, and pay on the honor system.

The traffic and people-watching go on twenty-four hours a day. Crowds were getting so big a few years ago that an annex kitchen and another parking lot had to be added. Both were shunned by the Tommy's regulars, who considered the additions a Siberia (restaurant lingo for the worst seating in the house). They preferred to circle the block waiting for space in the old lot, and line up at the original kitchen, no matter how long the wait there—or how short it was over at the new kitchen, just yards away.

Tommy's next move was to establish branch locations in suburban areas, like the San Fernando Valley. These also do business on a twenty-four-hour basis, but the plan failed as a device for slowing the crowds at the original stand.

Windy City Chili

Bishop's at 18th and Damen is the old-time chili joint of record in Chicago. The first Bishop's was opened in 1930, at 17th and Damen, by Mary (Grandma) Bishop and her son-in-law George Koritze. Mrs. Bishop had quit a chili parlor called Oly's when they asked her to stop making the chili her way and stick to theirs.

Son-in-law Joe Janouch came into the business in 1949, and opened a branch Bishop's in Forest Park in 1960. Another son-in-law, Jerry Klug, opened his own branch in Westmont in 1972. With the passing of Grandma Bishop, and then Klug, Janouch took over the supervision of all three places, which today are individually managed by the great-grandchildren of Mary Bishop, whose recipe is still the foundation of the success of Bishop's. Janouch personally blends the spices and superintends the cooking of the nearly 500 gallons of chili made each week for the three parlors.

Bishop's chili is served with either small pinto beans, pasta, or tamales, or over Thuringer sausage or frankfurters in buns. Janouch himself eats a bowl a day, usually spiced up with his own special hot sauce, or a squirt from a bottle of hot peppers steeped in vinegar. Both are available at all Bishop's, for the optional use of the customers. Filbert's root beer is the old-time Bishop's standby, but Janouch says that the Chicago and Westmont parlors also serve liquor with their chili.

After fifty years of popularity, the success of Grandma Bishop's recipe is incontestably clear. Oly's would have been better advised to have left Mary Bishop alone in their kitchen to create chili as the spirit moved her. Janouch describes Mary Bishop's chili as "Texas style," made with no tomatoes, and including thyme.

St. Louis Slinger

The popularity of chili in Illinois may have influenced the serving of chili aboard Illinois Terminal railroad dining cars, and this, in turn, may have something to do with St. Louis—the end of the line—

being a big chili town. Or it could be that the chili recipe hustler who sold his secrets to Charles O. Taylor of Carlinville scored again at the St. Louis Fair of 1904. It so happens that Otis Truman Hodge opened St. Louis's oldest surviving chili parlor the year of the Fair, on Pine Street, where it is today. The Hodge Chili Company of St. Louis, once connected with Hodge's chili parlor, has now been split away by marriage and new ownership. The canning operation began in 1905, which may make it an even earlier commercial effort than Gebhardt's.

As befits its age, Hodge's follows the old-time tradition of twenty-four-hour chili joints. Tile walls and floors, designed for quick maintenance right through the days and nights of continuous operation, so common in that earlier day, now make Hodge's and others like it unique, even though few still operate around the clock.

Frances Dolan Holloran has eaten chili all her life in St. Louis and remembers Hodge's as the place everybody went on a date or after a dance. Sitting in her formal dress with a wilted gardenia on her shoulder, eating Hodge's chili, which sold for a dime or 15 cents a bowl, is the picture that comes to her mind. Holloran also remembers that in St. Louis, it was the custom after funerals to go to the home of the deceased, where chili was served in cold weather; a bowl of warmth and consolation on a cold, sad day.

Hodge's chili is still made by the original recipe, which anti-tomato chili lovers will be happy to know contains no tomatoes. However, Hodge's chili, like many midwestern chilis, also has no garlic, an ingredient considered ungenteel by many Americans until the prejudice against it abated in the 1940s. Hodge's chili-mac is still the favorite midwestern way of making chili go further. A Hodge's customer who wanted to splurge could try the parlor's famous "Mac a la Mode," a chili-mac topped with a couple of fried eggs.

Even more popular at Hodge's nowadays, according to John Eirten, the present operator and a distant relation to Otis Hodge, is the Slinger, two cheese-topped hamburger patties, side by side in the center of an oval platter, flanked by a fried egg on one end and American fries on the other, the whole covered with a steaming mantle of Hodge's chili. The Super Slinger tops all of this with a tamale. Eirten says that an anonymous customer came up with this combination a few years ago, a circumstance that has changed the menu—and made chili history—at chili establishments around the country.

Many of Hodge's lunch regulars come from the nearby Switzer Candy Company, which has been in the neighborhood for nearly a century. They surprised Eirten one day by bringing him a recipe for a licorice-flavored chili.

Green Bay Super Bowl Chili

It could be a chili-world joke: "How well does a Lithuanian coal miner make chili?" In the case of "Chili John" Isaac, the answer is: well enough to keep people coming back to the Green Bay, Wisconsin, chili joint he founded almost seventy years ago. John Isaac was born in Lithuania in 1874 and his family emigrated to the Pennsylvania coal-mine area when he was four. His father worked as a miner and at nine, John was also working in the mines. During his young manhood, he moved west to the Springfield-Carlinville, Illinois, area and discovered chili.

When Isaac opened a saloon in Auburn, about halfway between Springfield and Carlinville, he offered a free chili lunch as a come-on. Over the years, he tinkered with the chili until he perfected his One-and-Only chili recipe. Customers told Isaac that he should forget the booze part of his business and just sell chili. When Auburn voted itself dry, around 1912, he did just that, but not in Illinois. He moved to Green Bay, Wisconsin, borrowed 40 dollars, and went into business near the Main Street bridge, calling his place Chili John's.

Chili John's, now the oldest restaurant in Green Bay, has been a local institution ever since. Today Harry Hoehne, Isaac's son-in-law, heads the establishment.

In Green Bay, John Isaac is credited with inventing the so-called oyster cracker. At Isaac's suggestion, a biscuit company began making the smaller crackers, which Isaac wanted because they were easier to keep on a spoonful of chili. (Why they aren't called chili crackers remains a mystery.)

Today, Chili John's offers chili, in rising degrees of strength—mild, medium, hot, and extra hot—served straight, with beans or spaghetti.

"When we say mild, medium, hot, or extra hot," explains Hoehne, "we simply mean putting more of the meat sauce in the bowl. We do not have different degrees of meat sauce, and we do not use tomatoes in cooking it, which, by the way, takes about five or six hours a batch. It's a slow, continuous cooking process, with myself doing all the cooking, and my wife, Dorothy, helping me on occasion. She made the chili all by herself in the past, but no longer does a solo."

It seemed only proper in Green Bay, which might be called the ultimate football town, that Hoehne decided to call his dish the Super Bowl. Oddly, it is not a Green Bay Packer but a former Minnesota Viking—Fran Tarkenton—who sings the praises of Chili John's the loudest in the pro football leagues. Tarkenton made it a tradition to eat a bowl of "extra hot" the night before every Viking-Packer game in Green Bay for fourteen years.

After thirty-one years at its location on Pine Street, the whole Chili John's operation was moved out of downtown to a branch on the West Side in 1978. The Pine Street Chili John's was just down the street from the hotel where visiting teams stayed when in Green Bay to play the Packers. So when the Vikings came to town in 1978, for the first time Tarkenton had to travel out to the West Side for his bowl of "extra hot" the night before the game. He went first-class in a rented limousine, and ended up paying the tab for everyone in the place.

Tarkenton's faith in John Isaac's chili was not invalidated; the Vikes managed a tie with the Pack the next day.

It has been a sad time for Hoehne, having to close the venerable Pine Street John's. "Many of our old-time customers in the downtown area—police officers, businessmen, secretaries—won't have time on their lunch hours to drive to the West Side for a bowl," he lamented.

It might take some of these downtown Green Bay chili lovers a vacation trip to California to get to a Chili John's again. The Burbank branch, now an independent operation, was founded by John Isaac's son Ernie about thirty years ago, and is operated today by Mickey Lamere, a relative by marriage. The chili is based on a recipe Ernie Isaac brought with him to California. The Burbank Chili John's menu features chili with beans and/or spaghetti, hamburgers, chili burgers, and a "chili sandwich." Like Hoehne in Wisconsin, Lamere turns out his chili himself. One batch uses 400 pounds of lean beef round, simmered for twenty-four hours. It is then stored in the walk-in refrigerator until it is needed.

Lamere uses the lean meat in a slow simmering process that produces a dark brown, almost grease-free chili. In Lamere's opinion, it is too rich to be properly savored straight, and for this reason, it is impossible to buy a bowl of straight chili at the Burbank Chili John's.

The principal diluting agent is the traditional bean. Lamere says he uses over three tons of fancy California pinks a year. Because of the house policy of serving no straight chili, those who prefer it beanless must buy chili to go, and feed their prejudices elsewhere.

There are valid reasons for having chili "in" at Chili John's. All the trappings that mark a superior chili house are within easy reach at the tables and along the horseshoe counter—bright red bottles of Tabasco sauce, bowls of John Isaac's "chili crackers," pickled yellow chiles, and fresh-chopped onions. And, the chili is very good.

Naturally, Chili John's recipe is unavailable from either Harry Hoehne or Mickey Lamere, but a recipe (page 137), over forty years old, for a chili meat sauce comes close, in that it may be too rich and pungent for some to eat straight.

The Alaskan Chililine

In downtown Anchorage in 1946 a place called the Chili Bowl was apparently a front for quite another operation. "One uninformed visitor walked into the Chili Bowl one morning," recalls retired airline pilot Bob Stevens, "slumped into a stool at the counter and called loudly for a bowl of chili." The sleepy-eyed madam finally appeared, looked at him coldly, and announced, "We ain't got no chili right now, but if we did it'd be twenty dollars."

Southwesterners who began to trickle to Alaska after World War II grew in numbers after Alaska was made a state, and began to flood in when work started on the pipeline. They brought with them the know-how for making a special chili that has earned them the lasting gratitude of Alaskan families. Southwesterners, accustomed to making chili with the deer they added to their family larders each year, adapted their chili easily to the meat on the hoof in Alaska— the moose. Hard put to find new ways to cook yet another moose steak, roast, stew, or mooseburger, Alaskan families quickly added the deliciously spicy, tenderizing, chili-making methods of the southwesterners to their own ways with this meat.

Frances Autry Jones and her husband Bill, known as B.J., moved to Alaska from El Paso in the 1960s. B.J. now works for Atlantic Richfield in Cook Inlet and they live in Kenai, where B.J. cooks the family chili (page 172). About moose, Fran Jones writes: "One winter we ate moosemeat continually, since B.J. had killed a big one that year and we were determined to learn to enjoy the stuff. The kids complained bitterly at first, but finally learned to eat moose steaks, roasts, tacos, and chili. Moosemeat is very healthful, but there's a certain wild smell when it cooks. I had to air out the house after cooking it, and that's hard to do in sub-zero weather."

The influx in recent years of oilmen, most of them chili lovers, has accelerated the spread of chili's popularity into the most remote areas of the state. "Chili is a sellout along the pipeline," says Beverly Ward, media representative for Alyeska, the Alaska pipeline company. "Everyone seems to have an opinion about its preparation—both customers and cooks."

Deadhorse, on Prudhoe Bay at the northern terminus of the line, is above 70 degrees north latitude, about as far north as Alaska goes. The Arctic Circle is 200 miles *south*. Dean Phillips, operations manager in Anchorage for Universal Services, the food service corporation at Prudhoe Bay, calls Rellis "Red" Skinner, who cooks at Deadhorse, the world's northernmost chili cook. Red grew up around a bubbling pot of chili. In 1941, he and his mother moved from North Dakota to Anacortes, Washington, north of Seattle. There Mrs. Skinner bought a place called the Chili Bowl from a man whose business it was, says Skinner, "to get a little empty store, set up a Chili Bowl, and then sell the place and the recipe and move on. His theory was that no one would do it right, anyhow, and just like the man said, my mother didn't follow the recipe."

"It was the standard chili for those parts," Skinner remembers, "with tomatoes, not a Texas recipe. I spent four years down there in San Antonio, and I know that a Texas chili can have goat, or skunk, or maybe snake in it, but it doesn't have tomatoes." Before he worked in the pipeline kitchens, Skinner cooked on fishing boats out of Kodiak and in the Bering Sea. He cooked chili aboard, but deprecates it, as "mostly made with hamburger."

For the pipeliners, Skinner cooks a good standard chili, sometimes using leftover roast beef, which he likes as a base for chili. "It comes apart in cooking into strings, and that's excellent chili," he says. In Alaska, pipeliner chili usually comes with beans, because the men want it that way, Skinner says. He speculates that they crave the extra starch because of the cold, just like they crave extra fat. "Any kitchen worth its salt up here has beans—and rice. Many of these men are Louisianans, and they eat more rice in Louisiana than the

41

Chinese do. We have nine holes on the steam table, and almost every meal, one of 'em has rice, and another has beans."

Skinner makes a special chili in a way he learned from an Athabascan—one of the far north Indian tribes—named Frank Sam. It was made with caribou, which Sam had to supply, since North Slope pipeliners, says Skinner, are not allowed to have guns or hunt. The late Frank Sam worked for Skinner as second cook for five or six months, on Foggy Island, in the Beaufort Sea. Sam told him, says Skinner, that he was a paratrooper during World War II, but he never did tell him where he learned to make chili (page 170).

Down East Chili

"I ate my first bowl of 'Texas chili' one cold night in the early 1940s in a small cafe adjoining the bus station in Gainesville, Texas," remembers Frank Hunter, who grew up in Maine. "It was love at first bite." Like many of his generation, Hunter was transplanted by World War II from his home in Maine to Texas, where he trained with the 86th Infantry at Camp Howze, near Gainesville, and spent his weekend passes in Dallas, where he devoured the chili he began to crave regularly.

After the war, Hunter returned to Maine, but he missed Texas and especially chili. So he tried his hand at putting together a batch at home in Brunswick. Like most American towns, Brunswick had its Italian and Greek neighborhoods, so Hunter remembers that "the garlic and *comino* were easy to find, but chile peppers in Maine were about as unheard of as clam chowder in Texas. I had to get a friend in Texas to send me some before I could get down to making chili."

Fortunately, Hunter's Texas friend was a considerate type who sent large, dry, blackish-red—and mild—chiles of the ancho variety. Hunter's first pot of chili therefore got high marks from himself and his Maine friends. Hunter, it developed, had a natural talent for cooking chili, as his "original" recipe demonstrates (page 121). It is one any Texan would be proud to have concocted on the first try or even the last. With Frank Hunter's help Brunswick, Maine, has become known in the Northeast as a chili town of some note. Hunter couldn't stay away from Texas—he lives there now.

In *Alice, Let's Eat*, Calvin Trillin reports on having been directed to "a diner just outside Brunswick that served chili spicy enough to charbroil the tongue." Trillin had two servings, which helped him counteract the effects of some health food he had been fed at a local fair.

Another who has made the pilgrimage to Brunswick is John Withee, of Lynnfield, Massachusetts, who admires the chili at the Miss Brunswick Diner. "It's a hotbed of chili down there!" Withee reports. There are at least a couple of places in Brunswick with "large signs offering chili dogs and 'chili bowl.'" But Ed Buckley, who operates the Miss Brunswick Diner, and makes its famous chili, told Withee when they met that he doesn't need a sign. "Everyone knows about my chili," he said, a powerful indication that Withee was in the presence of a confirmed One-and-Only chili-maker.

The Miss Brunswick Diner is "a small twenty-seat wood shack of a building—not a genuine railroad diner," says Withee, "about three blocks from the campus of Bowdoin College," probably the mainstay of its popularity. Withee describes Buckley as "about fifty-five, not outgoing, but with some tough humor." Buckley told Withee that he had acquired the Miss Brunswick after thirty years as a navy cook.

According to Withee, Buckley uses "hot, dry, green peppers, three or four inches long, which come from Florida in fifty-pound bags. His tomatoes are Brunswick grown, small, round, larger than cherry tomatoes, about an inch to an inch-and-a-half." Buckley marinates the peppers and tomatoes in cider vinegar for at least three months, Withee said, and then grinds that mixture for his chili. After simmering the tomato mixture with twenty pounds of braised ground beef, one pound of celery salt, one pound of garlic salt, and four pounds of chili powder, Buckley lets the chili simmer before adding ten six-pound cans of Maine shell beans. Withee said the shell bean is a fixture in Maine and Buckley would use no other. Withee should know about beans, being one of the world's experts on the subject (see Chapter 7).

A Fast Chili Gazetteer

With franchising, the chili business has come a long way from the one-man operations like the one "Uncle T" Emmons operated once upon a time in Baird, Texas, or the Squeeze-In ("Home of Good Chili") of Aurora, Missouri, where there is barely room for one cook and a hungry customer. It is the privilege of the old-timers, however, to believe that the best chili joints are those of memory.

There are many sources of reasonably good chili for the fan smitten with chili pangs on the road in unfamiliar territory. One franchise chain, Wendy's, offers a drive-in operation. The other, Bob's Big Boy, is in the family restaurant category. Of the two, Bob's has the best chili, served straight, with beans or spaghetti. Wendy's chili (with beans) can be made delicious with one or two of their "flavor packs," available on request. These contain added hotness and a good dose of cumin flavor in liquid form. At Bob's, call for the Tabasco, and some chopped onion. Bob "Yeller Dog" Marsh, who already has a chili mix on the market, has opened his flagship Yeller Dog's chili parlor in Leon Springs, Texas. He has also announced plans to develop a chain of franchises across the country.

In Atlanta, Georgia, there is the fifty-year-old fast-food institution called the Varsity that serves an estimated 15,000 daily customers who crowd into what the founder and owner Frank Gordy calls "the world's largest drive-in restaurant." Among other things, these 15,000 hungry fast-food devotees consume up to 25,000 hot dogs and 18,000 hamburgers a day, many if not most of them slathered with Gordy's no-beans chili. Jimmy Carter has been a Varsity fan since his days as a Georgia Tech student, and comedian Nipsey Russell worked as a carhop at the Varsity for five years. Nowadays, it takes up to 200 employees to keep things flowing during peak rush hours, like weekday lunchtime periods, or on weekends after football games.

In Kansas City, the Dixon's chain serves a mild, dry chili that can almost be eaten with a fork. President Harry Truman was known to amble in there for a bowl and a beer. (The beer had to be brought in from down the street.)

In Los Angeles, the Hamburger Hamlets serve a modern-day fast-food chili as does Buffalo Chips, in Santa Monica. At Philippe's, across from what is now the Amtrak depot on North Alameda in Los Angeles, the house specialty is the original (they say) French dip sandwich—a sandwich of sliced roast beef on a long French roll, with the top of the roll dipped lightly in au jus. This can be paired with a bowl of fair straight chili, plus a few pickled "eating" chiles, and a long neck beer, to make it seem almost like Texas. Although a barbecue pit would do Philippe's meat a world of good, the mustard is hot enough to scald the larynx of a champion chili eater. Philippe's mustard is the West Coast equivalent of the chilipiquín "peanuts" of Oklahoma chili parlors. Pots of it sit innocently on every table, waiting for the unsuspecting to slosh it on their sandwiches as they do at home. When this happens, the first bite has been rather neatly described as "purifying."

Barney's Beanery, which has been in West Hollywood for sixty years, serves what has been described as "L.A.'s second best chili." Also part of the chili legend in Los Angeles are Pink's on North LaBrea and Art's on Florence near Normandie.

A San Francisco chili place worth mentioning is the Roosevelt Tamale Parlor on 24th Street. Farther north, in Sonoma County, photographer-editor Mark Kauffman gives chili star billing on the menu in his Firehouse Cantina restaurants.

In Arizona, the downtown Phoenix Hyatt Regency Hotel is said to have good chili. Joe Jordan's, on North Central for over thirty years, and also on North Seventh, is recommended for red and green Sonora-style chili. In Tucson, there is Pat's on Grande Avenue, as well as the Grande Tortilla Factory, a takeout place worth visiting for Sonora chili.

Chili has always been a takeout food, by the way. The late Clarence Moon, of San Angelo, Texas, remembers an afternoon in 1901 when his family arrived in Texas with a cow and two wagons of possessions. The first thing his mother did was give Clarence a bucket and half a dollar and send him to Dave Mayo's Chili Parlor for a gallon of chili for supper.

"It was the first chili I ever heard of and ate," he says. "Naturally, I thought it was wonderful."

CHAPTER 5

When Chili Was Cheap: Food for Hard Times

New York newspaperman Ed Wallace claimed that the 5-cent bowl of chili "saved more lives in the Great Depression than the Red Cross."

Newspaper people should know. Like actors, entertainers, professional athletes, and other traveling people, they were usually underpaid, worked long and odd hours, and, as a result, were always hungry.

In those days, there was always an all-night chili joint down the block from the newsroom, stage door, or travelers' hotel, its lights shining brightly in the late hours, offering warm haven and a bowl of steaming chili after work on a cold night. The popular syndicated columnist of the day Westbrook Pegler was convinced that the best chili joints were near railroad stations, or depots as they were called then.

All the Crackers You Can Eat

Besides buying light and warmth, the price of a bowl of chili usually carried with it the right to all the free crackers it took to fill in the empty corners of the stomach. As times got worse and money got scarcer, the ratio of beans to chili grew steadily higher in chili pots both at home and in the chili joints. Straight chili lovers yearned for good times, when they could march into a chili parlor again and order a bowl "straight," and to hell with the cost, which could be as much as 25 cents.

Ptomaine Tommy's and the Chili Size

The problem confronted by a nameless but relatively affluent customer at Ptomaine Tommy's, a long-gone beanery on North Broadway in Los Angeles, was how to get some solid meat taste into his chili beans. In solving it, he created—in a left-handed way—the chili size. It was another of those inspired flashes that make chili history and forever enshrine the establishments where they occur—even if they have names like Ptomaine Tommy's. The late Fred Beck, who made famous the Farmer's Market, the Los Angeles fun park for food lovers, tried to document the tricky way this customer's solution to his dilemma came to be called a chili size. "When I arrived in Los Angeles in 1926," Beck recalled, "Ptomaine Tommy's was going good. I do not believe it was particularly a hangout for celebrities, but in those 'roaring twenties' slumming was a common late-night diversion and a few idiot types who thought they were right out of F. Scott used to show up there in tuxedos."

Perhaps it was one of these who prevailed on Tommy to cook a hamburger patty, and put a ladle of chili beans atop it. At Tommy's, this was afterward called, with more optimism than truth, chili con carne, but it caught on anyway.

Beck remembered that the ladle used to top off the meat patty with beans was a small one. A plain bowl of beans, on the other hand, was dished out with a larger ladle.

"Maybe a guy has only ten cents," said Beck, "so he asks for 'chili beans chili con carne size' and gets a small ladle of beans. Pretty soon, the regular hard-up customers—and panhandlers are usually taciturn—just climbed on a stool and grunted the word 'size.'" When Tommy chalked up on his blackboard menu the words CHILI SIZE 10¢, a new term entered the language. As happens, chili size has come to mean a beef patty smothered with chili. Almost no one—except people who hang on to such things, like Fred Beck—remembers that originally chili size referred not to beef, or chili, but the ladle used to dish up a down-and-outer's small order of beans.

Nowadays, when made with rich, straight chili, and a patty of good quality beef, broiled rare—as they do it at the Night Hawk restaurants in Austin, Texas—the chili size is the ultimate American short-order dish—meat on meat.

In the Army It's Still Free

A Pentagon survey of American soldier food preferences disclosed that chili ranked ninety-second in a field of 370 food items, barely making the top 25 percent. Another study revealed soldiers of the new army have been so thoroughly indoctrinated by "convenience" and fast-food styles of eating that they find it hard to relate to food—however appetizing—just sitting there naked on a plate or in a bowl. Apparently, food that isn't individually packaged, or doesn't come out of a machine at the touch of a button (and presumably *tastes* like it does), has a high rate of rejection among today's GI's. The army is working on this. At Fort Lee, Virginia, the army has created the Culinary Skills Division, to upgrade the quality of army cooking. As a result, army cooks have been walking off with top honors at cook-offs like the National Culinary Salon and Competition, held during the National Restaurant Association convention each year. But so far chili has not been added to the cooking events, and if it were, army cooks using the recipe currently specified in their GI recipe manuals would be in trouble in a match-up with skilled chili cooks.

The army's present chili recipe, designated in Pentagonese as TM 10–412 (page 102), lacks the force that would have set the moustaches of an old-time cavalry troop quivering. TM 10–412 and its forebears of recent times may have something to do with chili's drop in popularity with today's soldiers. Even in the military, chili cooks are chili cooks, and giving them a recipe, even an official one, would be like having given a paint-by-the-numbers canvas to Picasso.

Military service gave many of the men who fought in our wars, from the one with Mexico right on up to today, their first taste of chili. Such chili experiences undoubtedly contributed to the spreading popularity of the dish, not only in the United States, but in the areas overseas where war took GI cooks and chowlines.

A cook-off participant in California in 1977 said that when he was a pilot in China in World War II, his malaria was cured by the chili cooked by a buddy. In Vietnam, many GI's were lucky enough to encounter war correspondent Wick Fowler at his usual chore of cooking chili for as many people as he could, from what meat and pots he could forage. No doubt pods of the local chiles found their way into his 3- and 4-Alarm versions. He carried his own mix with him, of course.

CHAPTER 6

Chic Chili: Where the Elite Eat It

In Beverly Hills, chili costs upward of 10 dollars a bowl. This is because the chili Beverly Hills is noted for is dispensed at the famous Chasen's and the newer Rangoon Racquet Club. Old-time chili lovers might say that Chasen's has seen better days—days when ex-vaudeville performer Dave Chasen first opened an eight-stool diner at Beverly and Doheny, called the Southern Pit Barbecue. Then, the chili went for a quarter a bowl.

Even at the start, stars frequented Chasen's and dazzled the other customers. Chasen's is still famous for clients such as Jimmy Stewart, Henry Fonda, Jimmy Cagney, the late Spencer Tracy, W. C. Fields, Gene Fowler, Nunnally Johnson, Bing, Bogie—just to name a few. Harold Ross, the crusty westerner who created the *New Yorker*, was one of Chasen's original backers, along with a lot of show business people who had tasted Chasen's backstage cooking, and who put him into the restaurant business to assure themselves a good meal when they hit Hollywood.

The place is still as clubby as a star actor's boardinghouse. No credit cards are accepted (regulars are allowed to run tabs), and chili is still available, although it doesn't appear on the menu. The difference today is in the armies of well-heeled tourists who fight to get in— and pay the price—for the star-watching. Chasen's does a lot of high-level catering, and its famous chili usually goes along to charity, studio, and corporate events, where guests may include well-known chili lovers like Liz Taylor and Jack Nicholson. In the well-reported case of Liz Taylor, Chasen's has delivered chili by air to Rome and Puerto Vallarta.

It's all tacked on the bill, of course, but to a "regular" who gets a serious case of Chasen's chili pangs far from Beverly Hills, it's worth it.

Maude Chasen, who has taken over the operation of Chasen's since her husband's death, won't admit that the fairly consistent version of Chasen's chili which has been reported in newspapers and magazines for the past twenty years is true Chasen's chili.

The other Beverly Hills chili salon (joint or even parlor doesn't adequately describe these places) is the Rangoon Racquet Club, opened in 1975 on "little" Santa Monica Boulevard, in quarters formerly occupied by Au Petit Jean. C. V. Wood, Jr., one of the RRC's most visible backers, claims that his chili, which is the same served at the club, costs him around 10 dollars a quart to prepare at home. This makes the RRC's prices of 7 and 9 dollars a bowl for lunch and dinner, respectively, sound almost like a bargain. In 1976, Manny Zwaaf, the owner-host of the club, began cooking Wood-RRC chili at the Cannes film festival. "I had so many containers with powders that at the Nice Airport it took me twenty minutes to convince customs they were really mixings for chili," Zwaaf told Jody Jacobs of the *Los Angeles Times*. The chili proved such a success at Cannes that Zwaaf has gone back to make it since.

In 1979, Zwaaf also raised the flag for RRC chili on the Mexican west coast, when he delivered it to a movie company on location at Barra de Navidad, just north of Manzanillo.

Beverly Hills people go to Palm Springs to get away from it all, including high chili prices. Lovers of true chili, like Mary Martin, have discovered Sib's, an honest-to-goodness chili joint on East Palm Canyon Drive. Sib's is named for the former owner and present chili cook, Joe Marinko, of Czech ancestry, who comes from Swoyerville, Pennsylvania. "I didn't want to open another Joe's," says Marinko, "so I called the place Sib's, after my family nickname." Sib's chili has a respectable bite, and is made without salt. Marinko says that this omission serves to improve the flavor of his chili as it mellows with reheating. It is also good news to his customers on salt-free diets. (His prices help to keep the blood pressure down as well.) Star-watchers can forget Sib's; Palm Springs customers in this category usually send out for their chili, including one unknown chili lover who regularly dispatches his Rolls and chauffeur for large quantities of Sib's chili to go.

Los Angeles Times reporter Jody Jacobs, who has become the Boswell of this very social chili world, has noted society charity workers lunching on "chili and stem strawberries" in a Marina del Rey restaurant. At the Beverly Wilshire Hotel's "quiet hideaway . . . Don Hernando's," she reported Bernadette Peters "cooling off with hot chili . . . and chilled grape juice before taking off for London." On another occasion, Jacobs wrote that "Monte Kay, former manager of the Modern Jazz Quartet, hosted a chili party for the group, and some of their old friends, Sarah Vaughn, Carmen McRae, Diahann Carroll, Artie Shaw . . . and loads more."

In the San Diego suburb of La Jolla, the local chapter of the Wine and Food Society of London voted their chili supper to be the best affair of the year. A half-dozen members cooked their six versions of One-and-Only chili, which were tasted and judged by the membership and guests. An observer later commented, "There were more arguments over this than over many of the fine wines they have drunk in the past, and some of the also-rans refused to accept the decision."

Laid Back California Chili

The huge metropolitan area that is today's southern California is a world crossroads of foods, styles, products, fashions, and thought, particularly from around the Pacific basin. Southern California chili quite naturally reflects this. A fairly typical chili party would have some or all of the following displayed around the buffet chili pot along with the more traditional things: Tostaditos made of crisp, fried, quartered tortillas which are sometimes crumbled into the chili bowl like crackers; chopped super-mild (and super-expensive) Maui onions airlifted from Hawaii; chopped odorless Japanese garlic, peanuts, jalapeños, and cilantro; slices of avocado and ripe olive; lime quarters; tequila, sake, and Kahlua and honey; soy sauce, Mexican salsas, and bottled "chillie" sauces from Singapore and Penang; sour cream and one or more grated and shredded cheeses, such as Monterey jack, Tillamook Cheddar, or the "Italian goat cheese" Carroll Shelby reportedly uses.

Los Angeles magazine quotes another of the city's selected chili cooks, Bea Miller, as saying, "The fun of chili is making a personal statement with it." She starts off a pot of her Jazzy Snazzy Continental

Chili routinely enough, with a packaged mix like Shelby's or Wick Fowler's, but down the line she adds sliced mushrooms, canned green chiles, and black olives.

Mushrooms aside, the other added ingredients of Bea Miller's chili are descended from a California regional cuisine that goes back to Old California, and the missions and *asistencias* established by the Spanish padres. These missions, a hard day's ride apart, stretched north from San Diego—the first, established in 1769—to San Francisco Bay. In the mission gardens, along with garlic, spices, and chile, the padres planted grapes and olives. Wine and the olive are the foundations for California regional cooking, and still distinguish it from New Mexican and border cooking developed during the same period, just as the chile ties them all together.

Capitol Chili

Chili is served in the House cafeteria on Capitol Hill every March 2 in honor of Texas Independence Day. Its place in American history was also recognized during the 1976 Bicentennial celebration, when the Smithsonian Institution joined with the National Park Service to produce a summer-long Festival of American Folklife on the National Mall. As a part of these festivities, Stella Hughes, of Clifton, Arizona, who wrote the authoritative *Chuck Wagon Cookin'*, was invited to bring her Studebaker chuckwagon to the Mall for a week of cooking chili cow-country style, over hickory coals.

"The people lined up for hundreds of yards for a sample of chili and frijoles and about a quarter of a sourdough biscuit, touched with butter and prickly pear jelly," Mrs. Hughes reported. "The dudes kept asking why the chili did not have beans, and I kept telling them it was chili *con carne*, and not chili *con carne con frijoles*. The dudes also asked why I did not use hamburger. It's awfully hard to break popular habits fostered by fast food chains!" (See page 126.)

Texans have been bringing chili north to feed the have-nots in Washington for years. According to E. Aubrey Cox, the Wichita Falls chapter of the Texas Air Force Association began serving chili at annual AFA conventions in Washington in early 1970. The first year, Cox says, sixteen gallons of chili were dispensed in the Texas hospitality suite at the meeting; the next year, thirty-two gallons; and in 1976, one-hundred gallons of Texas chili, along with commensurate amounts of Fritos and Lone Star beer.

In 1977, Cox determined once and for all to satiate the throngs crowding the Texas suite in search of what Texans have always considered to be the Real Article. He reported in the *Goat Gap Gazette* that a three-stall carwash in Wichita Falls was taken over and set up as an assembly-line chili-making factory.

"Tables and chairs were set up and waiting for us to cut meat and onions, and measure ingredients," Cox continued. "Four cast iron pots were placed in the center stall for cooking and the third stall was arranged for placing the chili in gallon containers and then in cardboard boxes." The cooks—who included one retired and one active general, plus colonels and majors—arrived at seven in the morning, Cox says, and twelve hours later, "We had cooked up 615 pounds of lean beef and 100 pounds of onions, plus spices, into 110 gallons of Texas Red [and] the chili was placed in a huge freezer at a local McDonald's," to freeze it for the flight north.

After all this, Cox reported, the frozen chili got misrouted on its way from Dallas to Washington National Airport, and ended up lost at Dulles Airport outside Washington. By the time the chili finally was delivered to the Texas hotel suite, it had defrosted and the hotel management wouldn't allow it to be served.

"Our 900 dollars worth of chili was doomed," Cox told his *GGG* readers. But the Texans had promised to deliver chili to their Washington headquarters, and they were as good as their word.

They bought forty gallons of canned chili—with beans, the only kind available—at a local supermarket and doctored it up with "a basketful of ingredients with emphasis on cayenne pepper. I reasoned that if I couldn't make it taste like chili, I'd make it so hot they couldn't tell the difference," said Cox. The final blow may have been the hardest. Up in the Texas suite, the forty gallons of ersatz chili disappeared just as swiftly as the genuine article ever had.

"The damn Yankees and westerners apparently didn't know the difference," Cox fumed.

At the National Press Club in Washington, chili matters came to a head when Clyde LaMotte, a Texan and former president of the organization, noticed chili on the club menu one day. What it turned out to be, LaMotte said, was a "bowl of black-eyed peas with an ice-cream scoop of ground meat in the center." With laudable restraint LaMotte walked across the dining room to where Bob Baskin of the *Dallas Morning News* was sitting, to show him the evidence of what their club was calling chili. Naturally Baskin was as horrified as LaMotte, and a club chili society was the result, which made a cook-off inevitable.

A chili cook-off in Washington, D.C.— or anything else, for that matter—is never going to get very far away from politics and politicians. It was as easy as dropping a hint for LaMotte to get Senators Barry Goldwater of Arizona and John Tower of Texas good-humoredly throwing taunts at each other over the chili of their respective states. Once the ball got rolling, keeping other states out would have been impossible, even if anyone had wanted to. Robert Taft, then the senator from Ohio, aired his warm feelings about Cincinnati chili in the *Congressional Record.* Senator Pete Dominici of New Mexico also offered, in the *Record,* to mediate between Texas and Arizona from what he claimed to be New Mexico's superior and ancient position in the chili arts.

The 1974 National Press Club contest in Washington matched the winners of the elimination cook-offs at local press clubs around the country. The governor of the Tigua Indians, the El Paso press club entrant, demanded an iron pot and an open fire for cooking his concoction. It took an appeal over local radio to produce the pot, and on the day of the contest a fire was built for the governor in the club's ballroom fireplace. Iron pots in Washington went out with Andy Jackson and the Kitchen Cabinet, but the governor of the Tiguas didn't know this. He must have noticed, however, that the judges used an elegant atomizer of tequila as a palate cleanser between tastings. This should have offered a clue as to which way the chili winds blew. But despite all this, LaMotte said later, the Tiguan was furious when he didn't win, and departed in a huff, without divulging his recipe, as the contest rules required. "He wouldn't even tell the name of his chili," LaMotte says sadly.

Outgoing Democratic National Committee Chairman Robert Strauss threw a farewell chili party for the Washington press corps, before a short-lived return to "private life" in early 1977. His wife told *Washington Post* writer Jacqueline Prescott that their first chili party in Washington, four years earlier, was so small it was held in their one-bedroom apartment, and Strauss cooked the chili himself. Strauss's "farewell" chili party had well over one hundred guests, and was held in what Prescott described as "the plush rooms of a private Georgetown club, Pisces," with Strauss "advising" the club's chef on the preparation of the chili.

James Beard recommends a Georgetown place called the American Cafe, but not only for its chili. The American, Beard says, has everything from chili to tuna salad, which might put some chili people off, but probably won't. Chili lovers are drawn to an untried chili joint like moths to a flame. Also in Georgetown is Clyde's, which has served chili to actors, senators, and the White House staff for years.

Chili in the Big Apple

A legion of pessimistic New York chili lovers insist they are quoting from bitter experience when they say to forget chili in New York and learn to love Szechuan or Cuban food.

When pressed, New Yorkers mention the Lone Star Cafe on lower Fifth Avenue, or Anita's Chili Parlor, founded by Anita Carr Corey of Albuquerque, New Mexico. Anita's chili, as might be expected, has New Mexican overtones, and probably should be spelled with an "e." Famous for its meat and its ambience, P. J. Clarke's on Third Avenue has never gone to great lengths to publicize its chili, but Texans rate it highly.

Tad Adoue is one of those New York Texans who hold what might be called a dual citizenship, good in both places. On a recent trip to Texas, when Adoue ordered chili at a famous Dallas chili parlor, out of long Manhattan habit he automatically added "no beans," which every Texan learns to specify (usually in vain) when calling for chili away from Texas. The waiter, insulted, and taking him for a foreigner, snarled back, "If it had beans, mister, we'd call it stew."

Adoue has spread the word on chili among his many non-Texan friends in New York. One of these is the famous Bobby Short, who likes to describe himself as a "saloon singer and piano player."

Short loved the midwestern chili his mother made back in Danville. Since that time, Short has sampled the chili "as far afield as Paris and London," but, he says, it wasn't until Tad Adoue got the word to him in New York that he "discovered the wonderful world of the Texas stuff. When preparing it at home, I'm apt to want it done quickly, hence the Wick Fowler's mix. . . . I love every mouthful!"

Adoue has also tried to be of help to his chili-loving Texas friends traveling abroad. Mary Martin recalls Adoue's efforts the time she went visiting in Greece. She read up beforehand on the wonderful

Greek food she looked forward to having there. What she got, she says, was chili. Adoue had warned her Greek hosts to lay in a supply of Wick's mix and serve it often, if they expected to keep Mary from getting homesick for Texas chili.

A chili house of cherished memory which crops up in many stories of chili in New York was a place called El Rancho, on Seventh Avenue. It tickled Will Rogers that the proprietor was a Swede named Arvid Strom. As an Oklahoman, Rogers had trouble visualizing a Swede as a chili cook. He was right, because what Strom did when customers came in panting for a bowl of good old Texas chili was open up some cans of Gebhardt's. Columnist Westbrook Pegler often referred to El Rancho as "the Gebhardt Parlor."

During the 1950s, the Alamo Chile House on West 47th Street was a favorite lunchtime hangout for Texas-born staffers and their friends on the national weekly magazines. Established in 1929, the Alamo claimed on its menu to be "The Oldest Place in New York for Chile con Carne"—adding significantly, for those who may have had knowledge of El Rancho's failings in this department—"Made on the Premises."

The Alamo lost its lease and moved to West 44th Street, and then, sometime in the 1970s, faded into memory, like the *Life* and *Saturday Evening Post* hangovers treated there with Alamo chili and cold Mexican beer.

South of the Border

Mexico has long had a reputation as a place where it is impossible to find even a third-rate bowl of chili, but the situation is brightening. Texas chili fanciers flew deputations of chili cooks, like Wick Fowler, to Mexico City in the early 1960s to instruct the uninitiated at chili parties hosted by Mexico City's press club. In 1964, a chapter, or "pod," of the Chili Appreciation Society International (CASI) was formed there and by the mid-1970s cook-offs were being held not only in Mexico City, but in Guadalajara and Cuernavaca. Travel writer Horace Sutton has noted that a disco called Carlos Chili recently seemed to be the "in" place of the moment in Acapulco where "participants can gyrate in the main area and turn to an adjacent chili parlor for sustenance."

The Texans have done their work well, and chili relations are vastly improved over the days of the much-quoted Mexican definition of chili in the *Diccionario de Mejicanismos:* "detestable food passing itself off as Mexican, sold in the U.S."

Continental Chili

No matter where in the world they are, chili lovers are no longer afraid to ask, "Where can you get a good bowl of chili around here?"

Sandra A. Gustafson, of La Jolla, California, now Mrs. William Poole of Washington, D.C., spent 1978 and 1979 traveling in Europe, maintaining headquarters in Paris. She discovered a dozen flourishing chili dispensaries in Paris alone.

Gustafson's recommended chili spots range from Le Western at the Hilton Hotel on rue de Suffren ("ask for Chef Michael—he makes a big fuss over chili lovers"), to the place where Chef Michael goes after hours to eat chili, "a little nightclub in the Latin Quarter in St. Germain on rue des Cannettes. It is run by a Louisiana woman. Chili there is fiery hot!" Le Western's beef is imported weekly from the United States, M. Mastrouannopoulos, the *Directeur des Achats*, or food purchasing manager, for the Paris Hilton, told Gustafson; and its chili powder comes from Fauchon, the Tiffany of Parisian food stores. This means that it is probably Gebhardt's, the Texas-made world standby in this department, although M. Mastrouanno-poulos declined to specify the brand. Connoisseurs of cowboy food will be interested to know that Le Western has on occasion featured son-of-a-bitch stew, identified on its menu as *le bourguignon du Texas.*

Gustafson's own favorite Parisian chili joint is Mother Earth's at 66 rue des Lombards, "a tiny hole-in-the-wall, located in a dingy part of Paris, frequented by young models, photographers, Catherine Deneuve and Marcello Mastroianni. The chili is spicy . . . and they serve martinis—a rarity in Paris. There is a two-hour wait most week-ends." Conway's, at 73 rue St. Denis, run by a New York model named Avia, who presides at Sunday brunch, was recommended to chili lovers in *Vogue* magazine.

Near the Georges Pompidou art center is the Front Page, at 56–58 rue St. Denis. "The chili is good and comes with red beans, and, like any 'foreign' food in Paris, is expensive," reports Gustafson. For traditionalists there is a Dew Drop Inn, at 3 rue Solitaires; a Rosebud,

11 bis rue Delambre; and a Joe Allen, at 30 rue Pierre Lescot, a Parisian spinoff of the American chain. Most Americans in Paris recommend Haynes, one of the city's oldest American food establishments, at 3 rue Clauzel. Founder Leroy Haynes, a GI who stayed on in Europe after World War II, makes his own chili powder, the mark of a serious chili cook.

"You can get a bowl of chili at the American embassy in Paris," says Gustafson, "but it takes an official embassy pass to get in. For Paris—or anywhere—the price is right, 65 cents a bowl for what I hear is doctored-up Gebhardt's with beans. Everyone loves it and howls when it's not available." Finally, Gustafson lists La Louisiane, on Boulevard de L'Hôpital: "Don't know much about this one other than it's open *late* and a lot of bartenders wind up the evening there. The one who recommended it said it was the *best* chili he'd eaten."

Where there is chili activity like this, there are inevitably home chili-makers, but where do they get their ingredients? *The* place for out-of-the-ordinary food in Paris is Fauchon, at 26 Place de la Madeleine, which boasts more than 25,000 delectables, from champagne biscuits to chili beans from Gebhardt's of San Antonio. Edmond Bory, Fauchon's chairman of the board, confirms the availability at his famous food store of both canned chili and chili-making ingredients, including Jane Butel's excellent Pecos River brand of New Mexican chili products.

On her trips out of Paris, Gustafson reports finding chili at two places in Brussels (Rick's American Cafe, Avenue Louise; The Hard Rock, Chaussée d'Ixelles—the latter "run by an old Mexican woman from Chicago"), and one in St. Tropez and two in Monte Carlo, "one near the Casino and one on the beach," all run by a franchise fast-food chain called 23 Dayvilles. *W* magazine found chili off the coast of French Brittany, at Cafe Serghi, on Ile de Re, where, it reports, "the dish of the day" can be "anything from fish, of course, to chili or a traditional *pot au feu.*"

Americans who are unaware that Europe is a hotbed of chili activity continue to be surprised when they encounter it in their travels there. A Houston couple, sightseeing in London, was so bowled over when they discovered canned Texas chili (Gebhardt's again) at Fortnum and Mason, the "provision merchants" in Piccadilly, that they telephoned home with the news, and columnist Allison Saunders rushed the item into print in the *Houston Chronicle.*

CHIC CHILI: WHERE THE ELITE EAT IT

The Countryman, a British quarterly, published an "inquiry" in 1979 designed to gauge the modern British awareness of chili.

"I love the stuff," responded Jenne Hatton, of Saltdean, Sussex, who said she also "asked the first ten people I met after reading it if they liked chili con carne or not, starting with my milkman. Six said they'd never tried it; the window cleaner said he loved it; and the other three (all women) said they didn't care for it, but their husbands loved it." (Her own husband, Mrs. Hatton reports, does *not* like chili: "He had no idea of what it was before we married, ten years ago.") Mrs. Hatton says she discovered chili in undergraduate days in London, when she shared a flat in Hampstead with four other young women. Two of her roommates were Australian, and one of them made a mean bowl of chili, according to Mrs. Hatton.

Later, when she was working as a reporter in Norfolk, Mrs. Hatton remembers, she and a group of fellow newspeople came down with a mass-attack of chili pangs while "talking food" in the newsroom one night. Mrs. Hatton promptly made a batch of chili (page 175), which was an instant success.

CHAPTER 7

Chili Savvy

Chili basically consists of fat, meat, chile, and expertise—what an old-timer would call savvy. More than anything else, it's the savvy that makes one chili cook's efforts stand out from another's.

Taller, Suet, or Drippings

Chili-making begins with the oils or fats. "The flavor must ride on the agent of pure grease," one Texas traditionalist has declared. Old recipes call for what—to modern tastes—seems like a lot of suet or other fats, but this chili was cooked on open fires or wood-fired stoves, with uneven temperatures. To free themselves from almost constant pot-and-fire watching, cooks added plenty of fat, making it almost impossible for a dish to scorch or burn.

Hard work and freezing cold caused bodies on the frontier to crave fat. It is difficult for modern people, who have never lived on the edge of exhaustion or imminent frostbite, to comprehend this. When Texas folklorist J. Frank Dobie describes melted tallow "poured sizzling hot into a plate of blackstrap" as a "dessert as good as a hungry man ever flopped his lip over," only those who have been chilled to the marrow can truly grasp the intense craving he is speaking of.

Besides supplying meat with much of its flavor ("prime" meat is the fattest meat), some fat is essential to a balanced diet. The earliest frontiersmen, the trappers and buffalo hunters, always cooked the fat, which they called "fleece," along with their meat. Unlike many of the settlers and soldiers who followed them, they never had scurvy, even though they lived on fresh meat and pemmican for months at a time.

There are two kinds of fats in beef. Suet is the firm, waxy, white fat around the kidney. Some chili cooks confuse it with the hard fat called tallow—or "taller"—that borders the muscles. (Tallow is also called for in some chili recipes.) Uninformed cooks who believe suet and tallow are the same sometimes differentiate in their recipes by calling for "sweet" suet, referring to kidney fat. Most butchers will usually throw in a hunk of kidney suet with a meat order on request.

Drippings from the morning slab bacon or salt pork were carefully saved by cooks on the trail and in frontier kitchens, and often were used to start a pot of chili. Lard might make a good starter, when making chili with pork, or a bit of fat sliced away from the pork meat itself, before it is cubed, chopped, or ground. Excess fat can be skimmed from the pot after cooking, or the chili can be refrigerated until the fat settles on the top and then can be lifted off.

To cook chili without fat, particularly when ground meat is used, sprinkle a little salt on the bottom of the heavy chili pot as it heats. When the pot is hot, sear the meat. (Those who do this claim the meat will not stick to the pan.) Another alternative is to eliminate the frying altogether, putting the meat directly into liquid and braising it over a low heat or in the oven. Restaurant cooks often do this when cooking in quantity. Meat so cooked can either be prechopped or braised in the whole piece to the falling-apart stage.

Not So Prime Meat

The qualities considered desirable in a prime cut of beef, that it be well marbled with fat and remain tender and flavorful with brief cooking, are all disadvantages in chili-making.

Of all meats, some say, venison makes the best chili. If beef is used, good chili cooks insist that the best chili beef comes not only from the lower grades of steers, which contain the least fat and make for chili that's not greasy, but also from the parts of the steer that have worked the hardest and the longest, such as the rump and legs.

Not Older, but Better

The nationally known meat expert Merle Ellis of Tiburon, California, dispenses his meat savvy in his syndicated newspaper column, "The Butcher," in his books, and on television.

In a column on chili, Ellis says that the old-timers he's talked to claim that "the best beef to use, without question [is] a 13-to-15-year-old longhorn bull. But those are a little hard to come by."

"The second best," he wrote in his column, "is beef shank meat . . . the lower part of the leg. No muscle does more work and gets any tougher than the shank, which is loaded with connective tissue. This is not to be confused with gristle (another abomination of chili lovers). Gristle is as tough as a trail cook's saddle and it stays that way no matter what you do to it. With long, slow simmering, like a pot of chili gets, the connective tissue in beef shank virtually dissolves and makes a rich, beefy pot liquor that is the very essence of a good pot of chili."

Ellis recommends buying the center section of a beef shank, "the same cut you probably often have bought sliced in one-inch-thick slices for soup, but it's much easier to work with—for chili—if you buy it all in one piece." At home, the chili cook bones the shank, removes the tough outside membrane, and trims away fat and gristle, before cutting the meat into cubes "about the size of your thumb," Ellis said. "Do not grind it. It is almost as impossible to make a good pot of chili with a meat grinder as it is with a can opener!"

The son of a butcher and a butcher himself, Ellis calls his chili (page 157) Second Best Chili, because it is made with the "second best" shank chili meat, instead of "best" teen-aged longhorn.

Chili Grind vs. Hamburger

Unlike Ellis, who doesn't like ground meat, period, some chili cooks endorse meat ground coarsely with a grinding plate which has holes with a diameter of one-half to three-quarters of an inch. In the Southwest, this coarsely ground "chili meat," as it is labeled, shows up next to the packages of hamburger in supermarket meat cases. Some southwestern markets routinely grind and display chili meat year round; others wait for the first cold snap, and the onset of chili pangs which this inevitably provokes.

Some cooks can't see the necessity for all the uproar about the size of chili meat. But it is doubtful that any good cook would choose hamburger over coarsely ground meat if both were equally available. The improvement in flavor and texture gained in the use of coarsely ground meat in chili is unmistakable. While super-purists ban any type of ground meat from their chili pots, others condemn only meat put through electric grinders or food processors, which they claim frequently chop foods too fine, altering their textures. The old-fashioned hand-cranked grinder is acceptable among most purists so long as a coarse grinding plate is used.

But even the hand-cranked grinder sounds positively automated compared to the super-purist method of cutting chili meat to size by hand. With quantity recipes, this dedication to the highest standard can be an exhausting chore. But it was a method that many old-time chili joints never abandoned. Of the two Lang's chili parlors in Dallas, the one remembered as legendary cubed its meat in this fashion. A Dallas Junior League chili recipe suggests using "scissors to cut the meat into small pieces, instead of chopping it on a block or grinding it through a machine. This gives the meat an entirely different texture and adds juiciness to every morsel."

Recipes that call for meat in "small pieces" leave a lot of room for individual interpretation. Others, specifying meat of fingernail size, thumb size, finger size, medium size, and so on, are striving for clarification but not really achieving it.

Some cooks in New Mexico, Arizona, and farther west prefer inch-size or larger cubes of meat in their chili, although meat cut to this dimension makes what might more properly be called a chile stew, *carne con chile colorado* or *chile verde*—meat stewed with red or green chile.

The general consensus among top chili cooks is that chili meat should be cut, chopped, or ground into pieces approximately one-half inch in size.

Capsicum & Company

If all the claims made over past centuries about the beneficial qualities of the ingredients that make up chili were only minimally true, their merger in a bowl of red would make chili a miracle food.

The truth falls a little short of this, but only a little. Chili lovers can take comfort in the knowledge that chili is a minor miracle, nutritionally speaking, and can also be very good for them in other ways.

Though chili is not an aphrodisiac (nothing is), it does have acknowledged value as a hangover cure, in that the capsicum stimulates digestive flow. As a hangover preventive, the fat in an early-on bowl of chili *before* drinking slows the effects of alcohol.

Basically, chili is made up of meat and fat (usually beef), chile, garlic, cumin, and oregano. Individually, all of these have been highly touted as restoratives, curatives, and nutriments down through history. Meat is the principal ingredient of chili. Its dietary values are, if not undisputed, widely accepted.

In the 1880s, Dr. James Salisbury, a British physician, thought so much of meat, good English beef specifically, that he prescribed what has become known as Salisbury steak to his patients three times a day, as a cure-all for gout, colitis, pernicious anemia, pulmonary tuberculosis, rheumatism, and hardening of the arteries, among other afflictions.

Modern food scholar and encyclopedist Waverly Root says: "The most important elements that would be missing in an all-meat diet would be calcium among mineral salts and vitamin C among the vitamins. Meat, while an excellent food, is thus not a complete food. What is?"

Well, how about chili? Besides meat, the chile—capsicum—which is chili's other major ingredient, is loaded with vitamins A and C. A Hungarian scientist, Dr. Szent-Gyorgi, received a Nobel Prize in 1937 for his discovery that pound for pound, chile—in his instance, paprika—has a higher vitamin C content than citrus fruits, and in fact is one of the richest available sources of this vitamin. The Mayans used chile to cure cramps and diarrhea, and it is still used for these problems in the West Indies.

South American Indians used smoke from burning chiles as a weapon of war—a primitive but effective "poison gas"—in battle.

Nick Peirano, whose family has ranched in California's Ventura County for generations, now runs the hundred-year-old family store (a landmark building) in Ventura. Peirano remembers the time a ranch-hand named Juan Garcia asked his father for permission to plant chile in an unused Peirano field. His father told Garcia that the field did not have the moisture necessary to grow "sweet" (mild) chile, the rule of thumb being that "water keeps the fire away" when growing chile. But Garcia persisted, and the elder Peirano finally told him to go ahead. Nick remembers that when Garcia's chile got to the first—green-ripe—picking stage, he brought some baskets of it into the store. Ventura housewives snatched up the fresh-picked chile, but started bringing it back almost immediately. The chile was not only too hot to eat, but too hot to handle, they said.

"Well," Nick says, "my father told Garcia to plow that crop under, because it was just going to get hotter the longer it grew.

"So, Juan Garcia got out there with a mule, and started plowing. But he didn't get very far down the first row before that mule started kicking, and they both were burning up from the fumes of those chiles as they were crushed and plowed under.

"Then Garcia decided he'd burn off the field, and set it afire. Well, people downwind of that hot pepper smoke came in fast to protest.

"It ended up," Peirano said, "with that chile crop just standing there until it rotted away. Took over a year."

The aversion of the insect world to chile has been known for centuries. A spray made of dried red chiles steeped in water, used from ancient times to rid plants of bugs, has found renewed popularity with organic gardeners today. Sprinkled liberally on meat, powdered chile repels insects and works as a preservative. Indians of the American Southwest burned chile seeds—the hottest part of the chile—to fumigate their pueblos.

The TV quiz show "Hollywood Squares" has asked if it is true that a doctor says that gargling with Tabasco—the world-famous chile sauce made in Louisiana—is good for bronchitis. It is. Back in 1889, doctors were prescribing chile infusions for sore throat, and capsicum is an ingredient in throat lozenges today.

At the other end of the body, one herbalist has advised sprinkling a small amount of chile powder in your socks to keep the feet warm. A similar sprinkling in his bedclothes helped George Orwell get rid of bedbugs in a fleabag Parisian hotel where he was deposited by circumstance, described in *Down and Out in Paris and London.*

Garlic: Loved and Hated

Some chili cooks consider garlic almost as important to chili-making as chile. Some decidedly don't.

Others manage to love garlic and dislike it at the same time. Nelle Smith is one of these. For fifty years, she was the patient, loving wife of H. Allen Smith, the humorist and leader of the midwestern chili contingent. Allen's chili, she says, had "powerful, garlic-onion-meat-tomato aromas that were so pleasant and exciting that I could hardly wait to . . . lift the lid and get a strong close-up of that spicy herby fragrance. But now," she continues, "I have to tell . . . a secret. If we were having company and chili was to be the pièce de résistance, I asked Allen to make it a few days before so we could let it blend in the refrigerator. But the main reason I wanted it made ahead was I wanted every tiny bit of that garlic-onion-tomato-meat aroma to be out of the house."

As recently as World War I, the British army used garlic as an antiseptic for battle wounds. Garlic planted in among flowers (it's a lily, and has a lovely blossom) is said to intimidate garden pests, including gophers, and has been called "the systemic insecticide to end all others."

After twenty years of trying, a Japanese farmer is reported to have developed an odor-free strain of garlic. For most of those twenty years, the farmer, Toshi Nakagawa, was known as "the garlic nut" to his neighbors. But now, under the direction of the giant Mitsubishi Corporation of Japan, Nakagawa Number One garlic is being marketed around the world, at four to five times the price of the old-fashioned odorous kind. Recent studies indicate that eating garlic helps to keep the arteries clear. Among others, a West German researcher claims he has scientific proof that eating an average size clove of garlic a day helps rid blood vessels of cholesterol.

Beloved Cumin

Many people who like chili, but have not begun to cook it themselves, have wondered where that elusive tantalizing flavor comes from. It's cumin, one of the ingredients almost always included in the making of prepared chili powder.

A member of the parsley family, the fruit or seed of the cumin, used whole or ground, or in combination, is the flavoring agent perhaps most beloved of the great majority of chili freaks. Many cooks routinely add additional cumin to their chili mix or chili powder because they can't get enough of that flavor.

Like chile and garlic, cumin has been touted down through the centuries as a cure-all, a magic potion, and—of course—as an aphrodisiac.

Wild, Wild Oregano

The final traditional ingredient in chili is oregano, sometimes called "wild marjoram." Further confusion occurs because oregano comes in two main types, Mexican and European. The European type is related to mint, and the Mexican—preferred for chili—is a member of the verbena family.

Mexican oregano is the more pungent and flavorful of the two varieties. It is sometimes called "Mexican sage," and farther south in Mexico and Central and South America, just to compound the confusion, a plant with velvety-green sagelike leaves is called "oregano," and used that way in cooking, much like caraway is used for cumin in some chili recipes.

Options and Add-Ons

Other commonly used chili seasonings are: marjoram, coriander (which are the seeds of the piquant cilantro, but are not a substitute for it), bay, sage, thyme, cinnamon, nutmeg, clove, anise seed, and caraway. Less common, but appearing here and there in One-and-Only chili recipes, are: celery seed, cardamom, mustard seed, sweet woodruff, juniper berries (not to overlook the ever-popular Texas farkleberry), germander (a sagelike taste), fennel (finnochio), ginger, horseradish, mace (the outer seed of the nutmeg), and turmeric. Curry and mole powders (and pastes) bring a ready-assembled spice mixture to chili (and hopefully will be used with restraint).

Goat Gap Gazette publisher Hal John Wimberly says that he has in the past "added a teaspoon of basil to each pound of meat in his chili." Paul Burka, of *Texas Monthly*, also recommends basil. A Florida cook who uses allspice in the proportion of one third the amount of chili powder is reported—by a Texan—to produce a superior chili. Chili tradition would classify allspice users as being of the midwestern or Cincinnati school of chili-making.

To Bean or Not to Bean

The bean is what separates the Texas chili lover from all other chili lovers. Even in neighboring Arizona and New Mexico, both chili-loving states, the bean is never far removed from the chile. This is because beans and chiles have been partners in the pot there since ancient times.

Ray Shockley, of Wolf Brand Chili in Corsicana, Texas, has looked into the great bean controversy among chili eaters, and concludes that only in Texas do the straight chili fundamentalists outnumber the chili-with-beans libertarians. In Texas, the preference for straight chili runs about three to one, while almost everywhere else in the country, chili *with* beans is preferred by about the same three-to-one majority. Only in Oklahoma and the cities of New Orleans and Charlotte, North Carolina, are the pro- and anti-bean factions equal, says Shockley.

As the statistics show, Texas has always had a sizable pro-bean contingent among its chili fanciers. The very title of Joe Cooper's classic on chili, *With or Without Beans,* indicates the long-time Texas preoccupation with this question. Bob Pool, who operated one of the fondly remembered Dallas chili joints of the 1950s, never served his chili any other way than with beans, and, as he told Joe Cooper, "Nobody ever walked out because of the beans."

Looking at the controversy from the bean lover's point of view, J. Frank Dobie, the Texas author and lifetime bean lover, maintained that chili spoils the texture and flavor of a good pot of beans. Kent Finlay, of San Marcos, Texas, has written the anthem of straight chili lovers, *If You Know Beans About Chili, You Know That Chili Has No Beans,* which is played at every Terlingua cook-off. No chili-with-beans recipes are allowed to compete at Terlingua. Finlay, like Dobie, says he loves beans—and has written another song about this—but only as long as they keep their distance from chili.

It is the simple lack of choice that irritates most chili lovers. Cooking beans along with chili constitutes an irreversible act. Straight chili purists fret in the knowledge that while a pot of simmering chili, no matter how many times it is reheated, is getting nothing but better and better, any beans therein are getting worse and worse through overcooking. A solicitous chili host will cook and serve the beans separate from the chili, to be added or not, as guests desire.

John Withee, who is known worldwide as the Bean Man, adds a bean expert's concurrence to the separate-but-equal theory of cooking chili and beans. Withee, of Lynnfield, Massachusetts, has made a lifelong love of beans into a full-time retirement occupation. Through his nonprofit corporation, Wanigan Associates, Withee aims to preserve strains of what he calls "heirloom" beans sent to him from all over the world. He cultivates them, and if he is successful, distributes the resulting seed beans to his associates in other climates, to increase their chances of survival. Withee says that his interest in beans "sprouted from a try at finding a 'lost' baking bean recalled from a Maine childhood, when a full barrel of them started the winter in a cold pantry" at his home. Although he is of course a bean lover first and a chili lover second, Withee knows that chili which is frozen or otherwise stored for future use is best left beanless. However, when he makes his Big Bean Chili, with one of his most ancient bean varieties, the Aztec, he doesn't count on leftovers (page 165).

The Final Touches

Because Americans have always been dedicated to progress in all things, overachievement shows up in modern chili recipes with the same frequency that it does elsewhere in the land of the free.

So-called "secret" chili ingredients can be anything from farkleberries, buzzard's breath, rattlesnake sweat, and pineal nectar to cigar ashes. It goes downhill from there. Texas journalist Sam Pendergrast has judged many chili cook-offs, including the big one in Terlingua. He has seen and tasted a lot of chili, and says, "The problem seems to be that too many people who enter cook-offs try to do something unusual or exotic. And, frankly, armadillo haunches, rattlesnake ribs, carp eyeballs, and lizard's tongues just don't add that much to chili."

"Beer, wine, horseradish, cinnamon, peanuts, avocados, and spinach are some of the things we've seen added to chili," Barbara Hansen wrote in the *Los Angeles Times* in 1977. She was replying in her food column, "Border Line," to a man from Santa Barbara who had written in asking for a chili recipe using chocolate. Hansen recommended a much-published chili recipe created by Babs Bayer (Mrs. Bill Shoemaker), which calls for one square of baking chocolate to two pounds of finely diced meat and one pound of diced pork. Like Mexican chocolate and pure cocoa, baking chocolate is anything but sweet, and an objective and even mildly adventurous judge would concede that its rich flavor is interestingly compatible with meat. The French traditionally cook rabbit with chocolate, just as the Mexicans do turkey in mole poblano. In fact, the French recipe may have been the basis for the inspiration that struck the creator of mole, in the convent in Puebla. If so, the French were simply repaying the debt they owed for chocolate in the first place. The first cacao beans, from which cocoa and chocolate are made, were brought to Europe from Mexico by Cortés.

Paul C. P. McIlhenny of the Tabasco McIlhennys of Avery Island, Louisiana, says that he likes to add "a little instant coffee and a small bit of unsweetened chocolate, and of course, a lot of Tabasco" to his venison chili: (He also adds pork and pork fat "because the venison is so lean.")

Stella Hughes, author of *Chuck Wagon Cookin'*, puts brown sugar in chili because "I put some sugar in about everything I cook." B. C. Jefferson of the *Dallas Daily Times Herald* confessed to Joe Cooper that he always put a half teaspoon of sugar in his chili at Lang's, causing the waiters to "curl their lips in derision." The California Honey Advisory Board publishes a recipe for Honey Chili which calls for one-fourth cup of honey for one and a half pounds of meat. Those Texas cooks, like Jim Wright, who reportedly add mesquite blossoms to their chili, might want to consider mesquite honey for this purpose, and gain an extra dimension of flavor in the process. The pungent flavor of mesquite honey is favored in the Southwest where it is available in supermarkets.

Some chili cooks go to the opposite of sweet in their efforts to achieve the ultimate chili flavor. Jeannette Branin, who writes about food for the *San Diego Union*, can't resist the impulse to add a dash of vinegar to a bowl of chili before settling down to enjoy it. The vinegar's acidity cuts oily flavors and adds a tang of its own. The same could be said for adding wine or beer during cooking. Branin remembers that "we *always* had a cruet of vinegar on the table at home, and I think it was at Pop Hepner's Lunch Counter in Sterling, Kansas, that I started putting vinegar in chili to cut the thick coat of orange fat Pop's chili had on it: you had to eat it fast before it congealed and cracked into splinters." (See page 149.)

Famed food writer Craig Claiborne is from a part of the South where the vinegar cruet is also a familiar dinner table fixture. One of his chili recipes calls for a down-home teaspoon of vinegar, plus the gourmet touch of a couple of slices of fresh lime to be added to the pot during cooking. For those trying to cut down on salt, the flavor of vinegar or lime juice helps to make up for its absence, as do dashes of sugar and honey, although the latter two are less well known for this.

In various forms, the tomato is used to add acidity to chili, without the decisive sharpness of vinegar or lime. It has the added advantage of giving chili the rich, red color esteemed in some chili circles. Some chili cooks sneak a little extra spice into the chili pot by using canned tomatoes and green chiles, or one of the spicy bottled tomato drinks or a Bloody Mary mix. The additional hotness and color gained this way might justify the use of the tomato for those chili cooks who feel the need to explain this. With the possible exception of beans, no ingredient provokes more controversy among chili cooks than the tomato.

"Putting tomatoes in chili is the equivalent of dousing raw oysters with chocolate sauce," said one expert.

"Some cooks," Joe Cooper wrote, "apparently think tomato is the source of chili's distinctive complexion. 'Taint so, brethren. It's pepper that makes it red." Specifically, Cooper plumped for paprika, a tablespoon per pound of meat, to give chili a "real bloom," the deep-toned red that "most genuine chili lovers" want to see.

Wick Fowler and a woman famous in Texas for her cooking—and cookbooks—have been two champions of the use of the tomato in chili. Despite what anti-tomato Texas chili cooks seemed to be saying, Fowler went right on using tomato sauce as both a flavoring and coloring for his chili, and recommending that others do the same. The late Helen Corbitt for years reigned over Texas cuisine, as director of the Zodiac Room at Neiman-Marcus in Dallas. When it came to food in Texas, Helen Corbitt was the final authority, and no one disputed this, not even Lyndon Baines Johnson, who could be touchy about who had the final say-so. When Helen told LBJ that the chili being served at the White House was too spicy, it was toned down. Not only does Helen Corbitt's chili have tomatoes in it—whole canned tomatoes no less—it also has the rich flavor of whole dried chile pods plus chili powder (page 122).

After Jack Smith, the *Los Angeles Times* columnist, let it drop that his secret chili ingredient is peanuts, the *Goat Gap Gazette* took sharp editorial note of the disclosure: "Please stay in L.A., Jack, Texas is not ready for you." These are strong words for a publication with readers fond of pouring a nickel sack of peanuts down the neck of an open bottle of Dr Pepper, then savoring this mixture down to the last, salty sip. Combining the flavors of chile and peanuts was already an ancient cooking practice when the Spanish discovered the Incas—and peanuts—in South America. Along with the rest of their

American culinary plunder, the Spanish carried chiles and peanuts around the world with them on their spice and treasure ship routes. Today in Indonesia, peanut gravy, topped with crushed red sambal chiles in oil, is as commonplace on broiled meat as ketchup is in the United States.

Extenders are nothing new in chili-making. In hard times, everything from beans to corn to pasta has been used in chili to stretch its ability to feed hungry mouths. When the straight chili purist uses one of these extenders, it becomes a "thickener." In the Southwest, the traditional thickener is masa harina, the corn flour from which tortillas are made. Cornmeal also makes a good thickener (some cooks blend this, half-and-half, with white flour).

In New Mexico and Arizona, dried corn *(chicos)* added to the chili pot will absorb excess liquid and at the same time give chili a distinctive regional overtone. Fresh corn, scraped from the cob, also brings a wonderful flavor to chili, but doesn't absorb as much liquid as dried corn. Dried corn must simmer in chili long enough to become tender. Chicos will taste better if added and allowed to simmer in the chili before it is cooled and "rested" overnight in the refrigerator, then reheated and served.

Rice absorbs excess liquid without adding a lot of extra flavor. Some chili recipes call for a teaspoon or so of rice to be added for this purpose. Cracker crumbs, as previously mentioned, are a traditional Texas and midwestern thickener. They were first used to soak up the layer of excess grease that sometimes floated on top of the bowl of chili parlor chili. The term "greasy spoon" was not idly used in the days of 15-cent-a-bowl chili joints. Some cooks use a sprinkling of rolled oats to absorb the grease in a pot of homemade chili. The most refined thickeners are cornstarch, butcher's flour (powdered egg white), and bull flour (gluten flour—less fattening than ordinary wheat flour—nowadays available at health food stores). Almost anything, in short, that will absorb excess liquid in chili with (or without) added flavor has been specified in one chili recipe or another. There must be somebody out there using tapioca who has yet to report on this method.

The same thing is true with the liquids used in chili-making. The assumption that water was the liquid ingredient for the first chilis may not be exactly correct. Early water supplies, particularly in the arid, highly mineralized Southwest, were not as sparklingly pure as good-old-days propagandists claim. This is one reason cowboys drank a lot of coffee—and still do. Old-time cooks might have figured that if coffee helped make the water drinkable, it couldn't hurt the chili. Like chocolate, coffee blends with other flavors, adding a rich touch of its own without dominating the taste. Ham and eggs wouldn't be the same without coffee, and many a delicious red-eye gravy made from the juices of pan-fried ham steak begins with hot coffee poured into the skillet, after the sizzling ham is removed.

C. V. Wood, Jr., calls for chicken stock in his chili. Many chili cooks would rather add more flavor with the liquid they put in their chili than dilute the existing flavor with water. A flavorful broth results when the meat for chili is precooked Mexican-style by slowly braising it in a little water. The broth naturally finds its way into the chili pot, where it is often combined with the liquid in which dried chile pods are soaked. Canned bouillon or homemade stock can be used if additional liquid is required. Followers of this line of thought are also likely to fortify their chili with an added cup of dry wine or beer. There is a teetotaler in Atlanta who adds a bottle of Coca-Cola to his chili.

The practice of slipping booze into chili is a late development, doubtless founded on the growing interest in "gourmet" cooking, in which alcoholic flavoring plays such an important part. Beer is a less sophisticated tenderizer of tough cuts of meat but, along with wine or even sake, adds rich flavor to chili. The beneficial effect of bourbon on broiled meat—particularly beef—and its use in marinades undoubtedly account for the occasional inclusion of a shot (two ounces) of a good bourbon per pound of meat in chili. The first bourbon chili, however, could have come about during a spontaneous chili-making session following a party. The chili is always recalled as being the best anyone ever tasted, but it is always impossible to remember what went into it.

The recent surge in popularity of tequila in Texas and elsewhere has resulted in tequila finding its way into the chili pot. A Florida man named Stuart Cumming puts good Scotch whisky in his chili. He even did this at Terlingua, while wearing a kilt. What does Scotch do for chili? Well, Cumming says, the peat-cured malt used in making Scotch gives it a flavor "unlike that created by any other condiment in the world." The Scots themselves, Cumming says, have been cooking with their whisky for a couple of centuries. To test the truth of this claim, add a two-ounce shot to the chili just as it is put on the simmer. It just might be that, like chuckwagon coffee, whisky is used in cooking in Scotland—and in chili—simply because it is *there*. The same thing might be said for many other chili ingredients.

CHAPTER 8

Tools of the Trade

No longer limited to the iron pot, wooden spoon, and unpredictable heat of cookfires, today's chili cooks have a battery of modern cooking tools at their disposal. But preparing chili (or anything) well rests ultimately on the ability of the cook. Savvy is the one indispensable ingredient in the art of chili-making. The truly good chili cook knows that it is the end product that matters, not whether it is made in an iron pot over a cowchip fire or in a microwave oven.

Chili-making is based on the classic culinary technique of braising, which one dictionary defines as "to cook slowly, by sauteing in fat, and then cooking slowly with very little liquid." The object is to surround the cooking food with a slow, moist heat, and the cooking vessel has a critical bearing on just how efficiently this is accomplished. One of the best methods, which tends to be overlooked by many chili cooks, is the oven (page 177).

The basic cooking vessel for chili-making is, of course, the tried-and-true iron chili pot, but slow, moist heat is the basic requirement, no matter what is used. Gertrude Harris, in her informative book *Pots & Pans, etc.*, gives the best clue as to how to select a pot for this cooking purpose: "[It] should be of a thick gauge, just as heavy as one can afford and can lift without breaking a wrist." Ironware certainly more than meets the weight requirement, and is a highly efficient distributor and holder of heat. But by today's standards, iron cookware is hard to care for. Modern detergents and dishwashers will remove the seasoning so important to good iron pot or skillet performance. Also, ironware does not take kindly to the acid properties of some ingredients—like wine and tomatoes—called for in many modern chili recipes.

In addition to the traditional iron, other substances can be used. Listed in the order of their ability to distribute heat evenly, they are: silver, copper, aluminum, iron, steel, earthenware, porcelain, and glass. In this wide range falls most if not all of the cookware currently available to chili cooks from pressure cookers (page 179) to slow cookers. The pressure pan offers an excellent way to take already ground and frozen chili meat straight from the freezer to the pot without the usual period of waiting for it to thaw.

At the other extreme is the slow cooker (page 180) which takes all night to slow-simmer chili to the proper state.

Fortunately for chili lovers who are also microwave oven owners, dishes that call for the meat to be chopped, diced, ground, or cut in strips are among the most successful in adapting themselves to microwave cookery. Almost any chili recipe can be adapted to the microwave oven (page 178). Remember that microwave cooking does not require as much liquid around the food as conventional cooking does, since it is not evaporated in the cooking process. Nor is it condensed and made into the rich sauce chili cooks love to see in their finished product. So while the liquid should be reduced in volume, the chili should also be made richer at the beginning, to make up for this. Even though a microwave oven will zap through the first steps of chili-making, for best results the dish should receive an additional hour or so of slow cooking.

Where microwaves come into their own is in the fast reheating of already prepared foods. Traditionally made chili, frozen into individual servings, is a real microwave winner, using this method.

Chili Blends with the Times

While chili traditionalists opt for the old-time ways, others put progress to work in their chili-making with a flick of the finger.

Today, the blender is riding a crest of unprecedented popularity in Mexico, but not just for drink-mixing. In the modern Mexican kitchen, it has replaced the traditional *molcajete* and *tejolote* (mortar and pestle, made of volcanic rock), which have been used for thousands of years to hand-grind the chiles and spices.

With a blender, chili cooks can follow this lead, and make their own dry chili powder blends from scratch, using whole dried chiles and other dried spices; or they can liquefy them as a part of the chili cooking process. In the latter method, a base liquid is used and the spices are blended into it, before being added to the pot. Basically it is a simple method, which can be adapted to the cook's own preferences (page 186).

Another status tool of the serious cook—and few chili cooks are anything else—is the food processor.

On the East Coast, *Boston Globe* book editor Margaret Manning is one of the many fans of the food processor for making chili; on the West Coast it is Mark Kauffman, whom Mrs. Manning credits with introducing her to chili, via Wick's mix, back when they both worked in New York.

Kauffman is one of the world's top photographers, and like many of his trade, Kauffman likes to cook. For years he fancied himself as proprietor of his own restaurant. When he moved west, he finally found the time to take a shot at it, and opened his Firehouse Cantina in Rohnert Park, California. The main attraction at Kauffman's is his chili, which must be good (page 188) because now there is another Firehouse Cantina in nearby Santa Rosa. Both towns are in Sonoma County, north of San Francisco.

Airtights and Bricks

The first "cans," invented in 1810 by a Frenchman named Nicholas Appert, were actually glass. An Englishman, Brian Donkin, later came up with the less fragile "tin" cans, which cowboys call airtights.

Glass is what home canners (and savvy chili lovers) use today.

Instructions for canning chili can be obtained from canning supply companies, including the Ball Corporation and Kerr Glass Manufacturing Corporation.

These directions should be scrupulously followed when home-canning chili:

1. Chili must be pressure canned. Water bath canning will not reach the high temperature (240°F) absolutely necessary when canning chili.

2. Use only pint- or quart-size jars with the chili canning recipes—processing times are given for these two sizes only.

3. The processing times in the recipes must not be shortened. No shortcuts.

4. Beans should never be added to chili that is to be home-canned—repeat—*do not* can chili with added beans. If beans are wanted, add them when chili is served.

5. Visually examine home-canning jars for nicks, cracks, and sharp edges on the sealing surface before using them. Reject all imperfect jars.

6. Before use, wash and rinse jars, bands, and lids. Keep jars in hot water or on warm cycle of dishwasher until ready to fill. Place bands and lids in saucepan, cover with water, and bring to a simmer. Do not boil. Remove from heat but leave bands and lids in hot water until needed.

In the late nineteenth century and for the first several decades of the twentieth, brick chili could be found in almost every crossroads market and grocery store in areas where chili was popular. It was made locally, often by the storekeeper or butcher, from flanks and the chuck. It can still be found in chili-loving areas, usually displayed in a market's freezer or refrigerated food cases. Today's commercially made brick chili won't keep as long in a saddle bag heated from both sides by a working horse's rump and the hot sun. But it is favored by a special group of chili lovers who like their "store-bought" chili extra thick, or who like to choose their own liquids when they reconstitute it, since such liquids may be added to individual taste and volume. Some people just like the idea of brick chili; it has a sturdy, functional, *capable* look about it, as though it can get the job done on a cold day, indoors or out.

Today, shaping chili cooked extra thick into bricks is an excellent way to store it in the freezer. It is concentrated in size and volume and takes less freezer space. Some "brick" chili appearing in modern supermarkets comes in plastic cylinders of the type used for bulk sausage. When making brick chili, begin with a thicker than usual mixture and reduce it further in cooking. Be careful not to scorch it during cooking. Using less liquid will eliminate the need for thickeners. These can be added—if necessary—when the chili is reconstituted (pages 98–99). Although some people insist that freezing diminishes the flavor of chili, there is the advantage of storage which can safely stretch up to six months. When any chili is reheated, carefully bring up the heat to counteract the presence of any potentially harmful organisms, then lower the heat and simmer until served. Any subsequent reheatings should be handled in the same way.

CHAPTER 9

A Chile Primer

Of sixteen distinct species of capsicums, five were domesticated at least 2,000 to 3,000 (some say 7,000) years before Columbus blundered into the New World and bit into the fruit which was ". . . violently strong and growing on a shrub no bigger than a gooseberry bush."

Partly because it took years for the Spaniards to figure out that America wasn't the East Indies, and partly because of the chile's hot taste, the capsicum was lumped in with the small black peppercorns of the Spice Islands, *piper nigrum*, familiar to Europeans. The confusion this created seems likely to continue forever. Not only is chile almost always labeled a "pepper," it is usually necessary to hang an identifying word or two onto this, to indicate, however inadequately, which "pepper" is being referred to.

"Hot chilly pepper" is not exactly a model of clarity, when it comes to identification, but is in use as a description for chiles.

To complicate things even further, the Indians of the New World didn't agree on what to call the capsicum either. In South America and the Caribbean, the Indian name for the native capsicum ended up in Spanish as *ají*, or *agí*. In Mexico, the Spanish version of the Nahuatl Indian word for capsicum is *chile*. To an Inca, *tchilli* meant snow—which is where we get the word *chilly*—so the Spanish called their country Chile, still another confusion.

Add to all this the capsicum's almost diabolical ability to change its size, coloring, and character from seed to seed, plant to plant, field to field, and season to season, and the centuries-long problem of sorting out these little devils becomes apparent.

79

Of the cultivated species, Dr. Paul G. Smith, Professor and Olericulturist Emeritus of the University of California at Davis, says that *annuum* is "the species domesticated in Mexico and . . . commonly cultivated in the United States and more temperate parts of the world. There is a bewildering number of varieties. I would not want to guess how many."

Annuum is responsible for most of the popular varieties of chiles eaten in the United States, from the tiny, wild, berrylike chilipiquín, or chiltepín, to the meaty, mild bell pepper—along with most of the chiles that find their way into the chili pot. Nineteenth-century botanists named over one hundred distinct "species" which were later lumped into two, and finally a single, species.

The rule of thumb about chiles is: the smaller they are, the hotter they are. Greater size, meatiness, and girth usually indicate mildness in a chile. A small, skinny chile, tapering to a sharply pointed tip, will be hotter than a larger, fatter chile with a blunter tip. The mildest of all is the squat, blunt, no-tip-at-all bell pepper.

Because of the confusion in the names by which the same chiles are known in different localities, identifying them for the chili cook is easier done by size, shape, and color (even in Mexico a recipe often calls for *chile de la region* to avoid struggling with a long list of local names):

1. The tiny wild chile—like the chilipiquín—with its impressive international list of names. This is hottest of all.

2. The slender, sharply pointed, thin-skinned chiles, such as the green serranos and the bright red japonés, which run from about one to four inches long. These chiles are cultivated worldwide nowadays chiefly for their hotness, and everywhere there are different names for them: cayenne, Tabasco, Japanese santaka and hontaka, habanero, cascabel, arból, Bombay cherries, Louisiana hot. But wherever they are, whatever they are called, their ancestors all started their journey from America to the rest of the world with Columbus, like all chiles.

3. The larger, longer, wider, meatier chiles, with wider "shoulders" at the stem ends. The most common English-language name for them when green is simply "long green chile." When dried red—not as bright a red as some of the hot chiles—they are called anchos. In the United States they are also called Anaheim, Fresno, California,

Arizona, and New Mexico chiles. Dried, they will be colored somewhere from brick to brownish red to brownish black. Some of the darkening can be caused by commercial drying. (Native, sun-dried chiles—like those of northern New Mexico—will be smaller, less uniform in shape, brighter colored, and hotter, than the commercially grown and dried varieties.)

These milder chiles run from about five inches—for the natives—up to almost a foot in length for the extra-mild, uniformly shaped chiles developed by the agricultural schools for the chile industry. They are used in cooking primarily for their flavor.

4. The paprika-type chiles, used for color. Compared to the other chiles, these do not bring either pungency or flavor to a dish like chili. Their mild flavor is overwhelmed by both the hot and the flavorful chiles. Although bright red in color, hot chiles will not be used by most cooks in enough quantity to add much color to chili. If these cooks also shun tomatoes in any form in their chili pots, and they like their chili to be rich red in color, paprika is the answer. Where the big, flavorful chiles turn chili a brown-red (which some cooks admire), adding paprika gives it the red color some cooks feel a bowl of red should have, without adding pungency. Paprika, like cayenne, is pretty loosely used as a term nowadays, and commonly means a bright red powdered chile, without pungency. Cayenne, on the other hand, means a bright red powdered chile *with* pungency.

Although chiles are usually green at some time in their growth, they can turn every color from black to brown to purple to orange to yellow and the more familiar red when ripe. An added confusion is that many chiles change names in the process of turning from green to ripe. For example, the milder "long green" chiles are called anchos (among other names) when red-ripe and dried for use out of the growing season. The jalapeño, when picked red-ripe and smoke-dried to a rich, flavorful brown, is called a chilpotle. Bell peppers are called pimientos when red-ripe.

Many chile varieties, from the chilipiquín to the bell pepper, are eaten both green and ripe. They are used fresh and dried; whole, in strips, and diced; coarsely ground, powdered, and as pastes and liquids; canned, frozen, and pickled. In the American Southwest, dried red chiles are made into Christmas wreaths; in England, chiles are grown indoors in pots and in gardens as gaily colored ornamentals.

81

Taking Out the Fire

Hotness in chile comes from a chemical compound called capsaicin, found in the seeds and white membranes inside the fruit. Capsaicin is what gives ginger ale and ginger beer that "hot" taste. As little as one part capsaicin to a hundred thousand can be detected by human taste buds. This hotness intensifies as chiles mature.

Before use, much hotness can be removed from chiles, both fresh and dried, by removing the seeds and membranes containing the capsaicin. Even canned and pickled whole chiles can be reduced in hotness this way, and rinsing them inside and out in cold water will remove even more hotness. Some cooks like to leave a certain amount of seeds in, for just a little extra hotness, and some wouldn't dream of letting even one seed of that flavor they love go down the drain. They want it all.

Chile Know-How

Fresh green chile is prepared by removing the tough, transparent outer skin and cutting away and discarding the hot seeds and veins from inside the pod. One method is to blister the chiles by setting them on a wire mesh over the stove burner or an outdoor barbecue grill. *Chile*, the excellent booklet on the subject produced by New Mexico State University, cautions that "handling hot chile can burn hands and eyes. Protect hands with a thin coating of solid fat or by wearing rubber gloves. Keep hands away from eyes when working with chile." *Chile* gives complete instructions for preparing chiles:

"Slit one side of each chile pod. To lower the pungency remove seeds and veins before pods are blistered. Place chiles on a cookie tray or a pan, three to six inches below the broiler unit. Use high position of electric range or medium flame of gas range. Leave oven door open. Turn pods frequently for even blistering."

A few charred spots are okay, but take care not to burn the chiles in the blistering process. Another method is to put chiles on a foil-lined cookie sheet in a hot oven (450° to 500°F), turning them frequently until the skins blister.

Once the pods are blistered, plunge them into a pan of ice water to retain their crispness. Or put them into a plastic bag in the freezer for ten to fifteen minutes. For more thoroughly cooked chiles, place the blistered pods in a pan and cover with a damp cloth towel or wet paper towels (or put them into a brown paper bag) and let them steam in their own heat for ten to fifteen minutes. The steaming helps to loosen further the blistered outer skins which then can be peeled—starting from the stem end. When green chiles are especially pungent, even more heat can be removed after deseeding, roasting, and peeling, by washing the chiles under cold, running water or by soaking in cold water. (If soaked, thoroughly rinse again in cold water.) You can reduce the pungency in commercially canned green chile the same way, but the flavor will also be reduced.

Roasted and peeled green chile can be dried, like red-ripe chile, in the sun or the oven, or in a home dehydrator. It can also be home-canned or frozen. Dried, canned, or frozen roasted and peeled green chile is used in cooking just like the fresh. Dried red-ripe chile is sold in whole pods, crushed, or powdered. Sometimes commercially packaged chile is labeled hot (*picante* in Spanish) or mild *(suave)*, but such terms are relative and denote the tastes of the grower or seller, and not necessarily those of the buyer. Pure ground chile can be labeled *chile molido,* or more specifically, *chile molido puro sin ninguín especia*, pure powdered chile without added spices.

Crushed red chile (the peperone rosso used in Italian cooking has an identical texture) in Spanish is called *quebrajado.* In both ground and crushed red chile, the proportion of yellow flecks visible in the mixture indicates the hotness, since these yellow flecks are the capsaicin-containing seeds and veins that remain in the processing. Unpicked fresh green chile gets hotter as it matures toward ripeness, and the seeds turn from white to creamy white to yellow as this occurs, turning dark at full maturity, when the green chile is at a peak of hotness, just before it changes color.

Although the hot seeds and veins can be removed from ripe dry chile pods, dry red ancho-type chile is not usually peeled before it is ground or crushed. However, the skins can be removed by presoaking before the red chile is made into sauce, puree, or paste. Many chili recipes calling for dry red chile pods specify that the skins be removed (slipped) before they are added to the chili pot.

Red chile sauce or paste is marketed commercially in the Southwest. In New Mexico it is sometimes frozen, and often labeled "Chile Caribe." Like so many terms used in connection with chile, chile caribe is used interchangeably to identify both the sauces and the dry, coarsely ground chile used in making them. In Arizona, the Santa Cruz Chili & Spice Company, operated by Gene and Judy England, markets a powdered chile and a chile paste, both unspiced (page 192). The village of Chimayó (pronounced chee-my-OH), between Santa Fe and Taos, has earned a largely word-of-mouth reputation among advanced chili-makers as having New Mexico's most flavorful chile. These can be ordered by mail either as whole dried red chiles or as chile molido. At Casados Farms, on the Rio Grande at San Juan Pueblo, New Mexico, Peter Casados mail orders his chile molido and coarser chile caribe in two categories, regular and "local." The "local" type signals its extra hotness with yellow flecks of seeds ground along with the chile. Casados has developed a recipe using his own Casados Farms chiles, which he calls *Carne Adovada* (page 129), and subtitles *Carne en Chile Colorado.*

Canned red or green chile sauce, sometimes labeled "enchilada sauce," is more widely available outside the Southwest. Bottled red and green chile condiment sauces, or canned "salsas," containing tomatoes and vinegar, are not the same.

Red Dust

The perfect chile for chili-making would bring the best possible combination of hotness, flavor, and color to the dish. Unfortunately it doesn't happen that way. The formulas for commercially packaged chili powder are said to contain anywhere from one to two dozen (sometimes more) varieties of chile, blended together with spices, such as garlic, cumin, and oregano, or whatever the blender's instincts call for. A basic chili powder blend will include smaller portions of hot chiles, and larger portions of those chiles that give the mix its flavor and color. The first chilis may have been made exclusively with wild chilipiquíns, but good chili cooks weren't long in discovering that there's a lot more to chili's special zing than just hotness. This was not exactly a secret to Aztec and Inca cooks, either.

Chili powder—the already-assembled blend of ground chile and chili-making spices—is the product most Americans traditionally use in their chili. Commercial chili powders are blended to satisfy manufacturers' tastes and regional preferences. In Arizona and New Mexico, the customers like their chili pungent and bright red, and their chili powder straight, and they get it that way. Texans, who like their chili hot and flavorful, get chili powder from several national packers in specially blended lots, labeled "Texas Style." A darker-colored chili powder indicates that it has been blended with larger amounts of the darker, milder chiles. These darker mixtures sometimes have an almost sweet taste, much desired by some chili cooks.

Like a lot of chili recipes, chili powder formulas are closely held secrets. Many commercial chili powder makers buy their spices from the same wholesale spice houses located around the country, but their individual requirements for chiles and other spices are kept confidential. Most spice houses carry enough varieties of chile and other spices to satisfy any blender's needs. J. C. Cooley, who heads the family-run San Antonio Spice Company, offers nine chile varieties and nine molidos from which to choose. The chiles include El Dorado (medium), Packer's Special (dark), Rio Grande Red (light), S&S Fine (medium), and Santa Fe with extra heat (light). The molidos include Processor's Choice (dark) and San Juan Fancy (medium).

Either whole chiles or chiles molidos can be used in making chili powder. The same is true of the additional spices which may be used in whole or powdered form. A basic chili powder includes dried cumin and oregano, and dehydrated or powdered garlic, in proportions to suit the maker's tastes or his idea of what will sell. The chiles should include at least one dark, flavorful variety and one paprika for color. Name brand blends are generally made of far more complex chile and spice mixtures, of course, and this is where the fun comes in for students of chili powders. It is the same kind of fascination that draws one into a lifetime of blending wine, whisky, coffee, or tea.

Choosing the chile is only the first step in chili powder making. After that come the subsidiary spices, in proportions needed to make the desired blend. Since most One-and-Only chili recipes calling for a brand chili powder usually specify additional amounts of key spice ingredients, their authors already have a foot in the door when it comes to creating a personal chili powder blend.

Beginning chili powder blenders might use the following basic recipe as a starting point:

Basic Chili Powder

1 part pungent chile molido (look for a bright red New Mexico chile—Italian peperone rosso or even a "cayenne" will do)

4 parts mild chile molido (a dark red, brownish red, or almost black ground chile, no yellow seed flecks, labeled California, ancho, pasilla, or mild or suave)

4 parts paprika (sometimes called "sweet" paprika, since some imported paprikas are hot, but most supermarket brands are very mild); use less paprika if a less red chili color is desired

3 parts ground cumin

1 1/2 parts ground dry oregano

1 to 3 parts garlic powder, to taste

Mix or blend well (an electric blender is useful here) and store, tightly sealed, in a cool, dark, dry place (the refrigerator is best for this, and for all chile products, except unopened bottles and cans).

One to two tablespoons of this basic chili powder to a pound of meat will imbue that meat with the classic chili flavor. No dedicated searcher for the perfect chili will stop with the basics, however. The potential for chili powder is limitless. One advantage in using whole dried chile pods in making chili powder is that the hot seeds and veins may be left intact, or reduced to the desired proportion. And dried chiles bought in the pod can be more closely identified. Trying to classify packaged chiles molidos by color and the often vague labeling can lead to some unpredictable chili.

Sun-dried native and fresh red-ripe homegrown chiles are apt to produce *too* fresh a taste for lovers of traditional chili. This "raw" taste, common in the chili of New Mexico or Arizona, is what gives Mexican *carne en chile colorado* its "different" taste. The familiar taste of American chili comes from the commercially dried chile used in traditional brand chili powders. Chiles can be heat-dried in much shorter time than it takes even the hot southwestern sun to do the work. The "toasted" taste resulting from this process is what American chili palates are accustomed to. Many chili lovers around the world toast not only chiles, but other spices, like cumin seed as well. Chili cooks who use dried chile in the pod often give it a light toasting before use, whether it was sun-dried or not. To toast chile or other spices, follow the method given (page 82) or do this: after removing seeds and stems from dried chile pods, toast them on a heavy ungreased skillet over a medium-hot flame for a couple of minutes. Keep the chiles or the spices—especially oregano—moving to avoid scorching.

CHAPTER 10

Come and Get It

For nostalgic reasons, old-timers like their chili served in heavy chinaware bowls, like those used in diners and chili parlors. They are still available at restaurant supply houses.

The table at an old-timer's chili party would probably have a pot of beans beside the chili, for those who like them, plus a large bowl of freshly chopped onion; a small bowl of dried red chilipiquíns; a fresh, bright-red bottle of Tabasco sauce; yellow pickled "eating" chiles; crackers—preferably the little "chili" crackers—and plenty of cold beer in long-neck bottles.

There are as many accompaniments to chili as there are One-and-Only chili recipes. In the Southwest, the yellow chiles would be replaced with small, pointed serranos, or fat, blunt jalapeños, *en escabeche*—pickled in oil and vinegar. In the Midwest, where palates are not yet accustomed to the hotness of chiles, dill pickle spears serve the same purpose—as foils for fatty foods like chili. Many cooks pass wedges of lime at the table, while some like a dash of vinegar to add an astringent zing to chili in the bowl. In California chili takes on a more exotic and decorative proportion and is served with everything (and anything) from olives to avocados.

For all but the hidebound traditionalists, part of the fun of eating chili is adding the trimmings—building a bowl. In Cincinnati, for instance, you would build a bowl of Five Way Chili by starting with a base of beans, adding pasta, then chili, then grated Cheddar cheese, chopped onions, and finally, crushed crackers. The bowl could be built up even further according to taste and imagination. Texans with southern antecedents build a bowl by topping a split and buttered wedge of hot corn bread—Southern or jalapeño—with a generous dipperful of steaming chili. In many Texas homes, this combination is a cold-weather supper tradition, often accompanied by a pitcher of cold buttermilk.

Almost no Texan would fault the addition of a spoonful or two of fresh or bottled chile salsa to a bowl of chili. And there is that paradoxical love of anti-tomato chili cultists for ketchup in chili.

Although flashes of genius have been responsible for some historic breakthroughs in chili cuisine, not all have been winners.

Take the time that Ben K. Green recalls in his book *The Village Horse Doctor, West of the Pecos*. A stranger came into a west Texas diner just after dawn and ordered breakfast, shortly after Green arrived for his customary "ham-and." After much palaver between the stranger and the cook-proprietor at the other end of the counter, the latter stomped off and fixed an order of flapjacks topped with chili. After the stranger had eaten and departed, the disgusted cafe owner came over to Green and said he had refused payment for the chili-topped hotcakes. "I told him," the cook said, "that he was the first damned fool that ever had nerve enough to try to eat it, and he never owed me nothin'!"

There's a story in *With or Without Beans* about a Florida fight promoter whose training table menu for his two prelim fighters consisted of chili over pancakes for breakfast and chili-mac for lunch and dinner. This was a case of necessity, not choice, since few prelim fighters earn their keep, but they do require steady and substantial nourishment. The fact that a recipe for chili pancakes has appeared on the side of a box of all-purpose biscuit mix in recent years suggests that the appeal of chili pancakes may not be as rare as might be thought.

Believe it or not, a version of chili doughnuts appeared not in Ripley's, but in a *New York Times* cookbook.

Then there was a man in Denver who, in 1978, dreamed up a doughnut-shaped hot dog to make chili dogs neat to eat. The chili was spooned into the hole in the center, so it wouldn't drip out of a circular bun.

An idea the army might want to consider, for feeding chili to its fast-food-addicted enlistees, is the Hot-Smak. The Hot-Smak was invented and patented about twenty-five years ago by a Kansas City man. It was a saltine cracker cone, filled with four ounces of chili, and sold for a quarter. The inventor figured it would sell like hotcakes at football games and other cold-weather outdoor events.

Even though the Hot-Smak was a virtually litter-free fast-food item (the cracker cone disappeared inside the customer right along with the chili), the Hot-Smak turned out to be an idea way ahead of its time.

Cooling the Fire

Chili lovers insist on serving everything from cold milk and buttermilk to bourbon with their One-and-Only concoctions.

As with everything else connected with the subject of chili, the proper thing to drink with it is controversial. Beer is perhaps the most widely favored drink, as it is with other spicy dishes like curries and Chinese and Mexican food. A few high-livers in the crowd claim champagne goes perfectly with chili—which it does with anything. And then there's always water, a liquid commonly used to put out fires.

In California, they find a wine for every occasion, but the ultimate wine and chili story is probably the one told by Truman Capote in his introduction to his friend C. Z. Guest's book *First Garden*.

Capote vividly recalled the five-day, cross-country auto trip he and Mrs. Guest once made from New York to California, accompanied by his two English bulldogs and his cat Happy. The group, Capote says, subsisted almost exclusively on chili dogs, which he and Mrs. Guest, at least, "washed down with quaffs of Chateau Lafite Rothschild . . . straight from the bottle."

The continuing hot and passionate debate about chili—from what to put in it, to put on it, to how to spell it—seems to indicate that chili has roots not only in Texas, but has become a part of the entire American experience. The freedom of choice, so cherished by Americans, applies to all things and most especially to chili. The recipes that follow will probably keep the arguments and the choices going for many, many more years.

PART II
THE PRACTICE

RECIPES

Chili cooking basically follows one of two approaches. Some expert chili cooks keep their chili-making deceptively simple. Like the best athletes, they make it all look easy—until someone else tries it. Other chili cooks, just as dedicated, go in for studied complexity, an act equally hard to follow.

The following recipes cover the entire spectrum of chili cooking. In each case, the greatest care has been taken to follow the cook's directions as closely as possible, although where necessary, localized spellings and obscure cooking terms have been sacrificed in the interest of consistency and clarity. For cooking convenience, recipes have been adapted to a standardized format, with ingredients listed uniformly in order of use.

By any standard, chili-making is an inexact art. One chili cook's idea of piquant can be another's point of spontaneous combustion. And chili seasonings can differ wildly in degrees of pungency, freshness, and many other variables.

So, although it is probably unnecessary to say this to chili cooks— a maverick breed if there ever was one—the exercise of individual judgment, coupled with frequent tastings and the adding of seasonings in small amounts as the cooking proceeds, is the wisest and best way to cook chili—by anyone's recipe. When the point is reached, in the cook's opinion, where the chili achieves One-and-Only status, stop right there, and eat.

CHAPTER 11

The Old Ways and the Army Ways

DELUXE CAMP CHILI WITH JERKY

The word "jerky" comes from the Quechua word *charqui*, picked up by Europeans in South America. By whatever name, jerky is made around the world, another method of food preparation that seems to have come naturally to all those with a meat-keeping problem and no refrigeration. Besides its keeping qualities, jerky is also light, compact, and nutritious—a nearly ideal travel food.

Jerky is made by drying fresh, closely trimmed lean meat. In dry climates, this is done in the sun; where weather and high humidity make sun-drying chancy or impossible, the meat is jerked by smoke-drying it. Much of today's commercial and homemade jerky is oven-dried.

The word "buccaneer" comes from the French *boucan*, an adaptation of another Indian word for the grate used to smoke-dry meat in the humid climate of the Caribbean. The pirates of the region were called *boucaniers*, because they dried their sea rations in this native fashion.

The Indians of the Southwest used (and still use) a dusting of chile on their meat when jerking it, both as an insect repellent as it dries in the sun and as a preservative for afterward (chile cannot be called totally effective for either of these purposes, but it helps). Although the Indians washed or shook off much of the powdered chile before eating the jerky or using it in cooking, it is almost impossible to avoid classifying such jerky, boiled with water, as a form of chili. In addition, Mexicans in Sonora and Chihuahua sometimes sprinkle

94

the meat with salt and lime before sun-drying it, which gives their *carne seca*—literally, dry meat—a distinctive flavor.

It should always be kept in mind that improperly dried or smoked meat, fish, or sausage can result in poisoning when ingested by modern digestive systems, which have had the cast-iron characteristics of yesteryear bred out of them.

6 ozs. jerky	½ tsp. powdered cumin
3 Tbs. rendered suet, drippings, or oil	¼ tsp. garlic *powder* (not garlic salt)
1 tsp. whole cumin seed	water
4 to 6 Tbs. *unsalted* chili powder	flour for thickening (optional)
1 tsp. onion flakes	salt (if necessary) to taste
1 tsp. oregano	

Cut jerky into small bite-size pieces, remembering it will swell. In a heavy pot simmer jerky and cumin seeds gently in moderately hot fat for one to two minutes, stirring steadily to prevent burning. Add chili powder and continue to stir until well mixed. (Amount of chili powder will depend on hotness of the jerky and your taste.) Add onion flakes, oregano, powdered cumin, garlic powder, and enough water to cover generously. Stir. Simmer for one to two hours, adding water as the jerky takes it up.

Allow chili to cool, and reheat before serving. If a thicker chili is preferred, add a little flour mixed to a paste with hot liquid from the pot and cook to desired consistency, stirring frequently.

Author's Note: Chances are no salt will be needed at all, since there probably will be plenty in the jerky.

MACHACA CHILI

Today in Mexico and the border country, *carne seca* is prepared for cooking exactly as Coronado's historian Castañeda described the Plains Indians doing it in the sixteenth century, by pounding it to a dry, stringy fluff, variously called machacada, machaca, machacado (from the Spanish *machacar* and *machucar*, to pound or beat). Machaca makes a smoother, more gravylike chili than unpounded jerky, which can be tough. In Arizona and Sonora, machaca shows up in everything from *huevos revueltos* (scrambled eggs) to tacos.

6 ozs. jerky, pounded into ma- chaca	3 Tbs. flour or masa
2 to 4 cloves garlic	4 to 6 Tbs. *unsalted* chili powder
3 Tbs. suet, drippings, or other fat	water salt (if necessary) to taste

Pound jerky into machaca by using two rocks, a hammer and an anvil, a wooden mallet and a board—whatever comes to hand. (Some say roasting the jerky strips beforehand in a moderate oven for ten minutes or until it is soft helps speed the job.) Remove any fat and any nonmeat fiber that shows up during or after pounding. Garlic cloves can be pounded into the jerky during the machaca-making.

Melt suet or fat in a heavy pot, mince in garlic (if it isn't already pounded into the machaca), allowing it to saute for about a minute— do not brown. Then add machaca and mix well, frying gently for another minute or two. Blend in flour or masa, and fry for a moment, stirring constantly to keep from burning. Quickly mix in chili powder, stirring just long enough to bring heat back up throughout the mixture, then add enough liquid to cover generously, stirring to mix thoroughly. (Amount of chili powder used should be determined by the amount of original seasoning in the jerky, and your taste.) Simmer, stirring occasionally, and checking the liquid, adding water as the machaca takes it up, until desired consistency is reached and remains constant. (If it gets too loose, add more flour or masa.) This chili can be left thick, like a gravy, and served "sitting on top" of corn bread, tortillas, crackers, and the like, or it can be thinned down by serving it mixed with beans and some of their liquid.

GUISADO DE JERKY (serves 4)

This might properly be called a *carne con chile verde*, or green chili. It makes a nutritious, rib-sticking camp dish. *Guisado* is a Spanish word meaning stew, or ragout.

1½ cups beef or venison jerky, cut in small pieces	2 large ripe tomatoes, peeled and chopped, *or*
water	1 can tomatoes and green chiles
2 Tbs. rendered beef suet or other fat, or more to taste	4 green chiles—either canned or fresh—cut in strips, roasted,
½ medium onion, sliced	and peeled
1 Tbs. flour	salt (if necessary) to taste

Cover jerky with water and simmer (adding more water as necessary) until tender, about one and a quarter hours, depending on age of jerky. (If machaca is used, omit this step.) Reserve liquid.

Heat fat in heavy pot or skillet. Add onions, cook until clear, then add jerky and mix well. When it starts to fry, add flour, mix in well, and continue cooking until mixture starts to brown.

Add tomatoes and chiles. Cover and simmer for thirty to forty minutes, adding reserved liquid (it will be salty) if mixture gets too dry. Add salt if needed. Serve with hot flour or corn tortillas.

PEMMICAN CHILI

As J. Frank Dobie says in his western classic *The Longhorns*, "If dried properly, *carne seca* will keep indefinitely. . . . If it gets too dry it can be beaten into pemmican—though that word was unknown to the lean eaters of lean jerky." Dobie was speaking of southwesterners, and pemmican is a Cree Indian word. (The Sioux called it *wasna*.) Whatever they called it, the Plains Indians are said to have eaten on the average of a ton of pemmican each per year. In *Jim Bridger, Mountain Man*, Stanley Vestal noted that an Indian war party "always carried its pemmican packed in new moccasins to save weight, for as fast as the ration was consumed, new moccasins were needed to replace those worn out on the march." The white men who crossed the plains on trapping and trading expeditions looked forward to eating six to eight pounds of buffalo meat or pemmican a day for months on end, and almost nothing else.

The Hudson's Bay Company adopted pemmican as an inexpensive, portable, long-keeping, energy-rich ration for its men, and these qualities made it popular as an expeditionary ration. Admiral Peary, after reaching the North Pole in 1909, wrote: "Of all the food that I am acquainted with, pemmican is the only one that, under appropriate conditions, a man can eat twice a day, for three hundred and sixty-five days in the year, and have the last mouthful taste as good as the first."

When it has been beaten to the machaca stage, jerky is ready to be made into pemmican, which—if somewhat heavier than jerky—is also a condensed travel ration, and much more nutritious than jerky alone.

97

1 lb. best quality dry jerky,
beaten until stringy and fluffy,
or separated into fibers and
chopped fine, or ground fine.
(The first method is the best,
but tiresome to accomplish;
the third the least preferred.
It takes away the character of
the meat.) Up to a head of
garlic may be added during
the beating, chopping, or
grinding process, crushed and
well mixed into the meat.

1 lb. beef suet, rendered
1 to 4 Tbs. crushed chiles, or
more, to taste

Combine prepared jerky and melted fat and mix until the consistency of hamburger is obtained, and the mix is equal throughout. At this point the only other ingredient needed to achieve true, old-time chilipiquín pemmican is the berrylike chile, crushed.

Always remembering that the pemmican may be eaten as is, or diluted into a greater volume with liquid, the piquíns (which can be found in many U.S. Mexican markets and in the Mexican food sections of some supermarkets in cellophane packages marked "chiles tepínes") can be mixed into the jerky-fat mixture in amounts of 1/4 cup or more, to educated taste. Crushed red chile, like Italian peperone rosso, can be substituted for the piquíns, but chilipiquín freaks insist the flavor (and hotness, remember) will be inferior to the real thing. Hudson's Bay Company pemmican was rammed into buffalo hide bags, called parfleches, and melted fat was poured on top to seal the mixture in. The bags were then sewn shut.

CLASSIC BRICK CHILI (makes 3 bricks)

Like pemmican, brick chili has all the attributes of a highly efficient food for plains travel. In pioneer days, brick chili, like pemmican, was made from the meat and wild chile readily available on the southwestern frontier at the time. In addition, brick chili is much faster and easier to make than pemmican chili, since its principal ingredient is fresh instead of jerked meat. Properly packaged and stored, today's brick chili can be kept in the freezer for up to three months.

4 lbs. lean chili grind beef or venison

1 lb. beef kidney suet, coarsely ground

6 Tbs. chile molido or chili powder

4 red chile pods, *or*

2 Tbs. peperone rosso

1 large bay leaf

4 Tbs. whole cumin seed

6 cloves garlic, crushed or chopped fine

2 Tbs. paprika

salt to taste

2 to 3 Tbs. water if necessary

Brown meat with suet over high heat, stirring often to prevent sticking. Reduce heat and stir in chile molido or chili powder. If chile pods are used, grind them in electric blender or food processor along with bay leaf and two tablespoons of the whole cumin seed. (If peperone rosso is used, it is already ground.) Add to pot the ground chile or peperone rosso, bay leaf, and cumin, along with the remaining two tablespoons of whole cumin seed, plus the garlic, paprika, and salt to taste. Add small amount of water if necessary to blend all ingredients thoroughly. Cook slowly for two to three hours, stirring frequently, until meat is tender. Adjust seasonings to taste.

To prepare chili for freezing, line three small loaf pans with foil or clear plastic wrap, leaving several inches of wrap hanging over the sides of the pans. Pour about one-third of chili just warm enough to be unsolidified into each lined pan and let cool and harden. Carefully fold wrap over chili to seal, remove from pans, and freeze.

Excess fat from the suet on top of the bricks may be removed before reconstituting. To prepare for serving, add enough liquid (water, beer, wine, etc.) to the brick chili to make it the desired consistency when heated. When chili is reheated, it is wise to bring up the heat carefully at first, to counteract the presence of any potentially harmful organisms, then lower the heat and simmer until ready to serve. Any subsequent reheatings should be handled the same way.

"OLD" ARMY CHILI, 1896

Teddy Roosevelt's Rough Riders, who trained for the Spanish-American War in San Antonio, came away from there with a well-developed hankering for chili. Since Roosevelt's men were mostly newly recruited citizen soldiers, their introduction to chili may have occurred during their training days, as it has to citizen soldiers in every American war from the one with Mexico to Vietnam.

However, the "old" army, as its regular soldiers are called, had a handle on chili long before the Battle of San Juan Hill. This chili, listed under "Spanish Recipes," is from the Manual for Army Cooks, War Department Document #18, dated 1896.

1 beefsteak (round)	2 large dried red chile pods
1 Tbs. hot drippings	1 cup boiling water
1 cup boiling water	flour, salt, and onion (optional)
2 Tbs. rice	

Cut steak into small pieces. Put in frying pan with hot drippings, cup of hot water, and rice. Cover closely and cook slowly until tender.

Remove seeds and parts of veins from chile pods. Cover with second cup of boiling water and let stand until cool. Then squeeze them in the hand until the water is thick and red. If not thick enough, add a little flour. Season with salt and a little onion, if desired. Pour sauce over meat-rice mixture and serve very hot.

Author's Note: This recipe is designed for the use of one ration of beef. It could be cooked in a mess kit by an individual soldier, or the ingredients could be multiplied according to the number of beef rations available and contributed to the communal cookpot.

"G" TROOP CHILI (serves 10)

In his book published in 1909, titled *The Story of a Troop Mess,* Infantry Captain James A. Moss makes an important contribution to chili history. The army had its first skirmishes with chile con carne, Mexican style, in the Mexican War. By the turn of the century, as Captain Moss documents, honest-to-god American chili was an established army garrison supper tradition.

Here is the recipe as Captain Moss set it down in his book.

3 lbs. chopped fresh beef	1 tsp. cayenne
2 qts. water	2 Tbs. olive oil
¼ lb. butter	1 large onion, chopped fine, *or*
2 Tbs. Worcestershire sauce	pinch of garlic
3 Tbs. best ground chili powder	salt to taste
2 tsp. black pepper	flour and cold water

Boil beef three hours in the two quarts of water. Then add butter, Worcestershire sauce, chili powder, black pepper, cayenne, olive oil, and onion or pinch of garlic. Season with salt to taste. Thicken with flour and cold water to consistency of a stew. Cook slowly for one hour and serve hot.

CHILI CON CARNE (for 60 men)
War Department Document, dated 1910

This chili recipe, probably used through World War I, is a more basic and much simpler recipe than that of 1942 (World War II), using the same good chopped meat and bean thickener methods.

15 lbs. meat scraps, trimmed of all fat
rendered fat or oil
beef stock
3½ ozs. chile pods, ground

chili powder to taste (see *Cook's Note*)
salt to taste
3½ qts. small red beans, cooked

Chop meat into ½-inch cubes. Fry in the same manner as beef-steak but use a smaller amount of fat. Cover fried meat with about one inch of beef stock. Add ground chiles and chili powder, and salt to taste.

Run two-thirds of boiled beans through a meat chopper and stir into meat mixture. Add remaining third of beans whole.

While cooking it may be necessary to add more beef stock to replace that lost by evaporation. Simmer for one hour or more until meat is tender and mixture is proper consistency. When ready to serve, there should be just sufficient liquid to cover the preparation.

Cook's Note: "The definition of chili powder as given in the Manual for Army Cooks, dated 1910, reads, 'Red Sweet Pepper. Various preparations on the market sold as chili [powder] contain, in addition to the red pepper, garlic, and such herbs as cumin, oregano. . . .'"

ARMY CHILI TM 10–405 (serves 100)

Here is the way the army was cooking its chili in 1942, just after Pearl Harbor. This is the mess-hall chili that gave thousands of new army inductees their first taste of chili. It undoubtedly helps that the meat in this recipe is chopped, not ground. And the use of mashed or ground-up beans—two-thirds of the total amount called for—makes an unusual thickener that today's inflation-minded cooks might bear in mind. The identifying "TM 10–405" refers to the army way of cataloging its technical material, a system still in use.

8 lbs. small red beans
3 gals. boiling water
30 lbs. meat scraps, fresh pre-
    ferred, but may be cooked
2 gals. beef stock
6 ozs. dried whole chile pods,
    ground

2 ozs. chili powder
salt to taste
4 cloves garlic, crushed
9 cups tomatoes

Simmer beans in boiling water until soft. Run two-thirds of cooked beans through a food grinder.

Trim all the fat from meat. Chop trimmed meat into ½-inch cubes and fry until it loses pink color. Cover with about one inch of beef stock. Add ground chiles, chili powder, and salt to taste. Mix in ground beans. Then add the remaining third of the beans whole, and the garlic and tomatoes.

Heat and simmer for one hour or more, adding more beef stock if necessary to replace that lost by evaporation. There should be suffi-cient liquid to cover the prepared chili when ready to serve.

ARMY CHILI TM 10–412 (100 portions)

This is the army recipe currently in use.

8 lbs. dried kidney or pinto beans
3 gals. boiling water
4 ozs. salt
24 lbs. boneless beef, ground
1 oz. garlic, chopped
2 lbs. onion, chopped *or*
4 ozs. dehydrated onion
2 Tbs. monosodium glutamate
    (optional)
2 ozs. cumin (optional)
8 ozs. chili powder

2 ozs. paprika
2 Tbs. cayenne
5 ozs. salt
3 qts. canned tomatoes, crushed
3½ cups canned tomato paste
1 gal. hot water
1 cup sifted wheat flour for
    tightener (optional)
2 cups water or bean liquid (op-
    tional)

Wash beans and add to the boiling water. Return to a boil; remove from heat, cover, and let soak one hour or longer. Add salt and cook about one and one-half hours or until tender. Add water as needed to keep beans just covered. *Do not drain liquid from beans.*

Saute beef until it loses pink color, stirring to break meat in small pieces. Drain or skim off excess fat during cooking period. Add garlic, onion, monosodium glutamate, cumin, chili powder, paprika, cayenne, and the five ounces of salt. Mix thoroughly and bring to a simmer.

Add the canned tomatoes, tomato paste, and the gallon of hot water. Stir and bring to a simmer. Cook one hour. *Do not boil.* Add the cooked beans and liquid. Simmer for thirty minutes. To thicken chili, mix flour and water or bean liquid, and add to chili while stirring. Cook about five minutes.

Cook's Note: "Twenty-seven and a half pounds of canned kidney or pinto beans may be used instead of the dried beans. A 36-ounce can of tomato juice concentrate may be used in place of the three and a half cups of tomato paste."

CHAPTER 12

From Texas

ANNIE LITTLEJOHN'S CHILI

The church chili supper is a traditional cold-weather affair all over the United States. This is a church-supper recipe from *Texas Cooking Under Six Flags*, published in the early 1950s by the Holy Cross Episcopal Church Guild of Paris, Texas.

1 5-lb. beef roast
1 2-lb. soup bone, preferably knee bone
water
3 lbs. pinto beans, cooked until tender

4 ozs. Mexene chili powder
1 dessertspoon cumin seed
salt to taste
black pepper and cayenne to taste

Cook meat and soup bone separately until tender in enough water to keep covered. Dice roast, strain stock, and add the cooked beans. Stir in the Mexene and cumin seed. Add salt and pepper (black and red) to taste. Cook very slowly over low flame one and one-half hours.

Author's Note: Leftover roast beef will do a good job too, as will canned pintos.

MARVIN JACOBS'S (RESTAURANT SIZE) CHILI RECIPE
(makes 30 pounds)

Like Henry Poff, of the Oklahoma City Baxter's, Marvin Jacobs, the Dallas restaurateur, generously shared his chili recipe with all who wanted it. In this regard, Joe Cooper quoted Jacobs as saying, "If I can help anybody serve better chili, then I'll be happy." This quantity recipe utilizes both sauteing in rendered suet and oven braising, for which a heavy, covered, high-sided roasting pan, the kind used by professionals, is recommended.

6 lbs. sweet suet, ground through ¾-inch plate

2 lbs. onions, coarsely chopped

20 lbs. lean mature beef, chuck or neck meat, with all gristle and fat removed, ground through ¾-inch plate

2 large garlic pods (about 15 to 20 large cloves), finely chopped

6 ozs. dried chiles (about 12 large, 16 medium, or 20 small)

water in which pods simmered

1½ lbs. any good chili blend

2 ozs. powdered oregano

2 ozs. powdered cumin

3 ozs. salt, or to taste

3 ozs. good red paprika

1½ ozs. cayenne

1 to 1½ lbs. bull flour or cracker meal

Render suet in large pan, then remove the cracklins. Add onions and cook until clear, but not brown. Add meat, mix well, and cook about forty-five minutes, or until meat is half done, in a 300°F oven.

Add garlic and previously prepared chile pods along with water in which pods were simmered. This should be about one quart. Cook slowly until meat is well done, but not falling apart. Add remainder of dry ingredients, except bull flour or cracker meal, and cook ten minutes longer.

Remove from fire and stir in enough finely ground cracker meal, or bull flour, to absorb most of the suet which has risen to the top of the pan. (Amount of "tightener" will vary according to quantity of red grease on top, most of which must be absorbed.) Smooth surface and cool until chili has set. It may then be cut into desired size for storage in freezer or refrigerator. Bull flour is gluten flour used by professional chefs in making gravy.

BOB MARSH'S BUFFALO CHILI FOR 600

Knowing the powerful positive effects of chili on the human mental and physical systems, in San Antonio they waited until *after* the 1977

World Pentathlon Championships to feed visiting European athletes all the buffalo chili they could eat—along with all the Pearl beer they could drink.

The chili was prepared by Bob "Yeller Dog" Marsh, San Antonio's enterprising chili celebrity, who claims he leads the world in chili cooking—by volume. Marsh cooked a reported 2,593 pounds of chili in one giant pot to help pro-chili Texas legislators push their resolution to make chili the State Dish of Texas over the top. His subsequent petition to the *Guinness Book of World Records* for the "largest pot of chili ever cooked over a single fire" was disallowed, he says, for technical reasons.

For Marsh, cooking up a bait of "buffler" chili for six hundred famished athletes was child's play. Any little old sixty-gallon iron pot will do for this one, Marsh says.

25 lbs. dried ancho or Anaheim chile pods, boiled, skinned, seeded, and mashed to a pulp	10 cups finely chopped garlic
5 gals. water, including water in which chiles were cooked	10 lbs. lard or rendered kidney suet
300 lbs. coarse grind bison meat, diced or chopped, with fat left on	1 lb. mashed whole cumin seed, or ground cumin
	5 cups salt, or more to taste

Prepare chile pods and set aside. Put water left over from chile preparation into a 60-gallon iron kettle, adding more water to make five gallons. Bring to a boil.

Add meat and the chopped garlic, crumbling meat to avoid big chunks. Bring to a quick boil and cook for thirty minutes, adding additional water if necessary. Stir in remaining ingredients and cook for thirty more minutes, or until meat is just tender.

Cook's Note: "Recipe may be divided, to use two or more vessels. Serves 600 hungry athletes with plenty of pinto beans and hot corn tortillas—and Pearl beer—on the side."

MOUNTAIN OYSTER CHILI

An essential part of the cowboy mystique is the love of roasted or fried mountain or prairie oysters, or calf fries—all cowboy names for the testicles of bull calves. During spring roundup, as the annual crop of calves is branded, the bull calves are turned into meat-producing steers by castrating them. "The old-timers," Stella Hughes says in her book *Chuck Wagon Cookin'*, "can get a faraway and dreamy look in their eyes when they start reminiscing about tossing mountain oysters into the hot coals of a branding fire. . . . Time can improve any memory."

Will Rogers was reportedly fondest of a chili made with mountain oysters, a dish which had to have a sure appeal for Rogers, who was both a chili lover and a pure-dee cowboy all of his life. The particular recipe Rogers favored has not turned up, but Steve Cornett, information director of the Texas Cattle Feeders Association of Amarillo, has obliged with the recipe of Dr. Richard McDonald, a south Texan and executive director of the Association.

2 lbs. calf fries, washed, skinned, and minced	3 Tbs. chile molido or chili powder, or to taste
butter or margarine	salt to taste
1 large onion, chopped	water
2 cloves garlic, minced	flour for tightener (optional)
2 Tbs. whole cumin, or more to taste	

In a heavy pot, cook the fries in butter or margarine for a couple of minutes. Add onion, garlic, and cumin and continue cooking until browned. Stir in chile molido or chili powder and salt. Add enough water to cover and cook gently, stirring occasionally, for one and one-half to two hours. During this cooking, more water may be added, if necessary.

About ten minutes before serving make a paste of a small amount of flour and water and add to the chili if necessary, stirring until proper consistency is obtained.

E. DeGOLYER'S CHILI (serves 10 to 12)

E. DeGolyer was a serious student of the art of chili-making. One of his recipes calls for beef, with a note that he occasionally used one-third pork. This one specifies approximately two-thirds beef and one-third fresh ham—a tasty variation that comes from William

107

Weber Johnson, author of *Kelly Blue*, and long a student of the Texas mystique, including its chili traditions.

1 large onion, chopped
4 to 6 cloves garlic, minced
2 cups rendered beef kidney suet
2½ lbs. extra lean chuck beef, cubed
1 slice (approximately 1 lb.) fresh ham steak, trimmed and cubed

2 cups water
1 tsp. ground cumin
2 tsp. oregano
1 cup red chile pulp, *or*
6 Tbs. chili powder, or more
1 Tbs. salt, or to taste

Cook onion and garlic in rendered beef suet until onion is limp and yellow. Add beef and ham and cook, stirring often, until it is a uniform gray color. Add water, mix well, simmer one to one and one-half hours.

Add cumin, oregano, chile pulp or chili powder, and salt to meat mixture. Stirring frequently to prevent sticking, simmer for an additional hour.

JOE COOPER'S CHILI

For a seeker after the One True, Honest-to-God, Dyed-in-the-Wool Texas Chili, Joe Cooper was remarkably catholic in his chili tastes. His recipe calls for unorthodox ingredients like olive oil, bay leaves, and a touch of cocoa, and even tolerates hamburger. It also makes very good chili.

3 lbs. lean beef (neck or forequarter, free of bone, fat, and gristle), ground or chopped
¼ cup olive oil
1 qt. water
2 bay leaves (optional)
8 dry chile pods, *or*
6 Tbs. chili powder
3 tsp. salt
10 cloves garlic, finely chopped

1 tsp. ground cumin
1 tsp. powdered oregano
1 tsp. cayenne
½ tsp. freshly ground black pepper
1 Tbs. sugar
3 Tbs. paprika
¼ tsp. cocoa (optional)
3 Tbs. flour
6 Tbs. cornmeal

In a six-quart pot, sear meat in hot olive oil, stirring constantly over high heat until gray, but not brown. Add water and mix well. Add bay leaves now, but remove and discard after fifteen to twenty minutes cooking. Simmer covered one and one-half to two hours, stirring occasionally.

Add remaining ingredients, except flour and cornmeal. Cocoa should be added now. Simmer, stirring frequently for thirty minutes. Skim off any excess fat. Adjust seasonings and add flour and cornmeal blended with a little cold water to make a paste. Cook, stirring constantly to prevent sticking, until chili is desired consistency.

Cook's Note: "Of a certainty good chili has been made from finely ground meat if there is not ample time for hand chopping into small bite-size cubes. A butcher's mill with a ½ inch plate (¾ inch would be better, but seldom is available) will do a very acceptable job, thank you."

WICK FOWLER'S ORIGINAL CHILI

A few whole, dried red chiles *japonés*, about two inches long, used to be included with Wick Fowler's packages of chili mix. They were carefully floated on top of the chili pot in the final stages of simmering. As the pot was brought to the table for serving, their presence, riding wicked and red on top of the steaming chili, was highly intimidating to the uninitiated. This was their purpose—as long as the slender chiles remained whole and unbroken, and the fiery hot seeds were not released into the chili, they were harmless. Those in the know ate carefully around them—unless they liked them. This is Fowler's scratch recipe, from which his famous 2-Alarm mix evolved.

3 lbs. chili grind beef, mostly lean
1½ cups canned tomato sauce
water
1 tsp. Tabasco
3 heaping Tbs. chili powder
1 tsp. oregano
1 tsp. cumin seed or powder
2 onions, chopped

6 or more cloves garlic, chopped
1 tsp. salt
1 tsp. cayenne
1 Tbs. paprika
12 or more whole dried Japanese chiles (very hot)
6 to 8 chilipiquíns (very, very hot)
3 Tbs. flour for thickener

Sear meat in a large skillet until gray in color. Transfer meat to chili pot, along with the tomato sauce and enough water to cover meat about ½ inch, mixing well. Stir in the Tabasco, chili powder, oregano, cumin, onions, garlic, salt, cayenne, and paprika. Add Japanese chiles and chilipiquíns, taking care not to break them open lest the hot seeds escape into the pot. Leave this for each chili eater to decide, after serving. Let simmer for one hour and forty-five minutes, stirring gently at intervals.

About thirty minutes before the end of cooking time, skim off grease that has risen to the top. Mix flour with a little water to make it liquid without lumps. Add this paste to ingredients in the pot and blend in thoroughly. Adjust salt and seasonings. Unless you are chili hungry at the moment, let the chili remain in the pot overnight, then reheat and serve. Freeze any chili left over.

Serve with sliced or chopped onions and pinto beans on the side.

Cook's Note: "If you want to put out the fire, drink a pint of buttermilk; this is the drink that professional pepper-tasters use."

LBJ PEDERNALES RIVER CHILI (serves 8)

Some Texas chili traditionalists look askance at this recipe, which has been sent out by the thousands from the LBJ Ranch in response to requests. For one thing, it calls for no fat; and for another, it includes whole canned tomatoes. Maybe LBJ *liked* tomatoes in his chili (not as uncommon as Texas purists would care to admit). What is known for sure is that this recipe was tailored for Johnson by his doctor, after Johnson's first heart attack. Not only is it fat-free, it calls for lean venison, when available. Venison was Johnson's favorite meat for chili-making anyway, but he preferred it sauteed in a little beef kidney suet for flavor, before his doctor took charge of his diet. The local pronunciation of Pedernales (*pedernal* means flint in Spanish) is Purd-in-alice, and in this case local extends at least from Texas to Washington, D.C., and New York City.

4 lbs. bite-size or chili grind venison, if available, *or* well-trimmed chuck	2 cups hot water
	6 tsp. chili powder, or to taste
	1½ cups canned whole tomatoes
1 large onion, chopped	2 to 6 generous dashes of liquid hot pepper sauce
2 cloves garlic, minced	
1 tsp. ground oregano	salt to taste
1 tsp. cumin seed	

110

Place meat, onion, and garlic in large, heavy skillet or Dutch oven. Cook until light-colored. Add oregano, cumin, water, chili powder, tomatoes, hot pepper sauce, and salt. Bring to a boil, lower heat, and simmer about one hour. Skim off fat during cooking.

Author's Note: Even more fat can be removed if chili is stored in refrigerator, allowing fat to rise to top and solidify, when it can be easily removed. LBJ preferred venison in his chili, and so did his doctor, because it is so lean and fat-free. Ground beef heart is leaner still, and has a rich beef flavor with the added value of a high vitamin B content.

WOODY BARRON'S TEXAS CHILI

Chili, says Woody Barron, of Waco, Texas, "should be just that, chiles and meat, maybe with a little garlic and onions thrown in for flavor. This business of putting tomatoes in a dish of chili is an abomination, and anyone who would do such a thing should be forced to consume a whole fried chicken cooked in castor oil. Anyone who thinks they are making chili and adds tomatoes to the dish, will end up with a pretty good Italian meat sauce for spaghetti but a long way from true chili. I have tried cooking chopped beef in tallow, adding only ground chiles and salt and have found even this simple recipe a taste treat. Of course, you have to use a lot of chiles."

1 lb. suet	1 tsp. cumin
4 lbs. coarsely ground beef	½ tsp. oregano
4 Tbs. ground hot chile molido	salt to taste
1 large onion (to make ¾ cup ground)	hot water
	cornmeal (optional)
2 to 3 cloves garlic	

Use a large, heavy kettle, cast iron or aluminum. Slice suet thin and fry in kettle until about three to four tablespoons of fat are in bottom of kettle. Crumble the ground beef into hot suet and stir until meat is gray but not brown. Add chili powder to meat and stir. Simmer slowly for a few minutes to allow meat to absorb chili powder.

Put onion and garlic in blender and chop until very fine. Add to meat mixture. Add cumin and oregano. Salt to taste.

Add small amounts of hot water from time to time, but chili should remain thick. Simmer for two to three hours, stirring and adding water as needed. If chili appears to be thin, mix a small amount of cornmeal in water and add for thickening.

CHARLES PENDERGRAST'S TEXAS CHILI

After covering the history of chili ("the National Dish of Texas") in his brother Sam's late magazine *Oeste* (Sam returned to his first love, newspapering), Charles Pendergrast gets down to brass tacks on what goes into a One-and-Only chili, namely his.

The longhorns that provided the meat for early-day chili "bore little resemblance to the beef cattle of today," he says. "To make a proper chili, steer clear of the top grades and go to the bottom of the livestock quotations where you will find listed bologna bulls and chili bulls." Even for those who make chili with less than a whole beef, Pendergrast's meaning is clear: the tougher (and cheaper) cuts not only suffice, they are superior, in chili-making.

5 lbs. "lean muscle meat from an animal of maturity and character," ground coarsely together with	4 ozs. paprika 2 to 3 ozs. salt 1½ ozs. comino (cumin) powder water
1 to 2 lbs. suet or tallow 5 ozs. chili powder	2 ozs. garlic powder flour or masa harina (optional)

Place ground meat and fat together in biggest iron kettle or Dutch oven you have and fry, stirring occasionally. (Thousands of amateur cooks and hundreds of professionals would add liquid at this point, but I can only say this is my way and it will work.) After the meat has reached a grayish color, and the fat has melted, add chili powder, paprika, salt, and cumin. Having added spices, give mixture another brisk stir or two, add water—about a half a gallon should do it— and turn the fire to a very slow boil. Do whatever you like for the next three or four hours.

Then come back and add the garlic powder. At this point you will note there is a supply of rich red oil floating on top. There are several ways to deal with this, but you must not throw it away because it contains much of the flavor and the essence of the chili. The old-timers stirred it up and ate it greasy like that. If you like a thick smooth chili to pour over enchiladas or Frito pie, carefully lift the oil with a ladle into a small saucepot. Add an equal amount of flour or masa harina. Cook this for a few minutes and pour it back into the chili pot. This will make a thick chili gravy that tastes much better than it sounds. *Bon appétit* or—as they say—*mucho gusto.*

Author's Note: Expert chili cooks advise that one way to eliminate the "rich red oil" floating on top of a pot of chili, when there isn't time to let it cool, is to sprinkle oatmeal on the oil slick and allow this to absorb the fat, whereupon it can be removed with a slotted spoon.

MEL MARSHALL'S CHILI (serves 12)

In his book *Cooking Over Coals*, Mel Marshall displays a definitive knowledge of meat and what to do with it, not only over coals, but before and afterward. When a man with this kind of savvy talks about chili, wise people listen, and learn.

"Start with the toughest meat you can buy," Marshall advises chili-makers; "good grade meat makes mushy chili. Avoid ground beef, it produces inferior chili."

As an avowed traditionalist, it is not surprising that Marshall is anti-tomato in chili, but it does surprise when he adds: "Thickening chili with masa harina is a vice which should be discouraged."

3 lbs. (trimmed and boned weight) meat—shank, flank, or shortribs
chopped suet, trimmed from chili meat—or other
1 to 3 tsp. chile molido
¼ tsp. cumin seed, ground or crushed
1 tsp. oregano
2 cloves garlic, *or*
¼ tsp. garlic powder
1 medium-size yellow onion, minced
cold water
3 to 4 small hot dried red chiles—Japanese or chilipiquíns (optional)
1 tsp. salt (optional)

Cut trimmed meat into fingertip-size bits. It should be as nearly free of suet as possible. In a deep, heavy skillet, render suet until it is deep brown; it should yield enough liquid fat to cover bottom of pan to a depth of about ¼ inch.

Brown meat, stirring often. While browning, sprinkle over it the chile molido, ground or crushed cumin, and oregano. There is little consistency to the degree of spiciness a batch of chile molido will yield, or to how different molidos will respond to cooking heat. If unsure, start with a minimum of one to one and one-half teaspoons when browning the meat and add more later, if desired.

Add garlic and minced onion to meat, reduce heat to moderate, and stir until the onion is soft and transparent, about eight to ten minutes.

Add cold water to cover meat generously, stir until the water boils, then reduce heat to simmer. Taste liquid at this point and add more chile molido if needed. For a very spicy chili, add chiles and a modicum of salt.

Let simmer one and one-half to two hours, adding water as needed and stirring occasionally. When meat is tender, add enough water to cover, and simmer half an hour; add no more water. Remove from heat and let stand until fat rises, and skim off. Or refrigerate the chili in the pot overnight and remove the crusted fat from top before heating.

Cook's Note: "There are two schools of thought about cumin seeds *(cominos)* that traditional recipes call for. Some bake the *cominos* an hour in a low oven before crushing them, others say baked *cominos* are too hot [pungent]."

Author's Note: Mel Marshall's chili is not only well founded, it is also an excellent one for people who watch what they eat. It is relatively low in fat, calls for little or no salt, and is moderately pungent. In *Cooking Over Coals,* Marshall points out that plains hunters and trappers were apt to use little or no salt in their cooking, and got along without it entirely for weeks and months at a time. Those who did miss it, added a speck of gunpowder (the old-fashioned black powder type) or a touch of gall to the cookpot. The plainsmen of another hemisphere, the Bedouins, still get along without salt. It's a matter of taste (or doctor's orders).

SAM HUDDLESTON'S CHILI (serves 6)

Sam Huddleston's chili recipe is so close to being *the* basic, honest-to-god chili that this could well be its downfall when other experienced chili cooks start studying it. The American urge to improve on simplicity has always been a strong one, and chili cooks are far from being exceptions in this practice.

Don't do it, folks. Leave this one alone and taste the chili of the legendary chili joints of the past.

(Huddleston, who is from Brownsville, Texas, bills himself as "Part Owner of Texas" and is the author of *The Tex-Mex Cook Book*.)

2 Tbs. whole cumin	2 Tbs. paprika
2 medium onions, diced	6 Tbs. chili powder
3 cloves garlic, diced	water
vegetable oil	salt to taste
3½ lbs. lean beef, cut into ½-inch cubes	cracker meal or browned flour, for tightener

In a skillet slightly toast the whole cumin. To wake up flavors crush them with a rolling pin. Powdered cumin may be substituted, but do not toast. Saute onion and garlic in a little vegetable oil until transparent. In same skillet add a little more oil and sear meat until it has a grayish color.

Put cumin, onion, garlic, and meat in a large vessel. Add paprika and chili powder, stirring to mix all ingredients, as you add enough water to cover. Simmer for about one and one-half hours, adding salt to taste after the chili has cooked somewhat.

Make a paste of the cracker meal or browned flour by mixing with a little water. About ten minutes before chili is ready, stir in this tightener, and cook until chili is thick.

CATARINA RANCH CHILI (serves 16 to 20)

A deceptively simple, cumin-spiced chili, simmered in the old army (or *lavandera*) style, is the favorite at the Catarina Ranch, southwest of San Antonio. The ranch belongs to former Texas Governor Dolph Briscoe, Jr., and his wife, Janie, and it is not unusual for forty guests or more to put their boots under the dinner table. Governor Briscoe credits chili cook Bea Holmes with perfecting the Catarina recipe, and along with so many gourmet chili lovers, considers venison the ultimate meat for chili.

4 lbs. beef or venison, cut in
small cubes
water
salt to taste
3 large garlic cloves, chopped or
mashed

¼ oz. (approximately 4 tsp.)
comino (cumin) seed
1 4-oz. bottle chili powder
2 cups tomato juice

In a large, heavy pot cover meat with water and add salt, garlic, comino, and chili powder. Bring mixture to a boil, then simmer slowly for two to three hours, or until meat is tender, stirring as needed. About thirty minutes before serving, add the tomato juice and continue to simmer.

This recipe serves sixteen to twenty as part of a buffet, fewer as a one-dish meal.

MAVERICK CHILI

In the 1850s a Maverick ancestor, Sam Maverick—a signer of the Texas Declaration of Independence from Mexico—gave his name to the English language by his practice of not branding cattle on his ranch near San Antonio. Unbranded cattle became known as mavericks. As "special correspondent" to a San Antonio newspaper, Maury Maverick covered the historic cook-off at Terlingua between Wick Fowler and H. Allen Smith. His report was headlined *The Great Chili Confrontation.*

3 lbs. chuck or round steak,
cubed
4 cups water
⅓ tsp. cayenne
2 Tbs. cumin
5 Tbs. chili powder
2½ tsp. salt

5 cloves garlic, pressed
2 Tbs. oregano
3 tsp. sugar
3 Tbs. paprika
1 8-oz. can tomato sauce
2 Tbs. masa harina (optional)

Cook meat until gray in color. Add water and simmer for thirty minutes. Add remaining ingredients, except masa harina, and simmer for about two hours until meat is tender. Stir occasionally during cooking.

If you wish to thicken the chili, add the masa harina near the end of cooking time. Stir and heat to desired consistency.

Author's Note: Masa harina is a corn flour used to make tortillas, packaged and sold in the United States and Mexico by the Quaker Oats Co.

RICHARD BOLT'S CHILI

A real honest-to-god Texas chuckwagon cook, who learned the trade from his father, was the late Richard Bolt. In 1974, Bolt passed on his chuckwagon expertise in a small book he called *Forty Years Behind the Lid.* In it he tells how to cook everything from vinegar pie to green beans that "even cowboys will eat."

His chili, an authentic "deviled beef," cooked over coals in an iron pot, is basic and good.

¼ lb. finely chopped tallow (suet)	4 Tbs. chili powder
2 lbs. ground chili meat	1½ tsp. salt
water	¼ tsp. cumin
1 medium onion, chopped	¼ tsp. garlic salt

Place tallow and chili meat in iron pot. Cover with water about one inch above meat. Cook covered at medium heat until meat is tender. Add onions and cook ten minutes. Then add remaining ingredients and continue cooking about fifteen minutes. If moister chili is desired, add small amount of water and cook five minutes.

TEXAS PRISON CHILI (serves 100)

Because it offered such cheap consolation on a cold and lonely Saturday night, chili was a favorite food—on both sides of the bars—in many southwestern jails. This resulted in the inevitable controversy over which jail served the best.

The warden of the state prison at Huntsville, Texas, won—at least in showmanship—when he claimed that so many of his former boarders wrote in and asked for the state prison chili recipe that he had it printed up, so that his staff wouldn't have to be typing all day to fill the requests.

117

The warden lost, however, when it came to the popular name for this chili. Most people like the sound of Jailhouse Chili better than what the warden calls his, Prison Chili.

25 lbs. chili grind beef
4 ozs. chili powder
2 handfuls dried red chiles, crushed
8 ozs. cumin
2 ozs. paprika

8 ozs. garlic, finely chopped
water
2 handfuls monosodium glutamate
salt to taste

Place in a large, heavy cooking pot the beef, chili powder, chiles, cumin, paprika, and garlic. Add enough water to cover, close tightly, and cook fifteen minutes at high heat without stirring. Remove cover, add monosodium glutamate and salt. Stir and simmer for thirty to forty minutes. Do not add additional water. Correct seasoning to desired strength.

A. K. SWANN'S CHILI

The famous A. K. Swann chili recipe might have been lost to chili history if Susan and Jack Bush, now of Tucson, hadn't been determined to preserve it. The Bushes learned to love Swann's chili in Denver, and have carefully safeguarded Swann's original recipe ever since. The standardized, much-less-entertaining, but easier-to-follow version goes like this:

5 lbs. lean round steak, well-trimmed, either chili grind or cut in ¼-inch cubes
1 lb. kidney suet, rendered
6 ozs. chili powder
2 tsp. powdered cumin
2 tsp. paprika
1¾ cups solid pack tomatoes
1½ qts. water
4 to 6 garlic cloves, crushed or grated

6 to 12 serrano chiles, preferably fresh, chopped fine
2 to 4 jalapeño chiles, pickled in oil *(en escabeche)*, chopped fine
salt to taste
¼ cup cracker crumbs
½ tsp. flour, dissolved in small amount of water to make a paste

118

In a large, heavy pot saute prepared meat in rendered suet until gray, being careful not to brown. Combine the chili powder, cumin, and paprika and mix thoroughly.

Prepare canned tomatoes by rubbing through a sieve or colander. To this puree, add water and garlic. Also, stir in the combined chili powder, cumin, and paprika, along with serrano and jalapeño chiles. Removing seeds from the chiles before chopping and adding to the pot will decrease the hotness of the dish, without sacrificing the chile flavor. Pour this mixture over cooked meat in the pot. Mix well and cook slowly for two to three hours, stirring occasionally to prevent sticking. Salt to taste and adjust seasoning. Add cracker crumbs and flour paste, blending well. Cook, stirring frequently, for an additional thirty minutes or more. If chili is not thick enough, make up a little more flour paste and stir in, cooking chili to desired consistency.

Cook's Note: "Serve chili with or without cooked dried red beans, or even spaghetti or tamales. Do not cook beans, spaghetti, or tamales with the chili."

WALTER'S CHILI

Over many generations, many variations on the chili theme have evolved into beloved, handed-down family recipes.

A prime example of this kind of family culinary activity is the privately published (in 1966) *This Little Higgy Went to Market*, subtitled "An Album of Recipes Collected by the Family of Hattie and Rufus Higginbotham." The family chili recipe included in the book is called "Walter's Chili." It is named for Walter Bergstrom, a now-retired lawyer from San Antonio, and comes from Harriet Lang Worsham, by way of Mary Jane Higginbotham Wilson, both of whom are from Dallas.

4 lbs. well-trimmed beef round, cut into small cubes	15 to 20 dried red chile peppers
1 lb. pork round, cubed (optional)	1 No. 2 can tomato juice
shortening or oil	1 Tbs. cumin seed
3 to 4 onions, diced	oregano to taste
2 to 3 bell peppers, cut small	chilipiquíns or Japanese chiles to taste
3 to 4 tomatoes, peeled and diced	1 clove garlic, chopped (optional)
	salt and pepper to taste

Brown meat in small amount of shortening or oil. Remove from skillet to a large pot. Saute onions, bell peppers, and tomatoes until soft, but not browned, in the same fat. Add to meat.

Remove stems and seeds from dried chile peppers. Rinse well. Cover with water and boil fifteen to twenty minutes or until skin separates easily from pulp. Save juice and run pods through a coarse strainer. Discard skins. Add juice and pulp from the chiles to meat and vegetables. Add tomato juice, cumin, oregano, chilipiquíns or Japanese chiles and, if desired, the chopped garlic. Salt and pepper to taste.

Simmer for three hours or until done. If mixture gets too thick, add small amounts of boiling water.

GEBHARDT'S CHILI CON CARNE

The recipe for this lusty Texas chili has appeared on the back label of bottles of Gebhardt's Eagle Brand Chili Powder for generations. At one time someone at Gebhardt's decided to remove the recipe from the bottle label, and it disappeared—but not for very long. Letters came pouring in from irate chili cooks, and it went back on the bottle pronto, and has been there ever since.

1 lb. ground beef
½ small onion, chopped (optional)
⅓ cup flour
1 tsp. salt
3¼ Tbs. Gebhardt's Original Eagle Brand Chili Powder

3 cups water or tomato juice
1 15-oz. can Gebhardt's Mexican Style Beans (optional), *or*
1 15-oz. can Gebhardt's Pinto Beans (optional)

Brown ground beef (and onion, if used). Drain off excess fat. Add flour, salt, and chili powder. Mix well. Pour water or tomato juice over seasoned beef. Stir and bring to a boil. Add the optional beans if desired and simmer gently for twenty minutes.

Author's Note: Use only Gebhardt's Original Eagle Brand Chili Powder in this recipe. Gebhardt's sets the standard by which all chili powders are judged, as Tabasco does for hot sauce. Forget the beans and enjoy the flavor of chili, San Antonio style.

FRANK HUNTER'S NEW ORIGINAL CHILI

During World War II Frank Hunter learned about chili in Texas, then he moved to Texas in 1947, got married, and started making chili in earnest. The Hunters are both talented with food. Faye Hunter has done very well for herself with an outfit called Olde Tyme Foods, Inc., of Dallas, which produces a line of packaged mixes, like jalapeño corn bread. In 1972, Faye and Frank decided to bring out a chili mix, based on Frank's recipe, which is called—not surprisingly—Olde Tyme Chili Seasoning.

½ lb. green beef fat (suet)
water
3 lbs. chili grind lean meat
1 medium onion, chopped
9 dried ancho or mulato chiles
1 medium pod garlic (about 9 to 12 cloves)
1 Tbs. cumin seed
¼ tsp. cayenne
1 tsp. ground oregano

Cook suet in ½ cup water about five minutes, or until transparent. Add meat and enough water to cover meat by approximately one inch. Bring to a boil and cook, covered, for fifteen minutes.

Remove seeds and stems from chiles. Scald and drain. Run the scalded chiles, garlic, and cumin seed through a food chopper or grinder. Add to meat mixture. Bring to a slow boil. Add cayenne and oregano. Cover and cook thirty-five to forty minutes, or until meat is tender.

TOM ERWIN'S CHILI RICE

To publicize a client's interests, public relations experts Tom Erwin and his brother Jim once saw a chartered planeload of journalists off to the Terlingua chili cook-off from Dallas. Before the day was over, they sweated through reports of a forced landing and a missing newsman. In a second hastily chartered relief aircraft, the Erwin's weary charges finally made it back to Dallas at dawn next day. The Erwins soothe the frustrations of such a daily grind with chili from Shanghai Jimmy's when they can, and their own concoction when they can't.

white rice, cooked and kept
   warm
pot of chili (no beans), kept
   warm
bowl of finely chopped white
   onion
bowl of freshly grated cheese,
   preferably sharp Cheddar

sweet pickle relish (English pic-
   calilli)
shaker can of powdered American cheese
butter
Tabasco

In a bowl to suit the size of your individual appetite, put in a layer of rice and top with a layer of chili. Generously sprinkle with chopped onion and a layer of sharp grated cheese. Add another layer of rice, a tablespoon of sweet pickle relish, and top with more chili. Sprinkle lightly with rice, a bit more onion, and a more-than-generous amount of the powdered American cheese. Lay on a pat of butter and dot with Tabasco. Stir to mix all ingredients well for that special taste.

Author's Note: Try making Shanghai Jimmy's rice concoction with the San Francisco product Rice-A-Roni. Or try making a Cincinnati Three or Four Way with Rice-A-Roni and lots of grated cheese.

HELEN CORBITT'S LOW-CALORIE CHILI (serves 8 to 10)

For years, the late Helen Corbitt ruled over Texas cuisine as director of the Zodiac Room at Neiman-Marcus in Dallas. The position carried a lot of clout, and not only with the leading ladies of Texas society. Texas wives have been feeding their husbands Helen's low-calorie chili for years, guarding its fat-free secret. One husband who found out, and couldn't believe it at first, finally said, "The hell with it. It's not the calories, it's the flavor that counts." In Texas, that's clout.

The following recipe is taken from *Helen Corbitt Cooks for Looks.*

2½ lbs. lean coarse-ground beef
2 Tbs. chili powder
1 clove garlic, chopped fine
1 cup canned tomatoes, mashed

½ cup onion, chopped
¼ cup diced dried chile pods,
   stems and seeds removed
1 qt. boiling water

Cook meat in a heavy saucepan until brown. Add chili powder, garlic, and tomatoes and cook for ten minutes. Add onion and cook for ten minutes longer. Put the chile in water and boil until soft. Pour this onto meat mixture and cook slowly for twenty minutes, adding more water if necessary.

JESSIE'S CHILI (4 quarts)

Helen Corbitt was also responsible for making the food at the Driskill Hotel in Austin, the state capital of Texas, internationally famous. Shortly after she took over there, a member of the press club headquartered at the hotel asked if she would soon be serving some of that gourmet food she was so famous for. "Yes," said Helen. "What did you have in mind?" "Well, I was thinking of chili," the member said. He got it, in the form of Jessie's Chili, named for one of the cooks at the Driskill.

The recipe for Jessie's Chili is taken from *Helen Corbitt Cooks for Company.*

¼ pound chile pods (1 package)   ¾ cup chili powder
1 qt. water   2 cups chopped onion
1 lb. coarsely ground beef suet 2 cups canned tomatoes
5 lbs. coarsely ground beef   4 Tbs. cornmeal
3 to 4 cloves garlic, finely   2 Tbs. flour
   chopped, *or*   water
1 Tbs. garlic powder   salt
2 tsp. ground comino (cumin)

Boil chile pods covered in a pot with one quart of water for fifteen minutes. Remove pods, and save water they have boiled in. Remove pods' stems and slip off the skins. Chop pods. Saute suet, beef, and garlic until meat is thoroughly cooked, about forty minutes, with comino and chili powder. Add onions and cook ten minutes, then add tomatoes mixed with cornmeal, flour, and chopped pods. Cook another five minutes. Add chili water and enough water to make two quarts. Simmer for about forty-five minutes or until all the flavors are well blended. Correct seasonings.

Cook's Note: "When I substitute coarsely ground turkey or chicken for the beef, I add ½ cup butter or salad oil in place of the suet."

123

CHAPTER 13

From the Southwest

BAXTER'S CHILI MIX

This once carefully guarded spice mix recipe, the flavor secret of the legendary Baxter Chili Parlor chili, is given here exactly as Henry, Baxter Poff's brother, wrote it down in 1978.

80 lbs. ground dried red chiles	1 lb. dehydrated garlic
20 lbs. cumin	1 lb. dried oregano

Blend all ingredients thoroughly. Use one pound (2 cups) mix to 15 pounds of meat for chili.

BAXTER'S CHILI (makes 15 pounds)

Henry Poff was unusually generous, for a One-and-Only chili cook and chili parlor proprietor, in sharing his recipes with his customers. In the early 1940s Albert Elmore, a jazz musician working in Oklahoma City, showed up at Baxter's regularly after work for a bowl of chili. When Elmore told Poff that his chili was the best he had found in a long career of searching out the real article, Poff not only gave him the recipe, but threw in a starter of butcher flour and tallow, so that Elmore could duplicate Baxter's chili exactly. Elmore's widow still has the recipe.

15 lbs. chili grind beef	3 ozs. salt
1 qt. water	1 lb. Baxter's chili mix
3 lbs. tallow (suet)	1 lb. butcher flour or wheat flour

Put beef and water into flat-bottom pot. Cook over medium heat for one to one and one-half hours, stirring occasionally with spoon or ladle so meat will cook evenly. When meat is tender, add suet and salt. Heat to boiling and then reduce heat to very low. Stir in chili mix thoroughly. Simmer for fifteen to thirty minutes. Add butcher flour and stir in well. Let stand ten to fifteen minutes.

Author's Note: Butcher flour is dried egg white, used by master butchers in many ways; for example, to coat the seams of a boned roast before rolling and tying. The butcher flour, without adding any taste of its own, holds the roast together during cooking and carving. It also makes an inspired thickening agent for chili, as the Poffs knew. Butcher flour is not easy to find these days, but a wholesale grocer or meat supply house is worth a try. As a substitute, use all-purpose wheat flour, as Poff suggests.

GENE ENGLAND'S CHILI

Judy and Gene England operate the Santa Cruz Chili & Spice Company at Amador and nearby Tumacacori, in the beautiful Santa Cruz valley south of Tucson, Arizona, and mail order their products around the world. The Englands market both cultivated varieties of chile and the native, wild—and very hot—chiltepínes (chilipiquíns) gathered by hand in the mountains of Sonora.

One Santa Cruz product that will interest serious chili-makers is the pure, unspiced paste the Englands make from their cultivated chile (they also make an unspiced powdered chile).

"One of the virtues of our paste is that it stays pristine and delicious until you open the jar, whereas powder tends to lose its authority in time, although refrigeration helps," says Mrs. England.

The Englands are both very high on the chili made from their chile paste by Gene England's recipe, which is given to their customers to help them adapt to what might be a new way of making chili for them.

½ lb. beef chuck, cut into cubes
water
1 garlic clove
2 Tbs. oil
2 Tbs. flour

1 to 2 Tbs. Santa Cruz Chile
Paste
1 cup water or meat broth
oregano or cumin to taste
(optional)

Brown meat, add water to cover, and simmer until tender. Pound garlic and brown in oil with the flour. Remove garlic and add chile paste and water. (The broth from the cooked meat may be used in place of part or all of the water.) Cook until thickened and flavor to taste, using oregano or cumin, if desired. Pour this sauce over the meat, mix, and heat to serving temperature.

Author's Note: Chile paste, or pulp, is also popular in New Mexico, and can be found in supermarkets there, in both red and green versions. In New Mexico, instead of canning the paste, it is frozen in both red and green varieties, and put into pint ice cream cartons or freezer containers. The rest of us are more or less stuck with making a red sauce out of dried red chile pods, which is not going to taste the same.

STELLA HUGHES'S ARIZONA CHILI

Stella Hughes, the chuckwagon cooking authority from Clifton, Arizona, describes the week she spent cooking chili on the National Mall during the bicentennial as "the trip of a lifetime." Especially that last day, the Sunday "Hurricane Belle blew in and rim-wrecked our festival. It was cancelled about ten A.M., but old country folk are well started by ten A.M., so the fire [was] going, the beans a-boilin' and chili was a-cookin'!"

Stella knows her way around a story like she knows her way around a cookfire, and both talents are evident in her book *Chuck Wagon Cookin'*, published by the University of Arizona Press. Here is the way she made her Arizona chili for the dudes in Washington.

25 lbs. beef, cut in bite-size pieces
bacon drippings, oil, or shortening
3 to 4 lbs. onions, chopped fine
6 to 8 large cloves garlic, diced fine
2 gals. canned tomatoes, crushed
2 cups brown sugar
1½ lbs. Arizona chile molido
oregano ("damned little," Mrs. Hughes specifies)
freshly ground coarse black pepper
salt to taste
1 cup Ac'cent
hot water

Brown beef in a large 16-inch Dutch oven in a generous amount of fat. Add onions and garlic. Let simmer in meat until all is browned. Stir in crushed tomatoes. Add brown sugar, chile molido, oregano, black pepper, salt to taste, and the Ac'cent. Simmer, stirring occasionally, more than two hours. Add water when needed to keep from sticking, being careful not to add so much that the chili is too soupy when served.

Cook's Note: "Pure ground red chili (chile molido) is what I use, Santa Cruz brand from Amado, Arizona. This is a coarse ground chili made from good red chiles. You can get it mild, picante, or if you ask, a grind for sausage makers that is a little hotter than hot."

GARY NABHAN'S YAQUI DEER DANCER SALSA

The tiny chile that grows wild from Louisiana, Texas, Arizona, and Mexico right on down to Colombia, and probably flavored the first chili, has been around so long (some say 7,000 years) that it has acquired a bewildering array of local names. But all who know it agree that it is *hot*, perhaps the hottest of chiles, given its size and weight.

Joe Cooper found chilpiquíns growing wild in vacant lots in his native San Antonio before World War I. He remembers the time the family cow got hold of some his mother had potted up for kitchen use (the cow was not happy).

Texas cattle barons have long carried little boxes of chilipiquíns with them when they travel, to season their food to taste like home. In 1976, the *San Diego Union* society page carried a report about the unsuccessful after-party search for an "antique silver snuff box, filled with wild chile peppers," which had been lost. A Hawaiian lady, similarly hooked on them, reportedly steeps the tiny chiles in a "silver and crystal bitters bottle" filled with gin.

The Sonorans who go up into the sierra to pick the chiltepínes do not carry silver snuff boxes, but know the craving well. Most of them, says Gary Paul Nabhan, an agricultural botanist at the University of Arizona, who works at the famous Arizona-Sonora Desert Museum near Tucson, "just crush two to five chiltepínes atop their carne machaca or caldo [soup]." For fancier occasions, Nabhan gives a recipe for a salsa which will turn meat into a basic, incendiary chili that might well be called Yaqui's Revenge.

32 chiltepínes	½ tsp. salt
½ cup white vinegar	½ tsp. garlic powder
pinch sugar	

Crush chiltepínes in vinegar. Add sugar, salt, and garlic powder. Mix well, put in a stoppered bottle, and store in refrigerator. Use to taste as a condiment.

Cook's Note: "In Sonora (Mexico), the vinegar used is an alcohol vinegar made from sugarcane."

Author's Note: A "sweet" gin, like Old Tom, might suit for this, or a fruit vinegar.

MOM UNSER'S CHILI

Mom Unser's chili leans toward the New Mexican regional variety of *carne con chile verde*—green chili—but is on record as being a winner. Her son, racing driver Bobby Unser, ate a big bowl of his mom's chili before the 1975 Indianapolis 500, which he won. Although Mom Unser has since passed away, the Flying Unser Brothers have kept on eating her chili before racing and they've kept on winning. The recipe is supplied by Ortega, the chile-oriented subsidiary of Heublein, of Oxnard, California.

1 lb. lean pork shoulder, cut in
  ¾-inch cubes
2 Tbs. flour
2 Tbs. lard
½ cup chopped onion
1 clove garlic, minced
1 16-oz. can whole tomatoes,
  coarsely chopped

2 7-oz. cans Ortega diced green
  chiles, or more to taste
¼ tsp. oregano
2½ tsp. salt
2 cups water

Dredge meat in flour. Melt lard in large deep skillet. Brown meat thoroughly. Add onion and garlic, and cook until onion is soft. Add remaining ingredients. Simmer covered for one to two hours, stirring occasionally. Remove cover. Simmer, uncovered, five to ten minutes to desired consistency.

CASADOS FARMS CARNE ADOVADA
(Carne en Chile Colorado)

At Casados Farms, outside San Juan Pueblo on the Rio Grande north of Santa Fe, Peter Casados grinds his homegrown chile molido and coarser chile caribe in two categories, regular and "local." The "local" type signals its extra hotness with yellow flecks of seeds ground along with the chile. Made with any other chile, his chili recipe, which he calls Carne Adovada, and subtitles Carne en Chile Colorado, won't taste like the chili Mrs. Casados makes at the farm. But it will still be good, because of the interesting method she uses.

2½ to 3 lbs. pork, or other meat
1 clove garlic, mashed
1 tsp. salt, or to taste

oregano to taste
1 cup chile caribe
2 Tbs. shortening

Marinate meat approximately six to eight hours in a combination of garlic, salt, oregano, and chile caribe mixed with water. Put meat mixture in skillet with two tablespoons shortening to fry or bake. Fry or bake at 350°F for about one and one-half hours.

Cook's Note: "Remember, pork has to be cooked slowly! The sauce will eventually dry as you cook slowly. Serve with freshly cooked beans and warm tortillas."

CASADOS FARMS CHILE CARIBE SAUCE

At Casados Farms, they make a fine chile caribe sauce from their own ground caribe, which they mail order, along with their homegrown chile and chicos (dried corn). This caribe sauce makes a fine jerky chili (don't forget to omit extra salt when making it). Jerky shredded or cut into small pieces is added to the sauce about the time it starts to boil. The longer it simmers, the better the flavor.

3 Tbs. chile caribe	1 clove garlic, minced
1 Tbs. shortening	salt to taste
2 cups water	

Brown the chile caribe in heated shortening. Add water and boil to thickness desired. Add garlic and salt to taste.

Cook's Note: "A real delicacy is jerky (we prefer either pork or beef) that has been marinated in the chile caribe sauce and then hung out to dry, mmmmmm! To eat, place a few pieces in a flat pan, in the oven. Set oven at approximately 350°F. Keep turning the meat so that it is heated on all sides, approximately five to ten minutes."

TONY VELASQUEZ'S CHILI

T. J. Velasquez, now retired from the USAF, remembers that his father, who in his youth was a cowboy for a large ranch in New Mexico, told him that he "always carried beef or venison jerky in his saddle bags. When the time came to eat, and he was far from the ranch or chuckwagon, he would break up the jerky, boil it, add chile, make camp bread, and have a feast."

Tony's own chili recipe, which has spread around the world as he has traveled on assignment for the air force, shows more refinement.

1½ lbs. good quality beef, and
1½ lbs. pork, both cut in bite-
   size pieces
1 large clove garlic, crushed or
   minced
1 tsp. cumin seed
1 Tbs. oregano
1 medium onion, minced
1 medium bell pepper, chopped

3 stalks celery, minced
2 Tbs. flour
4 Tbs. New Mexico chile molido
   (ground)
2 Tbs. New Mexico chile caribe
   (crushed)
hot water
salt to taste

Brown beef and pork with garlic, cumin seed (rubbed between the palms of the hands), and oregano. Drain off all grease. Add onion, bell pepper, and celery. Cook until vegetables are soft and clear, then stir in the flour. Add chile molido and chile caribe and mix well. Add hot water slowly to the mixture, stirring until desired consistency is reached. Bring chili mixture to a boil, then simmer for at least three hours. Add salt to taste.

Cook's Note: "We serve beans separately. Then . . . guests can make their serving as spicy as they desire."

CHILE COLORADO CON CARNE
(from *Chile,* NMSU Cooperative Extension Service
Circular 463, February 1976)

Since chile is one of New Mexico's most important crops, the State Agricultural Extension Service has much information available on the subject. Their booklet titled *Chile* is highly recommended for both beginner and advanced chili cooks as a guide to the preparation and cooking of chile.

1 lb. lean pork or beef, ground
   or cut into 1-inch cubes
1 Tbs. flour
1 tsp. salt
1 clove garlic, crushed

1 to 2 cups red chile sauce
dash of cumin
4 to 5 coriander seeds, crushed
dash of oregano

Fry meat in heavy skillet on medium heat until lightly browned. Add flour and salt. Add remaining ingredients. Cover and simmer for thirty to forty-five minutes.

FRESH RED CHILE SAUCE (makes 1 to 1½ cups)
(from *Chile*)

14 to 24 fresh red chiles
1 tsp. salt
1 tsp. oregano
1 clove garlic

1 small onion, sliced
water
1 Tbs. butter or margarine

Remove stems, seeds, and veins of fresh red chiles. Cover with boiling water and let stand ten minutes. Remove chile to a blender container with salt, oregano, garlic, and onion. Add water, according to blender requirements, and blend until all ingredients are reduced to a smooth paste.

Put sauce in heavy pan. Add ½ cup water, or more, depending upon the amount used in blending. Add butter or margarine. Simmer about thirty minutes or until mixture has the desired consistency. Stir occasionally to keep from burning.

Author's Note: In southwestern and Mexican kitchens, this sauce is a much-used kitchen standby, for dishes like "red" enchiladas—"in-chies" in Tex-Mex—but it makes a handy base sauce for chili, too, and can be refrigerated or frozen. Chili cooks might want to add cumin, and replace the butter/margarine with kidney suet, rendered in the pan before the other ingredients are added.

DRY RED CHILE SAUCE
(from *Chile*)

Whole pods or chile powder may be used in making red chile sauce. Toasting the chile pods before sauce is made is optional. The pungency is largely in the veins of the chile, so for a milder sauce, remove veins.

SAUCE I

Remove stems, seeds, and veins from 14 to 24 chile pods. Wash in warm water. Place chile in a pan and cover with hot water. Heat to almost a boil. Remove pan from heat and let pods stand in water for one hour, or until the pulp separates easily from the tough outer skin. Put through a ricer or colander, adding enough water to remove pulp. If sauce is very thick, thin with water to desired consistency. Add salt to taste.

SAUCE II (blender method)

Remove stems, seeds, and veins from 14 to 24 chile pods. Wash and drain. Spread on cookie sheet and dry chiles in a warm oven (200° to 250°F), turning frequently. Leave oven door open. Chile burns easily—giving the sauce what some classify as an undesirable flavor. Remove chile to pan, cover with hot water, let boil for ten minutes or until pulp is soft and separates from skin. Use cooking water for the required amount of liquid. Blend until a smooth paste is acquired. Strain (optional). Add salt to taste.

SAUCE III

3 Tbs. olive oil or shortening
2 Tbs. flour
½ cup New Mexico chile molido
2 cups water
1 tsp. salt

Optional:
1 clove garlic, crushed and added to fat
1 tsp. oregano, blended with chile molido
4 Tbs. finely chopped onion cooked in fat before adding flour
Substitute tomato juice for 1 cup water

Heat oil or shortening, blend in flour, and cook until flour is done—three or four minutes. Add chile molido and blend. Use moderate heat, as chile molido burns very easily. Blend in water. Cook to desired consistency. Add salt. The quality of the sauce depends on the quality of the chile molido.

Author's Note: Dried red chiles sometimes become so brittle that they break up when handled. They will be much easier to stem and seed if they are "relaxed" first by heating them on a griddle or in the oven to make them more pliable.

133

CHAPTER 14

From the Midwest

H. ALLEN SMITH'S PERFECT CHILI

This is the version of H. Allen Smith's chili recipe that appeared in his last article about the subject, "The Perfect Chili," written shortly before his death in 1976.

4 lbs. carefully trimmed sirloin, or tenderloin tips, coarse grind
olive oil and/or butter
1 or 2 6-oz. cans tomato paste
1 qt. water
3 or 4 medium-size onions, chopped
1 bell pepper, chopped

2 to 10 cloves garlic, minced
1 Tbs. oregano
½ tsp. basil
1 Tbs. cumin seed or ground cumin
salt and black pepper to taste
3 Tbs. chili powder, or more
1 or 2 cans pinto or pink beans

Cook meat in olive oil and/or butter until gray. Add tomato paste and water. (Chopped fresh tomatoes, or canned tomatoes which have been sieved, may be substituted for the tomato paste.) Stir to blend, then mix in remaining ingredients except beans. (If available, chile pods may be used in place of chili powder.) Simmer covered for two to three hours, stirring occasionally. Taste and correct seasonings as needed. Add one or two cans of pinto or pink beans ten to fifteen minutes before serving time.

GEBHARDT'S CHILI LOVERS CHILI (serves 6)

Chili lovers from the arid Southwest get nervous in the presence of too much greenery, and the green peppers and celery in the chili of more verdant regions put them off, with mutterings of "spaghetti sauce!" and the like. Especially if the recipes call for tomatoes unaccompanied by lusty amounts of chile, garlic, and cumin.

Here is a typical midwestern way of making chili (or chilli). Like the chili recipes peddled at the St. Louis Fair in 1904, which led the way to chili's popularity in the Midwest, this modern recipe is also from San Antonio. It comes from Gebhardt's, and is specially tailored to midwestern tastes.

Traditional chili lovers are assured that the historic, lusty chili recipe that has appeared on the back of the Gebhardt's Chili Powder bottle for generations is still there.

1½ lbs. lean ground beef	2 cups water
2 cups chopped onion	2 Tbs. Gebhardt's Chili Powder
1 medium green pepper, chopped	1 Tbs. salt
	1 bay leaf
2 large garlic cloves, chopped	¼ tsp. Gebhardt's Hot Sauce
1 28-oz. can whole peeled tomatoes, broken up	2 15-oz. cans Gebhardt's Mexican Style Chili Beans
1 8-oz. can tomato sauce	

Cook beef, onion, green pepper, and garlic in large saucepan or Dutch oven until meat loses its red color. Stir in all remaining ingredients except beans. Cook over low heat, covered, for one and one-half hours. Add beans and cook thirty minutes longer.

"CINCY" CHILI

Although recipes for "authentic" Empress and Skyline chili are published regularly, they are actually closely held family secrets. Here is a version compiled from various efforts to satisfy the steady stream of requests for a Cincinnati chili recipe.

2 lbs. chili grind beef
2 medium onions, chopped
2 cloves garlic, mashed
1 8-oz. can tomato sauce (see
   Cook's Note)
2 cups water
1 Tbs. red wine vinegar
2 Tbs. chili powder, or chile
   molido
1 Tbs. paprika
2 tsp. freshly ground black pepper

1 tsp. honey, *or*
½ tsp. sugar
½ tsp. cumin
½ tsp. marjoram
½ tsp. allspice
¼ tsp. cinnamon
¼ tsp. cloves
¼ tsp. mace
¼ tsp. coriander
¼ tsp. cardamom
small piece of bay leaf, crumbled
salt to taste

Sprinkle some salt over bottom of a hot skillet or Dutch oven and add beef, onion, and garlic. When starting to brown (see *Cook's Note*), add tomato sauce, water, and rest of ingredients. Simmer at least two hours, stirring frequently.

Cook's Note: "To make Coney Island sauce, after browning beef mixture, put into blender for a few seconds (divide mixture into convenient blender portions), then return to skillet or pot and add remaining ingredients, substituting tomato paste for the tomato sauce. Simmer one to two hours until thick, adding water if necessary. Also good over spaghetti."

Author's Note: If the search for the Cincinnati chili of fond memory is important, add spices one at a time, tasting after each addition. When taste is right, stop adding ingredients. If the first attempt misses, the next time start adding spices from the other end of the list. Up to a teaspoon of turmeric may do it. Start off with ¼ to ½ teaspoon and work up.

LES FULLER'S CONEY ISLAND CHILI SAUCE

Les Fuller of Niles, Illinois, is a food scientist involved in product development who worked at one time for Wolf Brand Chili Company, owned by Quaker Oats Company. He has applied scientific methods and the know-how of years of eating Coney Islands to break the secret of Coney Island chili topping.

¼ cup olive oil
¾ lb. 70% lean ground beef
1 8-oz. can tomato sauce
4 dried chile pods, finely ground
3 cloves garlic, mashed
1½ tsp. sugar

½ tsp. turmeric
½ tsp. oregano
½ tsp. cumin
½ tsp. paprika
1½ tsp. cornstarch
¼ cup water

Heat oil in skillet. Fry beef for three minutes, breaking it up well. Add remaining ingredients, except cornstarch and water. Cover and simmer for twenty minutes, stirring frequently to prevent sticking or burning. Add just enough water to keep mixture flowable if necessary. Mix cornstarch with ¼ cup water. Add to meat mixture and simmer, stirring, for about ten minutes until desired thickness is achieved.

Author's Note: Most recipes that claim to duplicate Cincinnati chili call for cinnamon, cloves, allspice, etc. With turmeric, Fuller is right on the mark for that elusive flavor secret.

CHILI MEAT SAUCE

Harry Hoehne, of the Green Bay, Wisconsin, Chili John's, and Mickey Lamere, of the Chili John's in Burbank, California, don't even share their chili-making secrets with each other, much less anyone else. But here is a recipe for "meat sauce," as Chili John's straight chili is called, which is over forty years old.

It makes a chili too rich and pungent for some to savor straight— although some chiliheads are going to love it that way. It is actually a condensed brick chili (no water or other liquid except that from fat is used) and may be so employed if desired.

After examining the recipe, Hoehne wrote: "Our only comment to those who claim they know our recipe is: 'Often imitated, but never duplicated.' "

2 lbs. lean, closely trimmed chuck or beef shank, coarsely ground together with
1 lb. kidney suet
4 to 6 cloves garlic, crushed
1 tsp. chile caribe (coarsely ground red chile with seeds), *or*
1 heaping tsp. of crushed chilipi-quíns

1 Tbs. cumin seed
2 Tbs. chili powder
1 Tbs. paprika
1 Tbs. salt

Saute meat-suet mixture in heavy pot or skillet until gray. Add garlic, chile caribe (or chilipiquíns), and cumin seed and continue to saute, stirring regularly, until fat is melted.

Add remaining ingredients and mix well. Lower heat and simmer gently for at least three hours until all liquid except fat is cooked out. The fat will keep it from scorching, but check it regularly anyway.

Pour into a loaf pan or heatproof bowl and let cool. When mixture solidifies it can be frozen or refrigerated whole or cut into pieces that can be added to a simmering pot of beans, or reheated for chili, etc., as needed.

Author's Note: Do *not* use a tender cut of meat for this dish; it will cook down to mush. Use no thickeners. For straight chili, cut meat into small cubes, no larger than ½ inch. In this case render the suet in the kettle or skillet before adding meat, garlic, chile caribe or piquíns, and cumin.

CHAPTER 15

From California

CARROLL SHELBY'S CHILI (serves 40)

Carroll Shelby not only raced cars, he produced the legendary Cobra sports and muscle cars. At one time, he was an owner of Terlingua (and the source of the mysterious ads for the "Terlingua Racing Team" which appeared in *Road & Track* in the early 1960s). Shelby helped organize the first chili parties at Terlingua—at first they were Good Ol' Boy get-togethers with chili-making on the side—which evolved into the CASI cook-offs now held there each fall. Like many experienced chili cooks, Shelby's enthusiasm for chili-making rises in direct proportion to the number of people available to eat the result. About forty, he figures, is the right number.

20 lbs. coarsely ground round or chuck beef
12 large onions, finely chopped
6 green bell peppers, chopped
6 red bell peppers, chopped
rendered suet or oil
5 15-oz. cans tomato sauce
1 gal. water
10 Tbs. chili powder

2½ tsp. cayenne
5 tsp. black pepper
5 tsp. oregano
10 tsp. ground cumin
20 cloves garlic, finely chopped
salt to taste
drained canned kidney beans, (optional), as desired

Brown meat, onion, and bell peppers in suet or oil. Transfer to a large pot and add tomato sauce and water. Mix well. Stir in remaining ingredients, except beans. Let cook for one to two hours, stirring occasionally. If beans are desired, add for the last half hour of cooking time, or heat separately and serve as a side dish.

Cook's Note: "I don't like the taste of fresh green chiles in chili, so I use the green and red bell peppers."

C. V. WOOD, JR.'S CHILI (makes 6 quarts)

C. V. Wood, Jr., to hear Texas chili purists tell it, is the Bad Boy of Chili. Wood (who is originally from Amarillo, Texas) got so rambunctious at the CASI Terlingua cook-offs (which he won), with his airlifts of Hollywood starlets, hot-air balloon (he says he was only trying to give the party a lift), and other circuslike goings-on, that he was invited to cook chili elsewhere. Which he did. Wood went west and helped found the International Chili Society, California's answer to CASI. The ICS has its own "world championship" chili cook-off each year, coincidentally held in the fall, like CASI's, at the California ghost mining town of Tropico, which is mighty like Terlingua, but with a major difference. Tropico is within easy helicoptering distance of Hollywood, whereas Terlingua, in west Texas, has been correctly described as being "miles and miles of nothing but miles and miles" from anywhere. (Texans claim they like it that way.) Consequently, the ICS cook-off each year is rewarded with the presence of celebrities, who in turn draw thousands of spectators anxious to ante up, in the name of charity, in order to watch the celebrities watch the chili cooks at work.

What most annoys Texas chili cooks is Wood's chili recipe, which is equipped with every optional custom accessory known to chilidom, and a few extras that Wood may have thought up just to pop the veins in certain Texas foreheads. But like Bob Pool used to say about his own Dallas chili with beans, nobody is on record as having turned down Wood's chili (especially when they find out what it costs by the bowl at Wood's Rangoon Racquet Club in Beverly Hills).

1 3-lb. stewing chicken, cut up
1½ qts. water
½ lb. beef kidney suet
4 lbs. flank steak
5 lbs. thin, center-cut pork chops
¼ cup finely chopped celery
7 cups peeled, chopped tomatoes
2 tsp. sugar
6 long green chiles, Anaheim green or New Mexico No. 6
8 ozs. good light beer, preferably Mexicali
3 tsp. ground oregano
3 tsp. ground cumin
½ tsp. monosodium glutamate (optional)
3 tsp. fine black pepper
4 tsp. salt
5 Tbs. chili powder
1 tsp. chopped fresh cilantro
1 tsp. thyme
2 cloves garlic, finely chopped
2 cups onion, cut into ¼-inch pieces
2 cups green pepper, cut into ⅜-inch pieces
1 lb. jack cheese, grated
1 large lime

In a 2-gallon pot simmer chicken parts in water for two hours. Strain off broth and discard chicken. Let broth simmer while preparing remaining ingredients. Render suet to make 6 to 8 tablespoons of oil. Throw fat away and reserve oil.

Trim all fat from flank steak. Cut into ⅜-inch cubes (plus or minus ½₆ inch, but try to stay as close to ⅜ inch as possible). Trim all fat and bones off pork chops, leaving only center portions. Dice these into ¼-inch cubes.

In a 2-quart saucepan combine celery, tomatoes, and sugar. Simmer one and one-half hours, or until all ingredients are completely tender.

Prepare green chiles by holding over an open fire until skins are seared. Remove skins and boil chiles for about fifteen minutes until tender. Remove seeds and cut into ¼-inch squares.

Put the following into 8 ounces of light beer and stir until all lumps are dissolved: oregano, cumin, monosodium glutamate, black pepper, salt, chili powder, cilantro, and thyme. Add tomato mixture, chiles, beer mixture, and garlic to chicken broth in 2-gallon pot. Stir with a wooden spoon and bring to a low simmer.

Brown pork in a skillet with about one-third of the oil from the kidney suet. With a medium-size skillet, it is advisable to brown only half at a time. The pork should become white on all six sides and fully separated. (Do not overcook at this point.) Add pork to the 2-gallon pot and bring to a low boil for about thirty minutes—pork needs a half-hour head start on the beef.

141

With balance of oil, brown the beef—about one-third at a time in medium-size skillet. Let it get white on all six sides—but do not overcook. Add the beef to the 2-gallon pot and cook at a low boil for about one hour.

Add chopped onions and peppers and cook at low boil for about two to three hours, stirring with the wooden spoon every fifteen or twenty minutes. Caution: You don't want the meat to break down too much, but it should be just about to break down, having by now become very tender.

Remove the chili from the stove and allow to cool for about an hour. Then refrigerate for twenty-four hours to allow the spices to permeate the meat without hurting its texture or breakdown point. Then you can reheat the chili to serve it, or you can freeze it.

About five minutes before you are going to serve it, grate the pound of jack cheese and add to the chili. Stir with a wooden spoon until completely dissolved. If you are only reheating part of the chili, use ⅙ pound of cheese to each quart.

About a minute before you are going to serve the chili, add the juice of one large lime or two small ones; stir. Serve with little round soup crackers.

Author's Note: Cilantro, the fresh leaves of the coriander plant, is sometimes called Chinese parsley. There is no substitute for it— if it can't be found at your grocer's or in an ethnic market, omit.

RALPH BELLAMY'S CHILI

Ralph Bellamy has been demonstrating his highly memorable range as an actor on stage and screen for decades. Bellamy also has long been known as a talented chili cook. For years, when he mailed out orders of his chili mix, Wick Fowler included Bellamy's recipes for embroidering chili, based on Wick's Mix. Bellamy's pièce de résistance in this flyer is called "El 2-Alarm de Fowler en el estilo de Bellamy."

Nowadays, when he has the time, like so many cooks who were started down the right path by Fowler's ingredients and directions, Bellamy likes to make his own chili from scratch. He cooks the peripheral ingredients used in his "2-Alarm de Bellamy" chili as a side dish. Bellamy favors corn in his chili, and he keeps it in his scratch recipe.

2 lbs. ground sirloin
2 rounded Tbs. chile molido
1 rounded Tbs. paprika
1 rounded Tbs. cumin
1 level Tbs. oregano
2 cloves garlic, sliced

1 large onion, diced
1 sliced bell pepper
1 8-oz. can tomato sauce
2 cups dry red wine
1 can Green Giant Mexicorn
salt

Sear meat until grayish color. Add chile molido, paprika, cumin, oregano, garlic, onion, and bell pepper. Stir to mix. Add tomato sauce and wine. Cover and simmer one and one-half hours. Stir occasionally. Add Mexicorn, salt to taste, and a tightener if necessary, and let simmer for fifteen minutes before serving.

Cook's Note: "Serve with raw chopped onion, crackers, beer, and a cold raw apple.

"For breakfast on a cold morning: Break two eggs into an individual casserole. Cover to top of casserole with 2-Alarm. Put in preheated oven at 350°F for ten minutes."

BELLAMY'S CHILI "SIDE"

1 onion, chopped
2 cloves garlic, sliced
1 bell pepper, chopped
oil
1 medium-size jar pimientos, chopped

1 small can chopped black (ripe) olives
2 cans Green Giant Mexicorn
1 can kidney beans (washed in strainer)
1 can pinto beans

Saute onion, garlic, and bell pepper gently in a little oil until soft. Do not brown. Add remaining ingredients and simmer twenty to thirty minutes. Serve as a side dish to chili.

JOHN FORD'S FAVORITE CHILI (serves 4 to 5)

John Ford loved chili; his daughter Barbara remembers that they had it at home at least once a week for as far back as she can recall.

Olive Carey, widow of the famous movie actor Harry Carey, and mother of Harry, Jr., was one of Ford's "regulars"—a member of the cast and crew he called together many times over the years to work with him on his movies. She remembers that Ford especially loved chili when working outdoors on location. He had the caterers serve it so frequently, in fact, that its steady presence would finally get to some members of the company, and they would work discreetly on Ford to agree to a short breather in the chili diet. Ford's favorite chili was prepared by his niece, Cecil DePrida, and this is the recipe she used.

1½ lbs. stewing beef	1 6-oz. can tomato paste
1½ cups chopped onion	1 tsp. salt
1 shake (clove) garlic, mashed	1 whole bay leaf
1 cup green pepper, chopped	1-lb. can pinto beans, drained
2 cups tomatoes, broken up	2 tsp. chili powder
1 8-oz. can tomato sauce	

Cook beef the night before, covering with water in a heavy pot and simmering slowly for two and one-half hours. Next morning, remove all grease. Chop meat into small pieces. Reserve one cup of broth.

Put into a heavy saucepan the meat and a cup of broth from the pot meat was cooked in. Add onion, garlic, green pepper, tomatoes, tomato sauce, tomato paste, salt, and bay leaf. Stir in drained pinto beans and chili powder. Cover and simmer one and one-half to two hours. Remove bay leaf and serve.

Author's Note: Ford liked his chili made according to the old cow-country practice of cooking the meat a day ahead, so it was tender by the time the chili-making began. For this reason the meat used in making John Ford's chili should be as tough as the hero of one of his movies.

GLORIA PITZER'S CHASE SONS CHILI (makes 2 quarts)

When she was first married and the kids were young, says Gloria Pitzer, the family couldn't afford to go to restaurants. So she duplicated in her home kitchen the foods that the Pitzers couldn't afford to eat out. How successful was she? For openers, McDonald's accused her of wangling their "Big Mac" sauce recipe from a former employee. No way, says Pitzer, she did it all with her thinking cap and her kitchen range. Then, there are the recipe books she has produced, like her *Secret Restaurant Recipes Duplicated*, and her monthly *National Homemakers Newsletter* (Box 276, Pearl Beach, MI 48052). Sample recipe titles: Archer Teacher Fish Batter, March Done All's Spec'l Sauce, Stuck Ease Pecan Pie, and last but far from least, Chase Sons Chili. About the last, Pitzer says: "Finally had a chance to sample the chili that Liz Taylor and Richard Burton had flown to them wherever they were making a film. . . . Not at all like the recipes in print that claim to be the same." She and Maude Chasen are in agreement on that point.

1 28-oz. can tomatoes, undrained	½ cup Open Pit Barbecue Sauce
1 10½-oz. can Campbell's beef broth	1 Tbs. Worcestershire sauce
2 10½-oz. cans Campbell's chili beef soup	¼ cup cornmeal
1 16-oz. can kidney beans, undrained	½ tsp. garlic salt
1 16-oz. can chili beans in hot chili gravy	1½ tsp. cumin powder
	1 tsp. paprika
	1 Tbs. chili powder

In order listed, combine all ingredients in a 6-quart kettle on medium high heat, stirring until all ingredients are blended. Turn heat to simmer and cook on lowest heat for four hours.

JOHN NATION'S CHILI PIQUANTE

In his book *The Life and Legend of Gene Fowler* H. Allen Smith tells of the time that Fowler was assigned as a young reporter to interview the actor John Barrymore, known to be hard on those sent on such a mission. Barrymore insisted that the interview be conducted over chili and gin at the one-room apartment of a man known as the Baron. As happens at such times, the three men first focused their attention on the gin. The Baron's dog, Jim, got tired of waiting for his dinner. He gobbled the pot of chili, set on the floor to cool, down to the last lick. The Baron had made this chili the way Barrymore—a connoisseur of both chili and gin—liked it, which was *muy picante*, hot as the hinges of hell. Jim the dog discovered this fact about the time the Baron, Barrymore, and Fowler discovered the theft of their chili.

"Jim's rear end was on fire," Allen wrote, "and he was snapping in its direction as if he were being stung by digger wasps; he was baring his fangs and chasing his tail wildly and as Fowler later phrased it, 'plunging like a lassoed elk.'

"John Barrymore watched Jim's wild caracoling and listened to his jungle screeching (to which sounds was now added a resonant crackling flatulence) and finally issued a professional observation:

" 'Christ! What a performance! Perhaps I should have a serving of chili an hour before curtain time!' "

John Nation, an adept Los Angeles chili cook, has a remarkably similar story to tell about his chili and his dog, Rebel, but with an important difference. Rebel thrives on the stuff. John Nation calls his concoction Chili Piquante, and it is *muy picante*. Barrymore would have loved it.

2 lbs. chili grind beef stew meat
1 medium-size red or white
  onion, chopped
oil
1 15-oz. can tomato sauce
water
4 ozs. pasilla or California mild
  chile molido

2 Tbs. New Mexico hot chile
  molido
2 Tbs. ground cumin
1 tsp. paprika
1 Tbs. masa flour

If chili grind meat is not available, cut beef to thumbnail-size pieces. Sear meat and onion in a little oil until meat is a uniform gray color. Add tomato sauce and 1½ cans of water. Stir to mix, then add spices and stir again to mix thoroughly. Cover and bring to a bubbly boil. Reduce heat to very low and simmer for about one hour and fifteen minutes, stirring now and then.

Mix masa flour with just enough warm water to make a medium-thick paste. Add to chili and simmer another fifteen minutes uncovered. Masa thickens the chili and seems to add flavor. Taste and adjust seasonings. Chili should be salty enough for most tastes. Do not add salt until tasted.

Cook's Note: "The cooked chili is ready to eat; however, I like to let it 'steep' overnight to improve the flavor. This chili should be spicy enough for most, and not too hot for tender palates. Personally,

I add New Mexico chile to my serving at table. I like it straight; others prefer it over fluffy white rice, or with beans. The beans should be pintos, cooked separately and served on the side. Toppings can be chopped onion, grated sharp cheese, ketchup, even pickle relish— or, God forbid, all of them together."

JO LATHWOOD'S CHILI

Jo Lathwood's chili parties are famous. A clothes designer and artist, and great-niece of American painter Mary Cassatt, Lathwood has dressed, painted for, and fed the famous of Hollywood. Buyers come to her Santa Monica canyon studio from all over the world, and usually end up, she says, "sitting on the floor, eating my chili. I have a very special huge iron pot from Indonesia that I use . . . what a magnificent, bubbling mess it is to show to guests when they arrive!" With her chili Lathwood usually serves "avocado and sour cream, in big bowls, a bowl of cut red onions, and hot corn tortillas."

1 large red onion, chopped	3 buds garlic, crushed
3 Tbs. olive oil	celery seed to taste
¾ lb. lean beef, chopped	salt and pepper to taste
6 large ripe tomatoes, peeled and chopped, *or*	2 Tbs. red wine vinegar
	2 Tbs. brown sugar
1 large can stewed tomatoes	1 Portuguese sausage (linguisa),
3 Tbs. chili powder, or more to taste	peeled and chopped

Saute onion in olive oil until soft. Add meat and cook until reddish color is gone. Stir in tomatoes. Mix in chili powder, garlic, celery seed, salt, and pepper. Simmer for one hour. Add red wine vinegar and brown sugar, mixing in well. Add sausage and heat through.

Author's Note: Linguisa might be described as a Portuguese version of Spanish—not Mexican—chorizo. Spanish longaniza is even closer. A good garlic link sausage will substitute.

REBEKAH PRIZEWINNING ROSE BOWL CHILI (serves 80)

Shortly after dawn on New Year's Day, 1978, TV personality Ralph Storey appeared on the home screen, warming up to describe the upcoming Pasadena, California, Rose Parade for the millions who ritually tune in the parade each New Year's morning. Storey announced cheerily that he was still feeling a glow from the chili he had a few hours earlier, when he had been invited to join the workers on the Oddfellows float as they were taking a chili break. (The workers on the Oddfellows float went back to their task with an edge on their competitors that gained them a parade trophy.)

The job of provisioning the Oddfellows float workers was carried out by the ladies of the IOOF auxiliary, the Rebekahs, specifically the Monrovia, California, Rebekah Lodge. Mrs. Grace James of Arcadia, California, a chili cook and spokesperson for the lodge, says that the chili was made at home and driven out, heated, in insulated containers, to the Pasadena float-building area. It disappeared into the eighty-odd chilled, bone-tired workers in minutes.

6 large onions, chopped fine	3 tsp. black pepper, or to taste
¼ cup oil	3 tsp. garlic powder
12 lbs. ground beef	6 tsp. Lawry's Seasoned Salt
3 29-oz. cans tomato puree	2 tsp. Ac'cent
12 Tbs. chili powder, or to taste	11 15-oz. cans chili beans
5 tsp. monosodium glutamate	

Saute chopped onions in oil until clear. Add beef and brown lightly, breaking into small pieces with a fork. Mix in remaining ingredients, except beans, and simmer for three hours. Mix in beans and heat through before serving.

BILL WILLIAMSON'S CHILI

Bill Williamson, general manager of the chili products division of Universal Foods Company of Westminster, California, and past president of the American Spice Trade Association, goes back to the 1930s for his memories of good New Mexican chili: "During my college years, I played tenor sax and doubled on clarinet with a seven-piece band. . . . Way back in 1931, we booked a summer contract to play in the mining town of Silver City, New Mexico. After work, we always went somewhere to eat, as performers do, and there was a little open-all-night joint in Silver City where they made a tremendous bowl of chili. . . . I remember to this day how great it was, with its oyster crackers and chiltepínes (little round red balls)."

With memories like this to guide him, Bill Williamson's chili has distinct New Mexican overtones, including beans and green chile salsa.

1 Tbs. cooking oil	2 Tbs. garlic powder
2 lbs. *lean* meat, ground or finely chopped	1 tsp. oregano
1 onion, chopped	1 28-oz. can tomatoes, finely chopped
1 Tbs. flour	2 8-oz. cans green chile salsa
6 Tbs. chili powder	1 15-oz. can pinto beans, drained
1 tsp. monosodium glutamate	
1 Tbs. cayenne	

Saute meat and onion until meat begins to brown and onion is soft and transparent. Blend together flour, chili powder, monosodium glutamate, cayenne, garlic powder, and oregano. Combine these dry ingredients with water or some of the fat from meat, then add to meat. Add tomatoes, chile salsa, and pinto beans and simmer one hour or more. Serve with finely chopped onion sprinkled on top.

JEANNETTE BRANIN'S RAINY DAY CHILI

Jeannette Branin started putting vinegar in chili back in Kansas, where she grew up. The acidity cut the fattiness of the chili she got at Pop Hepner's, in Sterling.

In the South, particularly in Louisiana, vinegar cruets are often stuffed with inch-long red or green hot chiles—pricked with a fork before adding the vinegar. These give added zip to the dash or two put on everything from green beans to fried eggs—to chili.

1 lb. pink beans	¼ cup of the best chili powder
2 cans solid pack tomatoes	¼ cup dried oregano
2 lbs. lean ground round	1 Tbs. cumin seed
1 cup, firmly packed, ground suet	2 Tbs. ground cumin
2 large onions, finely chopped	salt to taste
2 cloves garlic, put through a press	

Soak beans overnight. Drain beans and put in a large kettle. Add tomatoes (juice and all) to beans and bring to a boil. Add remaining ingredients except salt, stirring until ground meat breaks up completely. Lower heat to simmer, cover, and cook most of the day. After cooking for several hours, add salt to taste. About an hour before serving, check seasonings and add more chili powder and ground cumin if needed.

Cook's Note: "Serve with a fresh spinach salad, soda crackers, and a cruet of vinegar."

MUZZY'S CHILI SUPREME

Ed Muzzy of La Jolla, once president of Almaden Vineyards, now heads the board of trustees of the San Diego Museum of Art. He is also food and wine consultant to various civic organizations. Muzzy's chili recipe begins with a solid foundation of chili tradition, and goes on from there to reflect—very subtly—his expertise in wines and cooking. The result is rich and provocative.

3 lbs. lean shoulder pork, finely ground
3 lbs. lean round steak, about ¼-inch dice
8 cloves garlic, minced
3 medium onions, diced
2 tsp. salt
1 tsp. black pepper
1 tsp. Ac'cent
2 cups Zinfandel wine
2 cups water
2 Tbs. Bovril

½ cup orange juice
1 tsp. sugar
7 Tbs. chili powder
3 Tbs. ground cumin
1 Tbs. ground thyme
1 Tbs. ground coriander, *or*
1 Tbs. ground oregano may be substituted
5 Tbs. masa harina
1 4-oz. can tomato paste
1 tsp. garlic powder
1 4-oz. stick butter

Brown meat with garlic, onion, salt, pepper, and Ac'cent. Simmer for about an hour. Add wine, water, Bovril, orange juice, and sugar and cook approximately one more hour. Carefully skim off all the fat. Add hot water, if necessary, to cover meat before skimming. Add the chili powder, cumin, thyme, and coriander—or oregano. Mix the masa harina in small amount of water and add. Then add the tomato paste, garlic powder, and butter. Check and adjust seasonings. Continue to simmer until done, adding water if necessary.

FATHER TOM WARREN'S OSO FLACO CHILI

Father Tom Warren is a modern-day mission father at San Buenaventura. His great-grandmother, Laureana Gularte, came around the Horn to California from the island of Pico, in the Azores, in the 1860's. His grandmother was baptized at Mission San Luis Obispo de Tolosa, and married at Mission Santa Ines. At the family ranch at Oso Flaco (Lean Bear) in the Santa Maria Valley, the family has kept the use of cumin, brought from the Azores, in its cooking. Along with this, Father Warren makes generous use of cardamom and locally grown and packed chile in his Oso Flaco Chili.

2 cloves garlic, diced
8 ozs. dried California red chiles, broken up and stems removed
4 Tbs. cumin seed
water
2 10-oz. cans Las Palmas red chile sauce
2 tsp. dried oregano
½ tsp. ground allspice
1 tsp. ground cinnamon
2 Tbs. chili powder
1 tsp. dried oregano
4 Tbs. ground cardamom
salt to taste
olive oil
2 lbs. ground round
Cabernet Sauvignon or other good California dry red wine

Place garlic, chiles, and cumin in a large stewing pot. Fill pot three-quarters full of water and let ingredients soak overnight. Next morning, bring to a boil. Add the chile sauce, spices, and salt. Cook over low heat for about two to two and one-half hours. In a little olive oil, lightly brown ground beef and add to pot. Simmer until seasonings are well blended with meat. To add a little zest, pour some Carbernet Sauvignon into the chili and heat to proper serving temperature.

PUNKIE'S CHILI

Nick Peirano's sister Virginia typed manuscripts for mystery writer Erle Stanley Gardner. This gave Gardner an excuse to drop by for some of Mother Clara Peirano's enchiladas or lasagna, when the word went out that she was making them. The Peiranos have adapted their Northern Italian cooking expertise to California-style dishes, like this chili, named for Nick's daughter Arlene, who is called Punkie.

1 lb. Italian sausage, bulk or links with casings removed, chopped
olive oil
1 large onion, chopped
2 lbs. lean chili grind beef
3 to 4 cloves garlic, minced
4 large fresh mild green California chiles, roasted and peeled with seeds removed, chopped; or
1 7-oz. can Ortega green chiles, diced
½ cup pure red California chile molido
1 Tbs. paprika
1 Tbs. fresh chopped oregano, or
½ tsp. crushed dried oregano

1 jalapeño chile, fresh or canned, seeded and diced
1 tsp. whole comino or cumin seed (optional)
3½ cups fresh or canned peeled Italian plum tomatoes, chopped
1 cup Cribari Vino Rosso red wine
salt to taste
freshly ground black pepper to taste
1 15-oz. can pinto beans, with liquid
1 15-oz. can garbanzo beans, with liquid
1 cup green or ripe whole pitted olives

Cook Italian sausage in a heavy pot until crumbly and beginning to brown. Remove sausage and add a small amount of olive oil to pot. Saute onion in the olive oil until clear, then add ground beef and garlic. Cook, stirring occasionally, for about twenty minutes. When meat is gray but not browned, add cooked Italian sausage, green chiles, chile molido, paprika, oregano, jalapeño, and cumin seed. Stir to blend, then mix in tomatoes, which have been chopped, and the red wine. Simmer, stirring frequently, for one and one-half to two hours, adding salt and black pepper to taste.

Add the pinto and garbanzo beans for the last thirty minutes of cooking time. Olives should be mixed into the chili a few minutes before serving, just long enough to heat through.

HARRIS RANCH CHILI

With good reason, meat lovers have long flocked to restaurants located at or close to stockyards. At Coalinga, in California's San Joaquin Valley, Ann Lee Harris and her husband Jack own and operate one of the best of these, the Harris Ranch Restaurant. They also run the Harris Country Store and Feed Company. The latter is one of the country's largest beef-feeding lots. It supplies the restaurant and the store with the beef which, along with the other good things, prompted *Gourmet* magazine to rave about the Ranch's "western food of quality and integrity," and to add, "There is nothing else comparable to this restaurant in California." Here is the Harris's chili recipe.

¼ lb. beef suet
½ cup chopped onion
2 lbs. lean chuck, coarsely
   ground
1 Tbs. chili powder
1 Tbs. flour

1 tsp. powdered cumin
cayenne to taste
1 Tbs. salt
1 Tbs. coarsely ground black
   pepper
water

In a heavy iron skillet melt down the suet, and discard. Add onions and brown. Add ground beef and stir until it has turned gray—do not brown.

Mix next six ingredients in a small mixing bowl. Add water slowly, stirring well to make a thick gravy. Add to meat, mixing thoroughly. Add enough hot water, gradually, to cover meat, and let simmer on low heat for approximately forty-five minutes. Stir frequently to keep from sticking, using a wooden spoon. If chili looks too greasy, mix a little more flour and water to thicken. Taste and correct for salt and pepper seasoning.

Author's Note: Like many stockyards restaurants, the Harris Ranch features mountain oysters. Fried *huevos de torito*—literally, eggs of bull calf—are a favorite hors d'oeuvre in La Cantina, the Ranch's bar.

HARRIS RANCH BEANS

Like Ann Lee Harris's chili, her bean recipe is a solid and simple one, with the all-important stipulation that the salt should be added only in the final stages of cooking, which keeps the beans firm and whole. And the beans are added to the chili only in the final stages of serving—if at all—which will gratify many chili—and bean—lovers.

2 cups pinto beans	1 long green chile, peeled and
water	seeded
1 smoked ham hock with lots of	1 pod of dried red chile
skin	salt to taste

Pick over beans for stones and stems and wash before putting into a 4-quart kettle. Add water to cover four to five times above the volume of the beans. Add smoked ham hock—the skin has the flavor—and let boil for approximately three hours. When beans are beginning to soften, add the green and dried red chile. Add salt to taste and continue to cook for another twenty minutes.

Let cool. Beans are always better if cooked ahead and reheated. Be sure there is plenty of liquid, but try not to add liquid unless necessary. If you need to add water, be sure it is boiling so cooking is not retarded.

Author's Note: Good cooks in the Southwest know the truth of Ann Harris's tip that pork skin "has the flavor." They get neatly rolled sheets of pork skin from their neighborhood markets for flavoring their frijoles (beans), chicos (dried corn), and posole (a stew of hominy and green or red chile).

HELEN GRESSETT'S RED WINE CHILI (serves 12)

Helen Gressett, a native Philadelphian, ate her first chili on a stop-over in El Paso, on a train trip from the East to California. She fell in love with the dish, and started teaching herself to make it. Now, husband Jess, who grew up eating chili in Texas, says that Helen could make a living selling her own concoction, while his wife modestly admits that she likes her own better than any she has ever tasted, the mark of the advanced One-and-Only chili cook. What gives Helen Gressett's chili its distinctive northern California touch is the sturdy red jug wine she uses as part of the liquid.

2 lbs. chuck, cut into ½-inch
   cubes
1 Tbs. rendered fat from
   trimmings
1 large onion, minced
1 clove garlic, peeled, minced
1 No. 2½ can tomatoes,
   including liquid
2 Tbs. chili powder, or to taste
1 tsp. ground cumin

1 tsp. oregano
1 bay leaf, crumbled
½ tsp. freshly ground black
   pepper
1 tsp. salt
1 cup good red jug wine, such
   as Burgundy or Barbera
1 cup water
4 cups dried pinto beans, cooked
   separately

Brown beef in fat, push to one side, and add onion and garlic. Cook until yellow. Break up tomatoes into small pieces and add with seasonings and spices to the pot. Stir well. Add wine and water. Simmer partially covered about one and one-half hours, or until meat is very tender. Cool, cover, and refrigerate overnight, if possible, to blend flavors.

Next day, add beans and additional liquid if needed. Adjust seasonings and heat just to boiling. Serve in bowls and top with sour cream, chopped fresh cilantro, and chopped raw onion.

Author's Note: Iron pots and long-simmering with wine are not compatible (see Chapter 8), so use something other than an iron pot when cooking this recipe.

OLD CALIFORNIA CHILI

Like the makings for the chili pemmican of the western prairies, all the ingredients for this early chili of California were available on the spot. Shortly after the missions became established, and their gardens, vineyards, olive groves, and cattle herds began to thrive, the coming together of beef, olives, chile, and wine in the same cooking pot were well nigh unavoidable. This recipe employs them all.

3 lbs. beef, cut into small pieces
salt and pepper
6 Tbs. olive oil
3 Tbs. toasted breadcrumbs
1 to 2 cloves garlic, mashed
1½ Tbs. red wine vinegar

1 qt. thick red chile pulp,
   prepared from dried red
   California ancho chiles (see
   Chapter 9 for methods of
   preparation)
1½ cups pitted ripe black olives

Season beef well with salt and pepper. Heat three tablespoons of olive oil, brown meat, then reduce heat. Simmer until meat is tender. Heat remaining three tablespoons olive oil in an iron skillet. Saute breadcrumbs and garlic in the oil, stirring constantly, until golden. Add vinegar and chile pulp. Simmer fifteen minutes. Gently stir meat and ripe olives into the sauce in skillet. Cook for about ten minutes, or until thoroughly heated.

LUCY MAYTAG'S ANCHOR STEAM BEER CHILI
(serves 4)

At one time during the gold rush days, San Francisco had more than two dozen steam beer breweries. (The steam beer process was developed to get around the city's lack, at that time, of cold storage necessary for lagering the pilsener-type beer preferred by Americans.) By 1965, San Francisco's unique steam breweries had dwindled down to one, the Anchor Brewing Company, and it was about to quit business when Fritz Maytag came to the rescue.

"Meet a Maytag Who Produces Suds That Will Not Clean Duds," the *Wall Street Journal* headlined its story about Maytag's getting into the steam beer business, describing him as the "scion of the Iowa washing-machine family."

It is only natural that Maytag and his wife, Lucy, have experimented with using steam beer in cooking. Lucy Maytag says that "cooking with steam beer is like cooking with wine. Steam beer adds a little something to the end product, but doesn't dominate it." Here is the result of some Maytag research into making chili with steam beer.

1 lb. ground chuck	1 or more dried pasilla chiles
½ onion, chopped	1 tsp. basil
4 cloves garlic, chopped	1 tsp. oregano
2 fresh tomatoes, peeled and roughly chopped	1 Tbs. cumin
	salt to taste
3 Tbs. tomato paste	1 or 2 bottles Anchor Steam beer
2 dried California chiles	1 15-oz. can kidney beans

In a 4-quart saucepan saute chuck together with onion and garlic until meat is just brown, stirring with a fork while it is cooking.

156

Pour off excess grease. Add all other ingredients except the beans, putting in only *one* bottle of Anchor Steam beer. Mix well. Cover, reduce heat to low, and simmer about forty-five minutes, stirring occasionally. Add beans with their juice and, if you like a soupy-type chili, a second bottle of beer. Continue cooking for another ten to fifteen minutes.

Cook's Note: ". . . [use] Anchor Porter for a darker, slightly richer flavor."

Author's Note: In California, the dried chile poblano is widely called a chile pasilla. They are dark, can be almost black, are roughly triangular in shape, and have a richer (and often more pungent) flavor than California or ancho chiles.

MERLE ELLIS'S SECOND BEST CHILI

Merle Ellis calls his chili Second Best Chili, because it is made with the "second best" shank chili meat, instead of "best" teen-aged longhorn. Another reason is that if he had claimed his chili to be "first best" in his newspaper column on the subject, he'd have been up to his neck in disputatious chili correspondence. In his private heart of hearts, Ellis, like every other chili cook, knows his chili is the One-and-Only. For the record, however, he stops short of confessing this.

4 lbs. lean tough beef shank, cut into cubes about the size of your thumb	2 tsp. dried oregano
	1 tsp. salt
	¼ tsp. pepper
¼ cup oil	¼ tsp. cayenne
1 medium onion, minced	1 tsp. paprika
2 to 3 cloves garlic, minced	½ tsp. sugar
1 15-oz. can tomato sauce	2 Tbs. masa harina,
1 12-oz. bottle beer	*or*
4 to 6 Tbs. chili powder	1 Tbs. flour mixed with 1 Tbs.
1 Tbs. cumin	cornmeal

Put meat in heated oil in a good-size heavy pot. Stir with a long wooden spoon so oil will coat the meat. Cook over low heat until the beef turns gray, stirring once in a while. Don't let meat brown. Add onion and garlic, cover, and simmer ten minutes. Add tomato sauce and beer. Cover pot and simmer for another ten minutes.

While meat mixture simmers, combine chili powder, cumin, oregano, salt, pepper, cayenne, paprika, and sugar in a small bowl. When the time is right, add all the spices to the pot and stir it up a bit. Put the lid back on, lower heat, and let it cook for one hour or so. Stir once in a while so it won't stick but keep lid on as much as possible so all that good rich pot likker stays inside. Just before serving, mix the masa or flour with cornmeal and with enough cold water to make a thin paste, and stir it into the chili to achieve just the right consistency.

Cook's Note: "Serve topped with chopped onions and accompanied with a cold beer!"

SYLVIA SEBASTIANI'S CHILI BEANS WITH WINE
(serves 4 to 6)

The northernmost in the chain of California missions, San Francisco de Solano was established in 1823 in the Sonoma Valley, north of San Francisco Bay. The nearby pueblo of Sonoma followed in 1835. The surrounding valley, called the Valley of the Moon by Jack London, who lived there, has since become a producer of some of California's finest wines.

The Sebastiani winery is in the forefront of Sonoma Valley wine producers. Sylvia Sebastiani is as famous for her cooking as her late husband, August, was for his wine. Her cookbook, *Mangiamo (Let's Eat!)*, is a collection of her family's favorite recipes, which have drawn many friends and guests to her table. The collection does not include this recipe for what Sylvia Sebastiani forthrightly calls chili beans with wine.

1 onion, chopped
4 Tbs. oil
4 Tbs. butter
1 lb. ground beef
2 cloves garlic, pressed
1 tsp. salt
1 package chili seasoning mix
(use all or part to taste)

⅔ cup California Burgundy or
Zinfandel
1 27-oz. can red kidney beans
2 8-oz. cans tomato sauce
pepper (optional)

Saute onion in a skillet in oil and butter. Add ground beef and garlic. Brown slightly and add salt and seasoning mix. Stir thoroughly and add wine, kidney beans, and tomato sauce. Add pepper if desired. Bring to a boil, lower heat, and cook thirty to forty minutes, stirring occasionally.

From the East Coast

ROSE MARIE BOGLEY'S CHILI

Nowadays, chili turns up in places that would curl an old-time chili cook's hair, not to mention his lip. Making its rounds among what it has called the "Powerful People," *W*, the chic semimonthly newspaper published by *Women's Wear Daily*, has discovered chili and chili fans about as far removed from chili's earthy beginnings as it is possible to get. For instance, Middleburg, Virginia, described by *W* as "the heart of the Hunt Country . . . where the smart set hides to escape its chauffeured limos, culture klatches and the bright glare of city lights."

At Peace and Plenty Farm, near Middleburg, *W* found Rose Marie Bogley serving chili to chilled riders of the fashionable Middleburg, Piedmont, and Old Dominion hunts after their weekly fall-and-winter cross-country gallops. No iron pot for this chili; it is served from an elegant silver punch bowl onto silver plates, after preliminary Bloody Marys in silver cups.

For tailgate affairs at race meetings, the Bogley chili appears in a large, homey-looking brown and black crock—the Bogley racing colors. This matches the color scheme of the Rolls parked alongside the buffet, set up on folding tables at the edge of the race course.

"I started making chili for hunt club affairs a couple of years ago," Mrs. Bogley told an interviewer. "We had one of those cold, blustery days, and I said, 'Oh, the hell with it, I'm going to give them something that will warm them up.' It's been a great success, and I've kept doing it. When the weather's cold, the chili just goes like mad. Everyone eats it first. It's amazing.''

The demand for the Bogley chili grew to where steps had to be taken. "When we give a hunt breakfast and the invitation is 'to the field,'" says Mrs. Bogley, "it means that with fifteen hunts going on the same day—that's every Saturday from October to March—you can get 150 guests, and, you know, that's a hundred and fifty pairs of boots in your house. Well, I just don't do that anymore, my hunt breakfasts now are 'invitation only.'"

A rancher might not be able to relate to jumping fences and frozen brooks for fun, just to work up an appetite for chili, but his wife will relate instantly to a trail of muddy boot prints in the house, all leading to the chili pot.

2½ lbs. top grade lean beef	1 tsp. freshly ground pepper
½ lb. pork	1 tsp. salt
2 Tbs. shortening	1 tsp. cumin seed
1 large onion, chopped small	1 tsp. oregano
2 cloves garlic, chopped small	½ cup fresh green pepper, finely
3 Tbs. chili powder	chopped
1 qt. ripe fresh tomatoes	1 large can red kidney beans,
3 bay leaves	drained and rinsed

Grind together beef and pork. Heat shortening in a skillet and brown meat, onion, and garlic. Add chili powder. Put fresh tomatoes through a sieve. If fresh tomatoes are not available, substitute one large can of tomatoes. Add to meat mixture.

Stir in remaining ingredients, except beans. Simmer for about two hours, then add the beans which have been very carefully drained and rinsed. Chili is better if made a day or two before serving.

Cook's Note: "If my chili's going to be served in the house, I make it thicker. If it's going to be served in the field, at one of the racing meets, I make it a little soupier, because I have big plastic cups for it. One good thing about chili is that you can freeze it. I like to pride myself on very seldom running out of anything, so sometimes we make it in stages for a couple of days beforehand, great pots of it. I think it's better after it sits for a while anyway, and if there are any leftovers, we freeze it."

LUCY WADE'S CHILI

Lucy Simounet Wade lives with her husband, Floyd, in Falls Church, Virginia. Her mother was English, her father French, one grandmother Spanish. Lucy's chili is an amalgam of all these cooking heritages, overlaid with several generations of family residence in Puerto Rico. Despite his Texas chili prejudices, Floyd Wade considers his wife's chili "infinitely subtler and more interesting to the palate" than some made with "heaping portions of Texas macho."

2 medium onions, finely chopped
1 small bell pepper, seeded and quartered
2 fresh ajicítos (tiny, round, button-shaped tropical chiles), optional
olive oil
3 large garlic cloves
2 tsp. salt
2 8-oz. cans Spanish-style tomato sauce

1 Tbs. Italian seasoning
1 lb. ground sirloin
1 6-oz. can Spanish-style tomato sauce
1½ Tbs. Goya achiotina, or substitute cumin
1 tsp. oregano
5 Tbs. chili powder, or to taste

Saute onions and bell pepper (and chiles, if used) in olive oil. Pulverize garlic cloves in a mortar with salt, and add with Spanish-style tomato sauce to onion and peppers. Work Italian seasoning into the ground sirloin. Blend in tomato sauce, Goya achiotina (or cumin), and oregano. Add to the onion-pepper-tomato sauce mix. Simmer for twenty minutes. Remove all trace of onions, garlic, and peppers from the pot. Mix in chili powder and heat to serving temperature.

Cook's Note: "Soak one pound of Goya habichuelas rositas No. 1 dried beans or pinto beans overnight. Drain, cover with water or chicken stock, and cook until tender, continually replacing stock as it evaporates."

Author's Note: In making her chili—and for much of her other cooking—Lucy Wade depends on a brand of Puerto Rican products called Goya, prepared by Puerto Rico Food Products Corporation, of Bayamon, PR 00619, and distributed in the eastern United States by Goya Foods, Inc., of Secaucus, NJ 07094.

Achiotina is the small, red seed of the annatto, much used as a coloring and flavoring by cooks of the Caribbean area and southern

Mexico. The seeds are soaked and ground to a paste, sometimes with other spices, before use.

CHARLES WILLEFORD'S TEXAS CHILI

Miamian Charles Willeford, whom the *Miami Herald* has described as "author, screenwriter, teacher, critic," and "sometime cook," teaches English at Miami-Dade Community College. He found his One-and-Only chili when visiting in Haiti. There he became friendly with a couple from Alvin, Texas. As it will, the subject of chili came up, and the wife gave her chili recipe to Willeford, who, of course, added his own embellishments to the concoction.

To feed twenty people, Willeford invites two of them over early, and together they make three pots of chili "with about four pounds of chili in each pot." As an appetizer he serves nachos before the chili course and afterward offers moon-pies and brownies for dessert. The drinks are "R.C. Cola, Dr Pepper, and Pearl Beer from San Antonio."

1 4-lb. chuck roast, cut into ½- to ¾-inch chunks
3 onions, chopped into ½-inch chunks
2 to 3 tsp. oil
salt and pepper to taste
2 heaping Tbs. cumin seed
6 cloves garlic
1 16-oz. can tomatoes
1 tsp. sugar
2 pkgs. chili seasoning
1 Tbs. chili powder
6 ozs. cold beer
4 Tbs. mole paste
Tabasco to taste
1 tsp. salt, or to taste
3 to 4 cups water
3 jalapeños, seeds and stems removed, chopped
⅔ cup masa flour

Brown meat and onions together in oil in an iron skillet. It is not necessary to cook meat thoroughly. Onions should be browned, but not caramelized. Season meat and onions with salt and pepper to taste and dump the skilletful into a large pot. Grind the cumin seeds in a mortar. Using the same pestle, mash up garlic. Add a little water. Remove cumin and garlic to meat.

In a blender, combine tomatoes, sugar, chili seasoning, and chili powder. Open a cold 12-ounce can of beer and pour 6 ounces into a glass. Drink the glassful and then pour the remaining 6 ounces from the can into the blender. Blend with tomato mixture and add to meat. Add mole paste, Tabasco, and salt, along with about a quart of water, to meat mixture. Add chopped jalapeños. Simmer about two and one-half hours, stirring occasionally.

At end of cooking time, make a runny paste of masa flour and water. Stir very fast as you add it to chili, or it will be lumpy. Cook thirty minutes more, stirring often. Serve hot.

MARGARET MANNING'S CHILI

Indefatigable *W* finds chili enthusiasts everywhere, even in Boston. In Cambridge *W* reports that Pulitzer Prize winning biographer Justin Kaplan makes the chili for the little dinners he and wife Anne Bernays have in town, and the chowder they serve at their place on the Cape.

In Boston's Back Bay, the Mannings, "Bob and Maggie," also like to give their dinner guests—who have included Julia Child—chili on cold, wet New England winter days.

The Mannings are both editors. Robert is editor-in-chief of the *Atlantic Monthly*, and his wife, Margaret, is book editor of the *Boston Globe*.

"I love chili," Margaret Manning says. "I make pounds and pounds of it and freeze it, and then make more." Mrs. Manning, who is from Nebraska, says that she was introduced to chili when she worked in New York City. Photographer Mark Kauffman gave her some packages of Wick Fowler's 2-Alarm chili mix, which has started many beginner chili cooks on their way to their One-and-Only chili. Mrs. Manning now typically makes her own, "from scratch, and so often that it's hard to remember, offhand, just what I do put in it." However, after some deliberation, Mrs. Manning came up with this recipe.

2 lbs. coarsely ground well-trimmed best beef
2 to 3 onions, sliced
chopped garlic, to taste
oil
3 Tbs. chili powder, or more
1 Tbs. cumin seed, or more
sea salt or kosher salt, to taste
cracked or freshly ground black pepper
2 Tbs. oregano

1 large can Italian peeled tomatoes, drained
1 or 2 4-oz. cans tomato sauce
cooked great northern or red kidney beans
Optional ingredients for flavor and added moisture, if needed:
red wine or beer
lemon juice
beef stock

Sear beef in iron skillet and remove to casserole. In the same skillet wilt onions and garlic in oil and add to casserole. Add chili powder, cumin seed, salt, pepper, oregano, tomatoes, and tomato sauce.

Simmer until all flavors meld, probably about four hours, adding wine, beer, lemon juice, or beef stock to taste as needed. If there is too much grease on top, counter with flour mixed with a little wine or water. And keep tasting.

When flavor and consistency are right, add the beans which have been cooked in beef stock with an onion. Heat beans and chili together until warm and serve with Italian bread and cole slaw.

Cook's Note: "My own chili is made up out of what I have in hand, so I'm afraid purists would shrink in horror . . . in summer when we have real tomatoes I might chop up a couple and throw them in."

JOHN WITHEE'S BIG BEAN CHILI

Expose a New Englander to chili and, chances are, a lifelong bean eater will be turned into a born-again One-and-Only chili cook.

It happened with the man who is perhaps the Numero Uno bean lover of the modern world, John Withee, of Lynnfield, Massachusetts. Withee turned his passionate love of beans into a full-time retirement occupation, complete with a nonprofit corporation called Wanigan Associates, Inc. Known widely as the Bean Man, Withee's interest in chili is naturally directed to the chili-with-beans sector, and he was inspired to try making chili using one of the oldest bean varieties, the Aztec, or Hava Supai, bean, which has been found in archeological digs in ancient Indian ruins in Arizona. The Aztec is a huge, white bean, and, says Withee, "made a bit of difference in the taste, but I thought the result was very good." Bean lovers, and chili-with-beans lovers, might want to try Withee's recipe.

3 cloves garlic, minced
3 medium onions, chopped
oil or fat
2 lbs. cheapest beef, cut into
  cubes
1 or 2 green bell peppers, minced
2 ozs. minced jalapeños

2 Tbs. celery seed
1 tsp. cumin
1 28-oz. can tomatoes, crushed
4 Tbs. flour
4 Tbs. chili powder
2 lbs. cooked fat runner beans,
  or fat lima beans

165

Lightly brown garlic and onions in a small amount of fat in a large skillet. Remove to a deep saucepan. Brown beef in skillet and then add it to saucepan.

Mix minced bell peppers and jalapeños with celery seed and cumin, and stir into the crushed tomatoes. Blend flour and chili powder and add to tomato mix. Place in saucepan with meat, onion, and garlic. Cook lightly to tenderize meat. When meat is tender, add cooked beans. Heat and adjust for thickness.

Cook's Note: "Serve with black Greek olives and corn bread."

NANCY BOTTCHER'S CHILI

John Withee, the Bean Man, found this unexpectedly lusty chili being served at the 1978 Merrimack County Fair in Hopkinton, New Hampshire. It was being sold in the "church eating tent" of the United Methodist Church of nearby Penacook.

The chili is Nancy Bottcher's, of Penacook, made from her mother's recipe, she says, which she "changed around" until she found the mixture of ingredients and seasonings she wanted.

1 lb. beef, chopped	1 28-oz. can whole tomatoes
6 onions, chopped	4 Tbs. chili powder
6 green peppers	3 tsp. garlic powder
1 15-oz. can kidney beans	salt and pepper to taste

Brown beef, onions, and peppers. Add beans and whole tomatoes. Cook for about ten minutes. Stir in chili powder, garlic powder, salt, and pepper. Simmer two to four hours.

Cook's Note: "Some chili powders give chili a sour flavor, not hearty as it should be. We use McCormick's."

Author's Note: McCormick also packages a "Texas Style" chili powder that is "heartier" still.

CHAPTER 17

Far Out and Far Off

CHILI MENDOW

One of the most imaginative and far out versions of chili and pasta ever devised is surely that of Hiram Z. Mendow of Minneapolis. Judge Mendow's recipe (he was a municipal judge in Columbia Heights) appeared in Virginia Safford's *Food of My Friends*, published by the University of Minnesota Press in 1944.

According to Safford, Mendow's father came from Rumania, and from him the Judge learned to make old-country dishes like mamaliga, a Rumanian corn bread created from the Indian maize first brought to Europe by Columbus. Corn made such a hit with the then-hungry Rumanians that corn bread quickly became a staple food with them.

Mendow's chili reflects these intertwined heritages, and is a prime example of the regional and ethnical influences that come to bear on dishes like corn bread and chili when they travel to far places, or when cooks from far places encounter them in this country.

2 lbs. ground beef
8 large onions, chopped fine
2 qts. canned tomatoes
2 cans red kidney beans
1 heaping Tbs. butter
2 tsp. black pepper
2 tsp. salt

3 Tbs. paprika
2 Tbs. sugar
2 to 3 Tbs. chili powder
½ lb. kosher salami, cut in small
  pieces
½ lb. wide noodles

167

Do not brown the meat. Put all but the last two ingredients in a large heavy kettle, and cook not less than two hours. About thirty minutes before serving, add salami and noodles.

Cook's Note: "This mixture is to cook down so it can be eaten with a fork—no lapping up from a bowl with a spoon. Pumpernickel is passed with the chili."

PASADENA JUNIOR LEAGUE APPLE CON CARNE
(serves 6 to 8)
(contributed by Mrs. John Bucklin)

Apples in chili. Kid stuff? Gourmet delight? Or something else? The recipe for Apple con Carne appears in *Pasadena Prefers II*, a cookbook produced by the Junior League of Pasadena, California. Apple chili is described as "suitable for feeding hungry children . . . hungry parents may join in, too."

Al O'Dell, interviewed about his chili ingredients at the 1977 chili cook-off at Goodfellow Air Force Base, near San Angelo, says that apples add a gourmet touch to his chili, and make it "aromatic."

The thinking behind the differing California and Texas philosophies could be redirected by a report issued from an Italian research institute, which claims that an apple can sexually excite a woman in seven minutes or less. The report didn't say *how*, but in chili is as good a bet as any other way.

2 Tbs. shortening	1 8-oz. can tomato sauce
1½ lbs. ground beef	1 20-oz. can kidney beans
1 tsp. salt	2 cups canned apple sauce
2 to 3 Tbs. chili powder	

Heat shortening in a 10-inch skillet. Add meat and brown quickly, stirring with a fork. Add salt and chili powder. Mix well. Combine remaining ingredients and stir into meat. Place in casserole and bake at 350°F until thoroughly heated.

GERMAN CHILI

The use of "Texas Gulasch" in Germany as a name for chili (there is no German word for chili) may be closer to the mark than Texas chili purists may want to know. Food writer Joseph Wechsberg's disgust at the Czech use of sauerkraut in his beloved *gulyás*—goulash—is nothing to a chilihead's reaction to its use in Texas chili. But a recipe for sauerkraut chili was one of those pressed on a writer for the Canadian magazine *Chatelaine*, which went to Texas to get a story about chili, as the bug began to bite north of the border.

2 Tbs. salad oil	½ tsp. cumin
1½ lbs. lean stewing pork, cut into bite-size chunks	½ tsp. crushed dried Japanese chiles
1 cup chopped onion	1 beef bouillon cube, crumbled
3 garlic cloves, crushed	6 Tbs. tomato paste
1 tsp. salt	2 cups beer
⅛ tsp. black pepper	1 15-oz. can red kidney beans, drained
2 Tbs. chili powder	
½ tsp. oregano	2 cups sauerkraut, drained

Heat oil in large saucepan or Dutch oven. Brown pork and saute onions and garlic. Add seasonings, crumbled bouillon cube, tomato paste, and beer. Stir well to mix. Cover and simmer about one hour or until meat is tender. Add beans and sauerkraut and heat through.

CHILI WITH PEANUTS (serves 8 to 10)

In Mexico, roasted *cacahuates* (as peanuts are called in Mexico) are coated with chile molido and served with drinks. In California, chopped peanuts and strips of roasted and peeled mild green chile are popular as a topping for hamburgers (as well as chili).

A booklet titled *It's Easy To Be a Gourmet with Peanuts*, published by the Oklahoma Peanut Commission (Box D, Madill, OK 73446), has an excellent recipe for peanuts in chili. Jimmy the Greek might give very long odds on its ever winning at Terlingua, but some people love an underdog—especially a tasty one.

½ cup peanut oil
2 cups onion, finely chopped
2 cloves garlic, finely chopped
2½ lbs. ground beef chuck
1 1-lb. can Italian plum tomatoes
⅔ cup coarsely chopped roasted Spanish peanuts

3 Tbs. tomato paste
2 to 3 Tbs. chili powder
1 Tbs. salt
1 Tbs. cumin seed
¼ tsp. hot pepper sauce
⅔ cup whole roasted Spanish peanuts
¼ cup chopped parsley

Measure peanut oil into large saucepan. Add onion and garlic, and saute until tender. Add ground beef and brown lightly. Stir in tomatoes, the chopped roasted peanuts, tomato paste, chili powder, salt, cumin seed, and hot pepper sauce. Simmer until sauce is thick, about thirty to thirty-five minutes. Stir in the whole roasted peanuts and chopped parsley. Serve over hot cooked rice, if desired.

Author's Note: As an alternative to the chopped parsley, use a half-and-half mixture of chopped parsley and cilantro, passed at the table, along with chopped onions, for topping individual bowls. A squeeze of lime juice would go well with this chili, also. To try peanut-flavored chili in a personal recipe, stir in ½ cup of chunky peanut butter per pound of meat, when the chili is simmering. Pass around a bowlful of chopped peanuts—or chili peanuts—along with other toppings, at serving time.

RED SKINNER'S NORTH SLOPE CHILI

There's not much between Foggy Island, in Alaska's Beaufort Sea, and the North Pole but a whole lot of very flat horizon. Even more than the rest of Alaska to the south, this could be called Ultimate Chili Pang Country. Rellis "Red" Skinner, the chief cook at Foggy Island, had to keep the chili pot bubbling for the oilmen who worked in the numbing cold of a North Slope winter. Skinner likes to know about the foods he cooks, and on the North Slope a man has plenty of time for study. To the story that chili powder was invented by an Englishman in San Antonio, Texas, trying to replenish his exhausted supply of curry powder by mixing local spices, he adds an interesting note. Skinner says the way he heard it, the Englishman was an engineer, who helped build the first railroad into San Antonio around

1877. His "curry powder" would have included chile molido, oregano, and the ever-popular San Antonio cumin, or comino, as it is called in Spanish.

2 lbs. slab bacon, diced	chili powder to taste
10 lbs. caribou meat, diced	2 No. 10 cans (about 25 cups)
5 large onions, chopped	tomatoes, diced
4 buds garlic, mashed	

Brown bacon, add caribou, onions, and garlic, stirring often, until caribou is brown. Add chili powder and tomatoes and simmer until meat is tender. If more liquid is needed, add water, or a good dry red wine or beer, as desired.

Cook's Note: "We use bacon up here because it's available, and there is no fat on a caribou. Suet or other fat can be substituted."

HAPPY VALLEY CHILI (makes 10 gallons)

To oilmen, any place is prime chili country, from the Gulf of Mexico to the Gulf of Aden to Alaska's Prudhoe Bay. Their cooks are either proficient in the chili-making arts, or they do not stay around long.

Beverly Ward, of Alyeska, the Alaska pipeline company, has supplied the recipe for the chili of Head Cook Richard P. Kannengieser of Happy Valley. Knowing that modesty is superfluous in a One-and-Only chili cook, Kannengieser says, "This is truly a camp favorite."

30 lbs. hamburger	½ lb. cumin
10 lbs. onions, chopped	6 to 8 ozs. chili powder, or to
½ cup all-purpose flour	taste
3 gals. diced tomatoes	2 gals. tomato juice
1 gal. tomato puree	1 gal. hot chiles
1 gal. water	½ lb. salt
4 ozs. black pepper	5 lbs. green peppers, diced
3 ozs. garlic	

Saute hamburger and onions. Remove excess oil from meat and add flour to tighten. Stir in diced tomatoes and tomato puree and let simmer for a few minutes. Add water and spices and let simmer for about one hour. Add tomato juice and chiles. Stir in salt and cook for another one and one-half hours. Add the diced green peppers and cook for about an hour longer. Taste the chili often and add additional seasonings until the desired flavor is obtained. The chili should be somewhat hot.

VALDEZ CHILI (serves 500)

This is the recipe used by First Cook Preston DeVallier at Valdez (pronounced Val-DEEZ) at the southern terminus of the Alaska pipeline.

100 lbs. ground beef	6 No. 10 cans tomato puree
5 ozs. garlic, chopped	(about 4½ to 5 gals.)
10 lbs. onions, chopped	8 ozs. monosodium glutamate
8 ozs. cumin	1 lb. salt
3 8-oz. bottles chili powder	flour and water

Cook beef in 80-gallon steam kettle, stirring to break into small pieces. Add garlic, onions, cumin, chili powder, tomato puree, monosodium glutamate, and salt. Simmer two hours. Skim off fat. Make a smooth paste of flour and water, add to simmering chili to achieve desired thickness.

Author's Note: To serve 500, DeVallier prepares 30 pounds of kidney or pinto beans to go with this chili. The beans are washed, then covered with boiling water and soaked for two hours. After soaking, the beans are simmered for one and one-half hours, or until tender, and one pound of salt is added to them.

B. J.'S MOOSE CHILI

Fran and B. J. Jones, now of Kenai, Alaska, are both from west Texas. The Joneses easily adapted their traditional Texas venison chili recipes to the annual moose B. J. brings home in Alaska. B. J. cooks chili in both red and green versions. This is routine in far west Texas, since El Paso is close to three western state capitals—all with their own Mexican-based styles of cooking. (Santa Fe cooks in New Mexican style, Phoenix in Sonoran, and Ciudad Chihuahua, of course, in the

Chihuahuan style.) El Paso borrows from all these to create a unique Tex-Mex style all its own.

2½ lbs. moose meat, ground	2 Tbs. minced onion
1 8-oz. can tomato sauce	dash Tabasco sauce
3 heaping Tbs. chili powder	1 chorizo sausage, removed from
¼ tsp. garlic salt	casing and chopped
¼ chopped onion, *or*	salt and pepper, to taste

Brown moose meat. Pour off grease, if any, and add remaining ingredients. Simmer for at least one hour. Serve with pinto beans and corn bread.

Author's Note: B. J. is calling for Mexican chorizo sausage in his recipe, which tends to have a higher fat content than Spanish chorizo, to be desired with lean moose meat. B. J. uses a brand of chorizo from El Paso, called Peyton's, which are packed in frankfurter-size casings, while most Mexican chorizo is packed in larger sizes. Use about 2 ounces of chorizo, or to taste, in this recipe.

U.S.O. CHILI CON CARNE (serves 20)

The name given to this chili tells a lot about its probable origins. It appears in a cookbook published by the Volunteers of the American Hospital in Paris, *Le Cookbook*, and was contributed by Mme Frederick Chartier. It is an interesting large-quantity recipe prepared in a large-capacity pressure cooker.

2 to 3 qts. tomato juice	6 lumps sugar
1 lb. dried kidney beans	1 12-oz. can tomato paste
2 lbs. sausage meat	10 Tbs. chili powder, *or*
4 lbs. ground beef	*substitute the following:*
margarine	2 Tbs. powdered caraway seeds
2 lbs. onions, chopped	4 Tbs. powdered garlic
salt	4 Tbs. powdered oregano
pepper	½ tsp. cayenne

Pour 2 quarts tomato juice into pressure cooker. Add beans and soak overnight. Next morning, saute sausage and beef in margarine and place in cooker. Saute onions and add with a good handful of salt, lots of pepper, sugar, tomato paste, and chili powder or the substitute mixture. Mix well. Add more tomato juice until mixture is swimming in liquid. Cook according to the pressure cooker manufacturer's instructions for mixtures using meat. If not using pressure cooker, cook for at least two hours, or until beans are soft.

Refrigerate overnight. Mix well. Add tomato juice if mixture is too thick. Add additional seasoning or cayenne according to taste. Reheat slowly, mixing several times.

Author's Note: The caraway seeds are obviously a substitute for look-alike cumin. Carroll Shelby, who has cooked a lot of chili in France, says he's done it—and it works out fine.

JENNE HATTON'S ENGLISH CHILI

Jenne Hatton says that one reason for the instant success of her chili at the *Lynn News* in King's Lynn, Norfolk, lies in the fact that "to get to Fleet Street, the national dailies [English journalists] make their mark on the local papers, moving extensively from place to place. Consequently, almost every journalist is prepared to try anything once." Which is added proof that newspaper people everywhere, not just in America, seem to have this affinity for chili.

English terms in Mrs. Hatton's recipe are explained as they come up.

3 rashers (slices) streaky bacon (about 4 ozs. salt pork), cut in ½-inch strips
2 tsp. corn oil
2 tsp. butter
3 English onions, chopped ("English onions are much smaller than Spanish onions and much stronger in flavour, size ratio is about an orange to a grapefruit.")
1 large green pepper, seeded and chopped
1½ lbs. Scotch beef, coarsely minced ("Scotch beef is superior, and is always labeled as such.")
1 or 2 bay leaves
freshly ground pepper
6 small tomatoes, plunged into boiling water, skinned, and coarsely chopped, plus a "squirt" of tomato puree [or 2 cups canned tomatoes, chopped, and their juice]

1 qt. (approx.) chicken stock
1 rounded tsp. freshly grated ginger
1 tsp. *each* oregano, cumin, turmeric, and paprika
2 cloves garlic, minced
2 tsp. Tabasco sauce
1 bottle Schwartz dried, crushed red chiles [A brand of British spices. Try 1 rounded Tbs. of chile quebrado or peperone rosso and increase amount to taste, *or* substitute 1 to 2 Tbs. chili powder, or more, to taste].
1 small carrot, grated
1 15½-oz. can red kidney beans
salt

In a heavy iron skillet or pot, allow bacon to frizzle until fat runs. Remove, add the oil and butter, then add onions and green pepper and let soften on a medium-low flame. Add beef, stirring to just start browning. Add bay leaf and several grinds of black pepper to taste. Add tomatoes, plus a spoonful of stock. Simmer.

Put a little stock in a small saucepan, add ginger and other spices, mix well, and allow to simmer for a bit. Add this plus garlic, Tabasco, and chiles, to main ingredients. Have more stock ready and heated in a separate pan. Remove the mixture to a casserole and stir in carrot and kidney beans. Add sufficient stock to prevent sticking, salt and pepper to taste, and cook covered for four hours at Gas Mark 4 (a moderate oven 350°F).

Serve with plain, boiled rice or chapattis (Indian wheat flatbread).

Author's Note: No doubt about it, English chili has an unmistakable kinship with the classic and ancient curry. But ginger is not absent from at least one Texas chili (Jim Wright's) nor is chicken stock (C. V. Wood's). Turmeric is claimed by one midwestern chili enthusiast to be the secret ingredient of Cincinnati-style chili, and rice is a welcome accompaniment to chili everywhere, including Texas. Chapattis are not more or less than the familiar Mexican flour tortillas (which are now made in some places with whole wheat flour, making them more appropriate for curry than Mexican dishes).

CHAPTER 18

The Newfangled Ways

OVEN BAKED CHILI (serves 6 to 8)

Iron-pot-and-wooden-spoon chili traditionalists will surely resist this thought, but the guiding rule about cooking chili—or anything—should be how good the end product is. Form should follow function, not tradition. An excellent—if untraditional—way to cook chili is in the oven. It eliminates a lot of tedious pot-watching, for one thing (and also eliminates a lot of fun chili-tasting during cooking, which is sure to turn a lot of chili cooks against it, for purely selfish reasons).

5 cups water	1 28-oz. can tomatoes, broken up
1 lb. dried pinto beans, washed	⅓ cup chili powder
2 lbs. ground beef	3 cloves garlic, mashed
2 onions, chopped	¼ tsp. paprika
1½ Tbs. salt, or to taste	2 tsp. ground cumin

In a Dutch oven bring water to boil. Add beans, return to a boil and simmer two minutes. Remove from heat, cover, and allow to soak for one hour. Saute meat in a skillet until it loses its reddish color; add to beans. Thoroughly mix in remaining ingredients. Bake, covered, in moderate oven (350°F) for three to four hours, or until beans are tender. Remove cover and bake additional thirty minutes.

Author's Note: This method also simplifies the making of straight chili (without beans). Use liquid sparingly in oven baked straight chili recipes; there will be little or no evaporation until the pot cover is removed for the final stages of cooking (which can also be done at a simmer on top of the stove).

ELECTRIC ROASTER CHILI (makes 6 quarts)

The electric roaster adapts handily to chili cooking, especially when quantity recipes are used. Williams Chili Seasoning—specified in this recipe from the *Junior League of Houston Cookbook*, contributed by Mrs. Richard R. Nelson—is an old-timer in the chili mix field. According to the company's present owner, Conrad Hock, Jr., C. L. Williams started packing his seasoning back in 1942, "in a garage in back of his house in Webb City, Missouri." The type billed "Hot Texas Style" on the label finds favor with a lot of good Texas chili cooks (see Appendix A).

10 lbs. lean chili meat, lean ground beef, *or* 5 lbs. each venison and beef
5 1-oz. pkgs. Williams Chili Seasoning
5 medium onions, chopped
2 cans condensed tomato soup
2 soup cans water
2 cloves garlic, chopped
2 or 3 bay leaves
6 ribs celery, minced
1 tsp. cumin seed
1 fresh hot red chile, chopped
salt to taste

Put meat *alone* in electric roaster on low, 200°F. Cook until meat is done, about three hours, turning meat often and removing grease as it appears. When meat is done, add all other ingredients except salt. Cook slowly for several more hours. Add salt to taste before serving. Electric skillet may be used for smaller quantities.

MICROWAVE CHILI

Because microwaves prepare food with the zap of a Buck Rogers (or Wilma Deering) rocket pistol, and thereby liberate the cook, they are priority items in modern American kitchens. But nothing is perfect. In dishes that require it, zapping is never going to do what long, slow simmering does for foods like chili.

To have the best of both methods, give chili the long, slow treatment the first time around, then freeze it; next time, zap it to steaming goodness in the microwave in seconds. This combines the very best technology of the past with that of the present, and that's savvy of a superior kind.

Which is not to say that zapping chili from scratch won't subdue an attack of chili pangs on a lowdown day. When moments count, get on with it.

2 lbs. lean chili grind beef
1 onion, chopped
2 cloves garlic, mashed
1 16-oz. can tomatoes, cut up
2 8-oz. cans tomato sauce, *or*
1 8-oz. can tomato sauce and
   1 cup beef broth or consomme

2 Tbs. chili powder
2 tsp. cumin seed
1 tsp. dried oregano
1 Tbs. brown sugar
¼ to ½ tsp. Tabasco
salt to taste

Combine meat, onion, and garlic in a large casserole. Cover, cook at HIGH setting for ten minutes, or until meat loses its reddish color, stirring once or twice.

Add remaining ingredients, mixing thoroughly. Cover casserole and heat until mixture comes to a boil. Reduce microwave temperature to SLOW or DEFROST and cook for about one hour, stirring a few times.

After cooking, allow chili to stand for a few minutes before serving.

Due to variations in microwave ovens, the cooking times and methods may have to be adapted to suit the particular oven. In microwaves with no SLOW or DEFROST settings, follow the steps for cooking meat, stir in remaining ingredients, and cook for fifteen minutes, stirring once. In microwaves with SLOW or DEFROST settings, a single portion of chili may be reheated in about five minutes.

PRESSURE COOKER CHILI

Pressure cookers offer two major advantages to the thoughtful, modern chili cook. First, they cook food quickly, which means less fuel is used—a major plus in these days of costly energy. Second, the tougher and more flavorful cuts of meat, preferred in chili, which normally take long cooking to tenderize, will be tenderized in a shorter time in a pressure cooker. Also, chili grind meat can be taken right from the freezer and put into the cooker without waiting for it to thaw first. The saving here is in time.

½ cup rendered beef kidney suet
2 lbs. chili grind meat, frozen
2 tsp. cumin seed, toasted lightly
½ cup water
1 tsp. instant coffee
2 tsp. Casados New Mexico chile molido (bright red)
2 tsp. Santa Cruz Arizona chile molido (bright red)
2 rounded Tbs. dark (California, ancho, pasilla, etc.) chile molido

1 rounded Tbs. paprika
3 cloves garlic, mashed
2 Tbs. minced fresh oregano, *or*
2 tsp. dried oregano
1 tsp. powdered cumin
1 scant Tbs. powdered mole mix (optional)
1 8-oz. can tomato sauce or Snap-E-Tom
1 8-oz. can water
1 scant tsp. salt, or to taste

Put suet, frozen meat, toasted cumin seed, and ½ cup water in pressure cooker. Cook at 15 pounds pressure for twenty minutes. Allow pressure to go down normally. Break up meat with a fork. Add rest of ingredients, stir in well, bring mixture to a simmer, and cook slowly for thirty minutes, or more, stirring occasionally.

SLOW COOKER CHILI

Going in the other direction from cooking chili "in no time at all," the slow cooker takes all night to slow-simmer chili to the proper state. Before using a slow cooker to cook meat, check its temperature range. The temperature must reach 185°F in order to kill any bacterial growth that occurs in the cooking process. Pour cold water into the pot, and set the cooker according to manufacturer's directions for cooking meat. After two or three hours, check the water temperature with a thermometer. It should be somewhere around 165°F, and after eight hours, it should be at least 185°F. A couple more things to remember about slow cookers: do not overload them with so much food that they can't reach a safe temperature, and do not leave food in a slow cooker after the heat has been turned off. Get any leftovers under refrigeration.

6 lbs. beef brisket or chuck,
  cut in ½-inch or smaller cubes
6 cloves garlic, mashed
1 cup (approximately) rendered
  beef suet
6 Tbs. chili powder
2 Tbs. dried oregano, *or*
6 Tbs. fresh oregano leaves,
  lightly toasted

2 Tbs. cumin powder
2 Tbs. cumin seed, lightly
  toasted
1 tsp. cayenne
2 Tbs. paprika
1 scant Tbs. salt, or to taste
1 scant Tbs. flour or masa harina
  for "tightener"
2 12-oz. cans of beer

Cook meat and garlic in hot rendered suet in a heavy, deep skillet over moderately high heat until meat is a grayish color. Stir to prevent browning. Add chili powder, oregano, cumin powder and seed, cayenne, and paprika, continuing to stir until thoroughly mixed. Turn into a 5-quart slow cooker. (If using smaller skillet, divide meat and suet into batches, adding the seasonings to the first batch, and mix in subsequent batches of cooked meat as they are added to cooker.)

When cooked meat and seasonings are all together and mixed in the pot, add about one tablespoon of salt, or to taste. Stir in a scant tablespoon of flour or masa harina, first mixed to a smooth paste with a little water. Stir well to mix in all the way down to bottom of pot.

Add beer to a depth of about one inch over the top of meat mixture and simmer for eight to twelve hours, or overnight, following directions for the type of slow cooker used.

CHAPTER 19

Saturday Night Specials

CANNED ROAST BEEF CHILI IN A HURRY

Many old-time chili recipes call for slowly braising the meat in the whole, in a little liquid, to the falling-apart stage, instead of sauteing pre-ground or chopped meat. When making chili in quantity, braising takes a lot of the work out of the job. An even quicker way to make chili for a crowd is to buy already cooked beef at a butcher or restaurant supply house. The meat comes cooked, wrapped, and refrigerated in the whole piece, and also steam-roasted and canned in its own juices. The approximately six-pound cans are the easiest to use for chili-making (besides being more economical in price). The canned meat is already in irregular-size pieces, and nothing needs to be added but chili seasonings and more liquid, if this is necessary. Then simmer. Quantity packages of chili mix and chili powder are also available at most food supply houses (make sure the mix or chili powder used in this recipe is unsalted, since the meat has salt already added). The canned variety of meat is often packed in Argentina, but be sure to get cans marked "roasted" and not "corned" beef (although the canned corned beef is not bad in chili, either, and is usually a little cheaper than the roasted).

A little chili savvy can turn this easy-to-make chili into a One-and-Only chili that will have people bidding for the recipe.

6-lb. can roast beef in its juices
3 pkgs. chili mix, unsalted, *or*
1 cup chili powder, unsalted

optional liquid and added spices, to taste

Heat beef slowly in heavy pot until all fat is melted. Add mixes and proceed as directed on chili-mix package, or add spices and desired liquid and simmer for at least one hour.

Author's Note: This chili can be stretched with beans (also available in restaurant-size cans at the supply houses) and is especially good over pasta or rice.

CHILI PIE

A popular speciality of many new generation chili parlors, like Chili's (in Texas, Colorado, and California) and the Chili Factory, in Santa Barbara, California, is Chili Pie. This is basically a casserole dish composed of a base of crushed corn chips, such as Fritos, covered with chili and a topping of grated cheese and sometimes chopped onion. It is a money-saver, since it stretches the chili base.

1 6-oz. pkg. corn chips, coarsely crushed	1 tsp. cumin
	½ tsp. oregano
1 15-oz. can straight chili or chili with beans	1 Tbs. chili powder
	¼ tsp. Tabasco, or to taste
1 tsp. salt	½ cup grated mild or medium
1 lb. ground beef	Cheddar
1 clove garlic, minced or crushed	

Cover bottom of an 8 × 8-inch baking pan or casserole with about two-thirds of the crushed corn chips. Spoon chili evenly over chips. Heat salt in a skillet and saute the beef and garlic until all the pink is gone from the meat. Add remaining ingredients, except cheese, and cook a minute or two more. Spread beef mixture over chili in the baking pan and top with remaining corn chips. Sprinkle the grated cheese over all and bake thirty minutes at 350°F.

Author's Note: Those who can find the California-made brand of chili called Stagg should try their Chili Laredo—a combination of beef, beans, and green chile—in this dish. If conventional chili is used, try mixing a 4-ounce can of diced green chiles in with the beef mixture before it goes in the casserole. Or two or three jalapeños, seeded and sliced in thin strips. In California, this Chili Pie might be served in regional Mexican style, with a topping of shredded lettuce, chopped tomato or salsa, and chopped onion and cilantro. A deluxe party version would also include sliced ripe olives, slices of avocado or spoonfuls of guacamole, and dollops of sour cream.

CHILI SALAD

A very similar—if simpler—recipe on Fritos bags in the 1930s and '40s was for a chili salad much like this one, combining Fritos, chili gravy, lettuce, and cheese—the whole baked in a casserole for fifteen minutes.

1 tsp. whole cumin seed
1 tsp. salt
1 lb. ground beef
1 clove garlic, crushed
1 Tbs. chili powder
½ tsp. ground cumin
½ tsp. oregano
¼ tsp. Tabasco, or to taste
1 15-oz. can straight chili
4 to 6 cups torn lettuce
1 medium onion, sliced in thin
    rings

12 tomato wedges
1 4-oz. can diced green chiles,
    or
2 to 3 canned jalapeño peppers,
    seeded and cut into thin strips
1 2¼-oz. can sliced ripe olives
1½ cups shredded sharp
    Cheddar cheese
corn chips

Put whole cumin seed into heated skillet and toast for one to two minutes to bring out the flavor. Keep it moving. When cumin starts to darken in color, gather at one end of the skillet and crush slightly with back of a spoon.

Add salt to skillet and then beef, and *brown* quickly (graying the meat won't do in this recipe). Add garlic, chili powder, ground cumin, oregano, and Tabasco, and mix thoroughly. Add chili, bring to a simmer, mixing well, and hold there.

In a salad bowl, combine the lettuce, onion rings, tomato wedges, chiles, and sliced olives. Bring to table along with bowls of the shredded cheese and corn chips, and the hot chili mixture.

Let each person serve himself first from the salad bowl, then top the salad with a generous portion of chili, shredded cheese, and a handful of corn chips, crushed like crackers in the hand.

Author's Note: This main-dish salad can be further gussied up,

California style, with slices of avocado (or guacamole), chopped cilantro, salsa, and sour cream.

CHILI AND BEANS WITH JALAPEÑO DUMPLINGS
(serves 6)

Jalapeño corn bread has grown into something of a fad dish in the southern and southwestern states. With the first chilly weather of the fall season, scores of recipes for jalapeño corn bread are published in newspaper food sections from Louisiana to California. From chile in the corn bread, it is only a step to chile corn bread in the chili.

1½ lbs. ground beef
1 Tbs. fat or oil
½ cup onion, chopped
1 to 2 cloves garlic, chopped
1 4-oz. can diced green chiles
1 Tbs. chili powder
1 tsp. cumin
1 tsp. oregano
2 11-oz. cans chili-beef soup
2 cups water (see *Cook's Note* below for variations)

1 8½-oz. package corn muffin mix
2 fresh or pickled jalapeños, seeded, deveined, and chopped
1 egg
⅓ cup milk
sliced ripe olives and chopped cilantro

In a large, heavy iron skillet, cook beef in fat until brown. Add chopped onion and garlic. When onion is soft and yellow, add the green chiles, chili powder, cumin, and oregano. To this mixture, stir in soup and water, blending well.

Meantime, combine corn muffin mix, jalapeños, egg, and milk, blending well. Carefully drop large spoonfuls of this mixture into gently boiling chili mixture, placing them around the edges of the skillet. Lower heat and simmer, covered, for fifteen minutes. Just before serving, sprinkle with olives and chopped cilantro.

Cook's Note: "Try using a mixture of water and beer, dry red wine, and/or tomato sauce in place of water in the chili."

185

SUPER "C" SUPPER (serves 6)
(Chili–chile–cheese corn bread)

A recipe as fancy as this one, which has the chili right in it, can't really be called corn bread, jalapeño or otherwise; it is a one-dish, meat-pie meal.

1 24-oz. can chili	2 pickled jalapeño chiles,
1 4-oz. can diced green chiles	chopped
1 3-oz. pkg. cream cheese, cubed	¾ cup cottage cheese
1 6-oz. pkg. corn bread mix	½ cup grated jack cheese

Heat chili, green chiles, and cream cheese in a heavy 10-inch skillet over medium heat, stirring often, until it reaches a low bubbly boil. Prepare corn bread mix according to directions on the package. Fold in jalapeños, cottage cheese, and jack cheese. Pour corn bread mixture over the hot chili in skillet. Bake at 450°F for about twenty-five minutes.

Author's Note: "Ye Olde Tyme" jalapeño corn bread mix has a recipe on its package for Chili Pie which calls for the chili to be spooned on *top* of the batter in the baking pan. In the cooking process the chili goes to the bottom and corn bread to top.

BLENDER CHILI

Blenders save time, money, and energy. It's no wonder that in Mexico—where cooking requires the use of chopped, ground, and blended ingredients virtually three times a day and seven days a week—the blender is hailed as the greatest invention since the bean.

2 Tbs. oil or other fat	3 Tbs. chili powder
1 medium onion, coarsely cut	1 tsp. cumin seed
1 to 2 cloves garlic, cut in half	½ tsp. dried oregano
1 lb. lean chuck, cut in cubes	3 Tbs. flour
2 cups canned tomatoes	

Heat oil or fat in a heavy saucepan or deep skillet. Blend onion and garlic until coarsely grated and put in skillet. Saute until onion is golden. Add meat and cook, stirring, until meat has lost its red color.

Place remaining ingredients in blender container. Blend until well mixed. Pour over meat and bring to a boil. Lower heat, cover, and simmer slowly for one to two hours, stirring from time to time. Adjust seasoning. Water or beef broth may be added during cooking if needed.

Author's Note: Whole dried red chiles may be used instead of chili powder or chile molido. Break up the pods and blend along with other ingredients. Remember when using whole chile that hotness is largely governed by the amount of seeds included. Similarly, fresh oregano can be used instead of dried. Use one and one-half teaspoons chopped fresh oregano for the half teaspoon of dried.

SIX POWDER CHILI

This recipe is a way to make chili and create a personal chili powder formula at the same time. The seasoning ingredients are all powdered, so that by keeping track of what goes into the chili pot, the final result is not only a One-and-Only chili recipe, but a chili powder blend that will make preparing future batches of chili simpler. Read the directions carefully before starting, and make sure all the ingredients are on hand.

½ cup rendered beef kidney suet
3 lbs. lean chili grind meat
4 Tbs. dark red (mild) chile molido
1 to 2 Tbs. bright red (pungent) chile molido
2 to 3 Tbs. paprika, for color (optional)

1 to 2 Tbs. ground cumin
1 Tbs. ground oregano
1½ tsp. garlic powder
salt to taste
tightener if necessary

Heat rendered suet in heavy pot or Dutch oven. Add meat and cook just through, stirring so it does not brown. Turn heat to low.

Add remaining ingredients in order and in small amounts, one at a time, until a satisfactory flavor is achieved. Then go on to next seasoning. When all have been added (don't forget to keep a record of the amounts), add enough water to barely cover the mixture, stir well, and taste and adjust seasonings if necessary. Heat mixture until it bubbles, reduce heat, and cook at a simmer for two and one-half to three hours, stirring from time to time, tasting and adjusting seasonings if necessary (and changing the record). Add more water if necessary, or a tightener if mixture is too thin. It would be valuable to let this chili—or at least a part of it—"rest" overnight in the refrigerator, then reheat it, and critically evaluate its flavor again. Some judgments may be altered in the chili powder recipe as a result of this day-later tasting.

Author's Note: The spice amounts given in the recipe are used for guidance to help you arrive at a personal preference level for each spice. Three pounds of meat are called for so that the spices will be used in amounts sufficient to work with and evaluate.

MARK KAUFFMAN'S CUISINART CHILI

Shooting photo assignments for the Time-Life Books series *Foods of the World* further sharpened Mark Kauffman's already active interest in food and cooking, and brought him in contact with people like Julia Child and James Beard, and introduced him to the food processor, which he has adapted to chili-making. "I make a damned good chili," Kauffman says, in typically modest One-and-Only chili cook fashion. He does. Don't let the lack of a food processor stand in the way of trying it at home, or at one of Kauffman's chili parlors, the Firehouse Cantinas, in Rohnert Park and Santa Rosa, north of San Francisco.

3 lbs. very lean beef, coarse chili grind using Cuisinart	4 ozs. chili powder
	1 tsp. cayenne
2 lbs. loin of pork, also ground in Cuisinart	1 Tbs. sugar
	1 tsp. ground cumin
2 to 3 Tbs. bacon fat or peanut oil	1 Tbs. dried oregano
	3 Tbs. coarse kosher salt, *or*
2 large onions	2 Tbs. regular table salt
6 to 8 cloves garlic	1½ tsp. monosodium glutamate
2 green bell peppers	1 Tbs. tomato paste
1 28-oz. can tomatoes	1 cup cold water

In a large, heavy pot lightly brown meat in fat. Using Cuisinart, finely chop onions and garlic. Add to meat. Coarsely chop bell peppers and add to pot. Drain (save the liquid) the canned tomatoes and puree in Cuisinart. Put pureed tomatoes and reserved liquid into pot with meat.

Put remaining ingredients in a quart jar, fasten top securely, and shake until well blended. Pour into pot. Bring to a boil, stirring often. Lower heat to a slow simmer, cover with a tight-fitting lid, and cook for forty-five minutes. Remove lid and stir, moving chili from bottom to top and around in the pot. Repeat this type of stirring two or three more times during cooking. Simmer for one hour and forty-five minutes.

Cook's Note: "I make my chili in the amount indicated simply because a heavy Danish pot I own is just right. I almost always cook the chili the day before serving. Then freeze about half and refrigerate the rest."

KERR AND BALL CANNED CHILI

As New York City's El Rancho and its proprietor Arvid Strom demonstrated for years, good canned chili receives a warm and deserved welcome from people who view it as a quick and convenient alternative to making chili from scratch, and to whom the decision between having canned chili or no chili at all is not ever going to be that hard to make.

Some particular chili cooks may want to can their own. Savvy chili lovers have been doing this for generations, and it's still a good way for those who agree with some experts who say that freezing spicy foods causes them to lose flavor. The majority of modern home "canners" use glass.

Home-canning is a straightforward operation requiring only careful attention to directions and proper equipment. The directions are available from many sources, including manufacturers of canning supplies, like Ball Corporation and Kerr Glass Manufacturing Corporation, both of which offer complete home-canning guides with excellent chili recipes. The canning directions on pages 77–78 should be scrupulously followed.

The first chili recipe for home-canning is from an early edition of Kerr's *Home Canning Book*. It makes a solid, basic, old-time chili that deserves to be remembered and eaten often, whether it is canned first or not. The latest edition of the *Home Canning Book* may be ordered at nominal cost from Kerr Glass Manufacturing Corporation, Sand Springs, OK 74063.

6 chile pods	2 tsp. cumin seed
1 lb. suet	4 tsp. paprika
2 medium onions, chopped	2 cloves garlic, minced
5 tsp. salt	½ tsp. pepper
5 lbs. ground (not too fine) beef	3 cups water
6 Tbs. chili powder	

Prepare chili pods by soaking for about fifteen minutes in hot water. Remove seeds and run pods through food chopper. Render suet to cream color and add onions and salt. Cook twenty minutes on low heat, stirring constantly. Remove onion and add all other ingredients.

Cook slowly for fifteen minutes. Pack into clean Kerr jars to within one inch of top of jar. Put on cap, screwing band tight. Process in pressure cooker at 10 pounds pressure: pints one hour and fifteen minutes; quarts one hour and thirty minutes.

The Ball chili recipe is from the latest edition of their famed home-canning guide, the *Blue Book*. It is a modern chili recipe, with tomatoes and a more watchful attitude about fat content.

The Ball *Blue Book* may be ordered at nominal cost from Ball Corporation, Muncie, IN 47302.

5 lbs. ground beef	½ cup chili powder
2 cups chopped onion	1½ Tbs. salt
1 clove garlic, minced	1 hot red pepper
6 cups cooked or canned tomatoes and juice	1 tsp. cumin seed

Brown meat. Add onion and garlic and cook slowly until tender. Add remaining ingredients and simmer twenty minutes. If meat is fat, skim off excess fat before canning. Pour, hot, into hot jars, leaving one inch head space. Place lid on jar with sealing compound next to jar, and screw band down evenly and firmly. Process pints one hour and fifteen minutes, quarts one hour and thirty minutes at 10 pounds pressure.

Appendix A-
Directory of
Sources

CHILI MAKIN'S—MAIL ORDER SUPPLIERS

Chili Mixes

Adkins Texas Style Chili Seasoning
Box 24855
Dallas, TX 75224

Best Yet Chili Mix
Thomson Food Co.
13830 White Heather
Houston, TX 77045

California Pride Western Chili Preparation
31348 Via Colinas, Suite 102
Westlake Village, CA 91381

Carroll Shelby's Original Texas
Brand Chili Preparation
Box 45303
Los Angeles, CA 90045

Chilli Man Chilli Mix
Milnot Co.
Box 190
Litchfield, IL 62056

Chill Lee's Chili Mix
Chill Lee Corp.
Box 462
Alief, TX 77411

Gebhardt's Chili Mix & Original
Eagle Brand Chili Powder
Box 7130 Station A
San Antonio, TX 78285

Hammett House Chili Seasoning
Hammett House Foods, Inc.
1616 W. Will Rogers
Claremore, OK 74017

Hoot 'n Holler Chili Mix
Yeller Dog Enterprises
Box 32134
San Antonio, TX 78216

Lawry's Texas Style Chili Mix
Lawry's Foods, Inc.
568 San Fernando Rd.
Los Angeles, CA 90065

Olde Tyme Chili Mix
Olde Tyme Foods, Inc.
Box 20129
Dallas, TX 75220

Original Chile Blend
Mexican Chile Supply
304 E. Belknap
Fort Worth, TX 76102

Original Chili Bowl Chili Seasoning
The Original Chili Bowl, Inc.
9016 E. 46th St.
Tulsa, OK 74145

Pecos River Chili Mix
Box 1600
Corrales, NM 87048

Ol' Hired Hand
Six Gun Chili Mixin's
Box 3966
Fullerton, CA 92634

Whitson's Moist (Canned) Chili Seasoning
Jetton Products
Box 1540
Fort Worth, TX 76101

Wick Fowler's 2-Alarm Chili Ingredients
Caliente Chili, Inc.
Drawer 5340
Austin, TX 78763

Williams Chili Seasoning
Williams Foods, Inc.
1900 W. 47th Place
Westwood, KS 66205

Chile Spices—Fresh, Dried, and Powdered

Bloomingdale's Delicacies Shop
1000 Third Ave.
New York, NY 10022

Casados Farms (also chicos, posole)
Box 852
San Juan Pueblo, NM 87566

New Mexico Chile Lovers' Supply
Box 2434
Las Cruces, NM 88001

Pecos River Spice Company
Box 1600
Corrales, NM 87048
or
Box 680
New York, NY 10021

San Antonio Spice Company (also spices)
Box 28125
San Antonio, TX 78228

Santa Cruz Chili & Spice Co. (also chile paste, chilipiquíns)
Box 177
Tumacacori, AZ 65640

Valley Distributing Co.
2819 2nd St. N.W.
Albuquerque, NM 97107

CHILE—CANNED

Britches of Georgetown
1247 Wisconsin Ave., N.W.
Washington, DC 20007

Clyde's
3236 M St., N.W.
Washington, DC 20007

Heublein, Inc. (Ortega Chile products)
Box 1348
Oxnard, CA 93032

La Flor del Sur Empacadores S.A.
(El Pato sauce)
Walker Foods, Inc.
237 N. Mission Rd.
Los Angeles, CA 90033

Las Palmas Chile Products (subsidiary of Tillie Lewis Foods, Inc.)
117 N. Ventura Ave.
Ventura, CA 93001

Mountain Pass Canning Company
(Old El Paso products)
Box 220
Anthony, TX 88021

Tia Mia, Inc.
Box 685
Sunland Park, NM 88063

SEEDS

Horticultural Enterprises (chile)
Box 34082
Dallas, TX 75234

Nichols Garden Nursery (pinquíto
seed beans, elephant garlic)
1190 N. Pacific Coast Hwy.
Albany, OR 97321

Reuter's Seed Company (Maui onion
seeds)
Box 19255
New Orleans, LA 70179

Rocky Mountain Seed Company
(NMSU chile varietals)
1325 15th St.
Denver, CO 80202

Vermont Bean Seed Company (red
peanut, pinquíto, bean seeds)
Garden Lane
Bomoseen, VT 05732

ODDS AND ENDS

Masa Harina
Quaker Oats Co.
Chicago, IL 61654

Fancy Dried Sweet Corn
John F. Cope Co., Inc.
Rheems, PA 17570

Andouille (Cajun pork sausage)
Tasso (pork jerky)
Oak Grove Smokehouse
Route 6 Box 133
Baton Rouge, LA 70815

CHILI MAKIN'S—LOCAL SUPPLIERS

Atlanta

Rinconcito Latino
Ansley Square Mall
1429B Piedmont Ave. N.E.
Atlanta, GA 30309

Boston

India Tea & Spice Co. (also mail order)
Cushing Square
9B Cushing Ave.
Belmont, MA 02178

Star Market
625 Mt. Auburn St.
Cambridge, MA 02238

Chicago

La Casa del Pueblo
1810 Blue Island
Chicago, IL 60608

Casa Esterio
2719 W. Division
Chicago, IL 60622

Denver

El Progreso
2282 Broadway
Denver, CO 80205

Houston

Rice Food Market (scratch ingredients)
3700 Navigation Blvd.
Houston, TX 77003

Los Angeles

El Mercado
First Ave. at Lorena
Los Angeles, CA 90063

Grand Central Public Market
317 S. Broadway
Los Angeles, CA 90013

Milwaukee

Casa Martinez
605 S. 5th St.
Milwaukee, WI 53204

New York City

Casa Moneo (New Mexico chile)
210 W. 14th St.
New York, NY 10014

San Francisco

La Palma
2889 24th St.
San Francisco, CA 94110

La Fiesta
2737 20th St. & York
San Francisco, CA 94110

Seattle

Mexican Grocery
1914 Pike Place
Seattle, WA 98146

Washington, D.C.

International Safeway
1330 Chain Bridge Road
McLean, VA 22101

Casa Peña
1636 17th St., N.W.
Washington, D.C. 20009

Arlington Bodega
6017 N. Wilson Blvd.
Arlington, VA 22205

BRICK CHILI

Dallas

Neiman Marcus's
Red River Brand Chili

Epicure Shop
Neiman Marcus
Main and Ervay
Dallas, TX 75201

Appendix B—
Directory of
Organizations
and
Publications

Organizations

Chili Appreciation Society Inter-
national (CASI)
Box 31183
Dallas, TX 75231

International Chili Society (ICS)
Box 2966
Newport Beach, CA 92663

International Connoisseurs of Green
& Red Chile (ICG&RC)
Box 3467
Las Cruces, NM 88003

Wanigan Associates, Inc. (a nonprofit organization of bean lovers)
262 Salem St
Lynnfield, MA 01940

Lovers of the Stinking Rose (a garlic
lovers' society)
526 Santa Barbara
Berkeley, CA 94707

American Spice Trade Association
580 Sylvan Avenue
Englewood Cliffs, NJ 07632

Publications

Goat Gap Gazette
5110 Bayard Lane #2
Houston, TX 77006

Garlic Times
526 Santa Barbara
Berkeley, CA 94707

Wanigan *Newsletter*
262 Salem St.
Lynnfield, MA 01940

Luckenbach *Monthly Moon*
218 Acacia
San Antonio, TX 78209

195

Glossary

ADOVADO, or ADOBADO—meat or chiles marinated or pickled in a thick sauce of chiles, vinegar, and other seasonings.

AJÍ, or AGÍ—Spanish, from a Quechua Indian word for the capsicum, used in South America and the Caribbean islands.

ANCHO CHILE—the long green chile when picked red-ripe and dried to a brownish-red. Sometimes called chile colorado, also called California, Arizona, or New Mexico chile. Used for flavor rather than hotness in cooking. In Spanish, *ancho* means broad, wide.

ASCM—American Society of Chili Makers, proposed by Dallas printer Will C. Grant in 1952, but never officially activated.

ASTA—acronym for the American Spice Trade Association, headquartered in New York City. Organization of chile and spice growers, processors, and wholesalers.

BRICK CHILI—a condensed, long-keeping chili made from fresh rather than jerked meat, reconstituted with liquid when eaten. Comes in "bricks," loaves, or packed in plastic tubes like bulk sausage. Latter sometimes called "chilistick" in the Midwest.

BULL FLOUR—gluten flour, used by chefs in making sauces and gravies. Used in chili as a "tightener."

BUTCHER FLOUR—powdered egg white, used by butchers to "glue" meat-cuts together. Used in chili as a tightener.

CANNED CHILE—mature green pods of long green chile, canned in a brine solution, ready for use in cooking just as fresh green chile is used. Some Spanish terms used on canned green chile labels: *rescolados*—roasted; *pelados*—peeled; *desvenados*—deveined; *enteros*—whole; *rajas*—strips. The hotter chiles are usually canned and bottled as pickles or condiments, labeled *en escabeche*—pickled in oil and vinegar; and *encurtidos*—pickled in vinegar.

CANNED CHILI—USDA specifies that any canned product labeled "Chili" must contain at least 40 percent meat.

CANNED CHILI WITH BEANS—USDA specifies that any canned product labeled "Chili with Beans" must contain at least 25 percent meat.

CAPSAICIN—a chemical compound, the chief source of "hotness" or pungency in chile—and chili. Found principally in seeds and membranes in chile pods. Gives ginger ale and root beer their "hot" taste. One part capsaicin in 100,000 can be detected by human taste buds.

CAPSICUM—plants indigenous to the Americas, now grown worldwide. Pods, used in cooking and condiments, run from cranberry-size up to a foot in length, with pungency decreasing as size increases. The *annuum* furnishes the principal seasonings for chili.

CARNE CON CHILE—Spanish for meat with chile.

CARNE SECA—literally, dry meat—jerky.

CASI—acronym for Chili Appreciation Society International, begun as an informal get-together of Dallas chili lovers around 1939, formalized in either 1947 or 1951, depending on the source consulted.

CHILATOR—Dallas printer Will C. Grant's proposed term (circa 1952) for chili expert and member of ASCM.

CHILE—Spanish, from a Nahuatl Indian word for capsicum, used in Mexico, the U.S., and, with variations in spelling, around the world.

CHILE CON CARNE—Spanish for chile pods—green or red—stewed with meat for flavoring. Chili con carne is a bastardization having no real meaning, since chili *is* meat, flavored with chile. Adding con carne—with meat—is redundant

CHILE POWDER, or CHILE MOLIDO—pure, unspiced powdered chile, sometimes labeled in Spanish *chile molido puro sin ninguín especia*, or pure powdered chile without added spices.

CHILI—*Annuum* furnishes the principal plants used for chili seasoning. usually including garlic, oregano, and cumin. In the Midwest, sometimes spelled CHILLI.

CHILI BEANS—beans flavored with chile and optional meat.

CHILI BOWL—used as a synonym for chili in parts of the U.S. outside the Southwest, as in "Let's go have some chili bowl."

CHILIBURGER—chili-topped meat patty on a bun.

CHILI COOK-OFF—the steadily proliferating chili-world activity in which One-and-Only chili cooks travel widely and pay stiff entry fees to shoot it out gastronomically with their peers. Today, winners of "sanctioned" cook-offs accumulate "points" toward competing at one of the "world championship" cook-offs held each fall by CASI at Terlingua, and ICS at Tropico, California. At whatever level,' judging a cook-off between One-and-Only chili cooks has got to be the most thankless and potentially dangerous job since the days of Shirley Temple look-alike contests.

CHILI CRACKERS—John Isaacs, who founded the Green Bay, Wisconsin, Chili John's around 1912, is credited with inventing the small cracker also known as an oyster cracker, to go on his chili. (He also sold oysters in season.)

CHILICRAT—a term coined by Joe Cooper in *With or Without Beans* to indicate a chili lover or expert.

CHILI DOG—frank or wiener in a bun topped with chili. Also called a coney or Coney Island.

CHILIHEAD—a knowledgeable chili lover.

CHILI JOINT or PARLOR—eating place specializing in chili. Cincinnati, Ohio, with over thirty chili parlors of the Empress, Skyline and Gold Star chains, plus dozens of others, qualifies as the chili parlor capital of the U.S.

CHILI-MAC—pasta topped with chili, a steady midwestern and hard times favorite. In Texas, called Spaghetti Red.

CHILI MEDIUM—an order of chili with beans at the old Lang's, in Dallas; still used at Chili John's, in Green Bay, Wisconsin.

CHILI MIX—chili seasoning ingredients in convenience-style packaging.

CHILI PEMMICAN—see PEMMICAN.

CHILIPIQUÍN or CHILTEPÍN, etc.—very hot, tiny, wild chile, indigenous to the U.S. from Louisiana to Arizona. Pods, about the size of cranberries, are eaten both green and red-ripe.

CHILI POWDER—principal chili seasoning. Ingredients include powdered chile, garlic, cumin, oregano, and other spices. The first commercial chili powder was probably that made by William Gebhardt, who founded the San Antonio chili products firm now controlled by Beatrice, the food conglomerate. Gebhardt first called his chili powder Tampico Dust, later changed the name to Eagle Brand. Some support DeWitt Clinton Pendery's Chilomaline (once produced in Fort Worth) as the first chili powder.

CHILI QUEENS—the legendary chili-makers whose open-air stands in San Antonio's plazas were a city institution from (according to one source) 1813 until World War II.

CHILI RICE—rice topped with chili. The legendary Shanghai Jimmy, now of Dallas, is famous for this concoction.

CHILI SIZE—broiled beef patty, topped with chili.

CHILISTICK—wooden implement used to stir a pot of chili and nothing else. Also, a midwestern term for supermarket brick chili.

CHILI STRAIGHT or STRAIGHT CHILI—the real article, without extenders.

CHILI WITH—chili with beans. The preferred chili everywhere but Texas.

CHILPOTLE or CHIPOTLE—a red-ripe jalapeño, smoke-dried, or sometimes pickled adovado.

CILANTRO or CULANTRO—fresh leaves of coriander, also called Chinese parsley, used in Mexican, Portuguese, and Oriental cooking. Chopped leaves used as a chili topping.

CUMIN—in Spanish, *comino*. A vital chili seasoning. An ancient superstition held that cumin was a wrathful plant, and in order to thrive had to be cursed and vilified when sown. More peaceable caraway is an infrequent substitute for cumin in chili.

FORSCP—acronym for Fellows of the Red Squeezings of the Chile Pod, a name for a chili society proposed by Joe Cooper in the early 1950s.

FRIJOLES—Spanish for beans. The preferred bean for chili is the pinto, followed by the small Louisiana red or western pink. The small pinquíto, grown in the Santa Maria Valley of California, midway between Los Angeles and San Francisco, is the gourmet's chili bean. Cowboys call beans prairie strawberries. Frijoles refritos are cooked beans mashed and fried in hot fat. A society of bean lovers, Wanigan Associates, is headquartered in Lynnfield, MA.

GARLIC—in Spanish, *ajo*. A principal seasoning ingredient of chili. Mature bulbs, or heads, can be separated into small individual bulbs, also called cloves, pods, buds, tooths and shakes. There is a society of garlic fans (Lovers of the Stinking Rose, in Berkeley, CA) and an annual garlic festival in Gilroy, CA.

HOT SMAK—a fast-food chili item invented in Kansas City in the 1950s, consisting of four ounces of chili in a patented saltine cracker cone.

ICG&RC—International Connoisseurs of Green & Red Chile, an organization of chile—capsicum—lovers, formed in New Mexico in 1973.

ICS—International Chili Society, an organization of chili lovers formed in southern California in 1975 by a group of expatriate CASI members.

JALAPEÑO—a dark green chile, about two inches long, with a blunt shape and tip, from medium hot to hot in pungency. Used fresh in cooking and salsas, but in U.S. usually found pickled en escabeche (pickled in oil and vinegar). When red-ripe and smoked, called a chilpotle. Sam Lewis, of San Angelo, Texas, markets jalapeño lollipops and ice cream.

JERKY—from the Quechua Indian word *charqui*—meat jerked or dried either in the sun, or, in cooler climates, by smoking. Also called carne seca, tasajo, biltong, basturma, pipikaula, squaw candy, etc.

199

LONG GREEN CHILE—the most common American name for the ancho chile when green. Next to the green bell pepper, the mildest of chiles. Also called Anaheim, Fresno, and Numex, and in Mexico, Poblano.

MAC A LA MODE—chili-mac topped with two fried eggs, as served at Hodge's in St. Louis.

MACHACA—carne seca or jerky, pounded into a stringy fluff. Much used in Arizona-Sonora cooking, and for making chili.

MASA FLOUR—the moist corn dough used for making tortillas. Masa harina (Spanish for flour) is the dry packaged version, used as a chili tightener.

MOLIDO—Spanish for ground. Used with chile, it means pure, unspiced, ground or powdered chile.

MOUNTAIN OYSTERS—also called prairie oysters, huevos, or calf fries. The testicles of bull calves or lambs. Considered a delicacy among stockmen, when fried or roasted. Principal ingredient of mountain oyster chili, said to be a favorite of Will Rogers.

NATIVE CHILE—the name given to traditional varieties of chile, grown in northern New Mexico. Usually sun-dried. Considered by many gourmets to have more flavor and character than commercially grown and dried chile. The area around Chimayó has the reputation for growing the best native chile.

ONE WAY, TWO WAY, THREE WAY, etc.—chili specialties at Cincinnati chili parlors, and used throughout the Midwest as terms for, respectively, straight chili, chili-mac, and chili-mac with a cheese topping. Also used at Shanghai Jimmy's in Dallas, to denote similarly escalating chili-rice combinations.

OREGANO—Mexican is preferred over European for seasoning chili—but which Mexican? Diana Kennedy reports in *Cuisines of Mexico* that when she asked Mexican botanists about oregano, they gave her a list of thirteen varieties in popular use around that country.

PEMMICAN—a Cree Indian word meaning jerked meat pounded together with fat and berries to make a highly nutritious, long-lasting, portable trail food. The Sioux called it wasna. Made with wild chile—the chilipiquín "berries" of the Southwest—chili pemmican was very likely the first chili.

PICANTE—Spanish for hot or pungent. Used with chile.

POBLANO CHILE—Mexican name for long green chile.

QUEBRAJADO—applied to chile, means cracked, crushed, or coarsely ground. Peperone rosso is the Italian equivalent.

RISTRA—Spanish for string. In New Mexico, red-ripe chiles are strung together each fall for sun-drying, then hung inside for use during non-chile-growing months. The strings of chile are called ristras. In Arizona, these are called sartas, another Spanish word meaning string. Both Double Eagle I and II, the balloons which tried (I) and then accomplished (II) the historic flight across the Atlantic, had ristras of chiles hanging from their gondolas, along with the U.S. and New Mexican flags.

SALSA—Spanish for sauce. A chile salsa can be fresh-made, bottled, canned, or frozen. The hotter chiles are made into condiment—topping—salsas, sometimes with vinegar and tomatoes for acidity and tang. Salsas come in red and green varieties. Fresh salsa is often called salsa fresca or salsa de cocina (kitchen). Bottled chile salsa is sometimes labeled taco sauce. Condiment salsas run from mild to nerve-deadening. A salsa called El Pato (The Duck), canned in Los Angeles, is labeled on one side Tomato Sauce, and on the other Salsa de Chile Fresco. Believe the Spanish. Long green chile and its red-ripe counterpart, the ancho chile, are also made into sauces, primarily for cooking. They are used for flavor rather than hotness and might more accurately be called chile gravies. Called green and red chile sauce, or enchilada sauce, etc., they are fresh-made, canned, or frozen.

SERRANO—literally "mountain" chile, about an inch and a half long, narrow, tapering to a sharply pointed tip. Used fresh or pickled when green, and in salsas. Also used red-ripe and dried. Hot to very hot.

SLINGER—two cheese-topped burger patties served on an oval platter, flanked by a fried egg and American fried potatoes, all covered with chili, as served at Hodge's in St. Louis. A Super Slinger is a Slinger topped with a tamale.

SON-OF-A-BITCH STEW—also called S.O.B. and son-of-a-gun. Another cowboy favorite, made of the "innards" of a fresh-killed calf or steer, including the marrow-gut—everything, as one chuckwagon cook put it, but the "hair, horns, and holler." Some say chili evolved from a Tex-Mex border son-of-a-bitch.

SPAGHETTI RED—Texas term for chili-mac.

SUAVE—Spanish for smooth, gentle. With chile, means mild, not pungent.

SUET—the white, waxy fat encasing the beef kidney, preferred for chili-making. Also called "sweet" or "green" suet.

TALLOW—the fat bordering the muscle meat used for chili-making. Specified in some chili recipes.

TERLINGUA—Spanish for Three Tongues. Remote ghost mining town in west Texas Big Bend country, about eighty miles south of Alpine. The site, each fall, of the CASI "world championship" chili cook-off. In recent years, CASI cook-offs have been held in Arriba (Upper) Terlingua.

TEXAS RED—another Texas way of saying chili—hottest of chilis.

TROPICO—Spanish for tropical. Southern California ghost mining town, located on the "high desert" about five miles northwest of Rosamond, which is eighty-five miles north of Los Angeles. The site, each fall, of the ICS "world championship" chili cook-off.

WET SHOES—an order of french fries smothered in chili, as served at Chili West in Oxnard, CA. The dish reportedly originated in Atlanta.

Bibliography

Adams, Ramon F. *Come an' Get It*. Norman, OK: University of Oklahoma Press, 1952.
————. *Western Words . . . A Dictionary of the American West*. 2d ed., paperback. Norman, OK: University of Oklahoma Press, 1974.
Arnold, Sam. *Fryingpans West*. 7th ed. Denver: The Fur Press, 1969.
The Autobiography of Will Rogers. Selected and ed. by Donald Day. Boston: Houghton Mifflin, 1949.
Ball Corporation. *Blue Book*. Muncie, IN.
Bainbridge, John. *The Super-Americans*. New York: Doubleday, 1961.
Beck, Fred. *Second Carrot from the End*. Foreword by H. Allen Smith. New York: William Morrow, 1946.
Beck, Neill and Fred. *Farmers Market Cookbook*. Foreword by M. F. K. Fisher. New York: Henry Holt & Co., 1951.
Benet, Sula. *How to Live to Be 100*. New York: Dial, 1976.
Bierschwale, Margaret. *Fort McKavett, Texas*. Salado, TX: A. Jones Press, 1966.
Bolt, Richard. *Forty Years Behind the Lid. Chuckwagon Grub*. Guthrie, TX: 1974.
Bolton, Herbert Eugene. *Coronado, Knight of Pueblos and Plains*. Albuquerque, NM: University of New Mexico Press, 1949 and 1964 (hard & paperback).
Boy Scouts of America. *Handbook for Boys*. New Brunswick, NJ: Boy Scouts of America National Council, 1948.
————. *Scout Handbook*. 8th ed. New Brunswick, NJ: Boy Scouts of America National Council, 1972.
Brandon, William. *The American Heritage Book of Indians*. New York: American Heritage Publishing Co., 1961.

Brown, Dale. *American Cooking*. Foods of the World. New York: Time-Life Books, 1968.

Bushick, Frank H. *Glamorous Days*. San Antonio, TX: The Naylor Co., 1934.

Chase, A. W. *Dr. Chase's Recipes, Or, Information for Everybody*. Ann Arbor, MI: R. A. Beal, 1872.

Chile. Ed. by Ruth Sneed. Las Cruces, NM: New Mexico State University, 1966.

Chile. Revised by Mae Martha Johnson. Las Cruces, NM: New Mexico State University, 1976.

Cincinnati Companion. Cincinnati, OH: Tom Tuttle & Assoc., 1979.

Claiborne, Craig. *New York Times Guide to Dining Out in New York*. New York: Atheneum, 1964.

Clark, Amalia Ruiz. *Special Mexican Dishes*. Tucson, AZ: Roadrunner Technical Publications, Division of Desert Laboratories, Inc., 1977.

Clark, Morton Gill. *The Wide, Wide World of Texas Cooking*. New York: Bonanza Books, 1970.

Cleveland, Bess Anderson. *California Mission Recipes*. Rutland, VT: C. E. Tuttle, 1965. Adapted for modern usage.

Cleveland, Terah Lynn. *Frontier Texas Recipes*. San Angelo, TX: M. H. Cleveland, 1970.

Coleman, Arthur and Bobbie. *Texas Cookbook*. New York: Wynn, 1949.

Condon, Richard, and Wendy Bennett. *The Mexican Stove*. New York: Doubleday, 1973.

Cooking Recipes of the Pioneers. Printed by *Frontier Times*. Bandera, TX: Bandera Library Assoc., 1936.

Cooper, Joe E. *With or Without Beans*. Dallas: William S. Henson, 1952.

Corbitt, Helen. *Helen Corbitt Cooks for Looks*. New York: Houghton Mifflin, 1967.

————. *Helen Corbitt Cooks for Company*. New York: Houghton Mifflin, 1974.

David, Elizabeth. *French Provincial Cooking*. New York: Harper & Row, 1960.

Davis, Adelle. *Let's Cook It Right*. New York: New American Library (Times Mirror), 1970.

Dawson, Charlotte. *Recreational Vehicle Cookbook*. Beverly Hills, CA: Trail-R-Club of America, 1970.

De Baca, Margarita C. *New Mexico Dishes*. 10th printing. Sante Fe, NM: The Rydal Press, 1968.

De Gouy, Louis P. *The Gold Cook Book*. New York: Greenberg, 1947.

Delgado, Lucy. *Comidas de New Mexico*. Santa Fe, NM: 1967.

De Stewart, Doña Eloisa Delgado. *El Plato Sabroso Recipes*. Santa Fe, NM: 1940.

Diccionario de Mejicanísmos. Francisco J. Santamaria, ed. Mexico City: Editorial Porrua, S.A., 1959.

Dobie, J. Frank. *The Longhorns*. New York: Little, Brown, 1941.

Drury, John. *Rare & Well Done*. Chicago: Quadrangle, 1966.

El Molino Best Recipes. 8th printing. Alhambra, CA: El Molino Mills, 1953.

Evans, George W. B. *Mexican Gold Trail, The Journal of a Forty-Niner*. Ed. by Glenn S. Dumke with a preface by Robert Glass Cleland. San Marino, CA: The Huntington Library, 1945.

Everett, Donald E. *San Antonio, The Flavor of Its Past, 1845–1898*. San Antonio: Trinity University Press, 1975.

Favorite Recipes of Colfax County. Colfax County, NM: Colfax County Home Demonstration Clubs, 1946.

Fergusson, Erna. *Mexican Cookbook*. Garden City, NY: Dolphin Books, 1961.

Ferrell, Retta, ed. *The Best of Concho Cookery*. 2nd ed. San Angelo, TX: San Angelo Standard-Times, 1976.

Fischer, Al and Mildred, eds. *Arizona Cook Book*. Phoenix, AZ: Golden West Publishers, 1974.

Fisher, M. F. K. *The Art of Eating, The Collected Gastronomical Works of M. F. K. Fisher*. Cleveland & New York: The World Publishing Co., 1954.

Forbis, Wm. H. *The Cowboys*. New York: Time-Life Books, 1973.

Frontiersman's Pocket-Book, The. Comp. and ed. by Roger Pocock ("On Behalf of the Council of the Legion of Frontiersmen"). London: John Murray, 1909.

Gerarde, John. *The Herball or the General Historie of Plants*. London, 1597. (Huntington Library, San Marino, CA).

Gilbert, Fabiola C. *Historic Cookery*. Reissued. Santa Fe, NM: "THE SHED," 1965.

Gorman, Marion, and Felipe P. de Alba. *The Tequila Book*. Chicago: Henry Regnery Company, 1976.

Great Green Chili Cooking Classic. "New Mexico Prized Recipes." Albuquerque, NM: *The Albuquerque Tribune*, 1974.

Green, Ben K. *Horse Tradin'*. New York: Alfred A. Knopf, Inc., 1967.

———. *Wild Cow Tales*. New York: Alfred A. Knopf, Inc., 1969.

———. *The Village Horse Doctor, West of the Pecos*. New York: Alfred A. Knopf, Inc., 1971.

———. *Some More Horse Tradin'*. New York: Alfred A. Knopf, Inc., 1972.

Green Chile Recipe Fiesta: A Cookbook for Green Chile Chefs. Las Cruces, NM: New Mexico State University Alumni Assoc., 1973.

Harris, Gertrude. *Pots & Pans, etc.* Preface by M. F. K. Fisher. San Francisco: 101 Productions, 1975.

Herter, George Leonard and Berthe E. *Bull Cook and Authentic Historical Recipes and Practices.* 11th ed. Waseca, MN: Herter's Inc., 1967.

Hesse, Zora Getmansky. *Southwestern Indian Recipe Book.* Vol. I. Palmer Lake, CO: The Filter Press, 1973.

Holiday Book of Food and Drink. New York: Hermitage House, 1952.

Holy Cross Episcopal Church. *Texas Cooking Under Six Flags.* Paris, TX: 1953.

Howerton, P. and Peavy M. *Turkey Trot Cookbook.* Cuero, TX: Cuero Publishing Co., 1934.

Huddleston, Sam. *Tex-Mex Cook Book.* Brownsville, TX: 1971.

Hughes, Stella. *Chuck Wagon Cookin'.* Tucson, AZ: The University of Arizona Press, 1975.

Humphrey, Sylvia Windle. *A Matter of Taste.* New York: The Macmillan Co., 1965.

The Institute of Texan Cultures. *The Melting Pot, Ethnic Cuisine in Texas.* San Antonio, TX: The University of Texas at San Antonio, 1977.

Johnson, Ronald. *The Aficionado's Southwest Cooking.* Albuquerque, NM: University of New Mexico Press, 1968.

Jones, Evan. *American Food.* New York: Dutton, 1975.

Junior League of Charleston, Inc. *Charleston Receipts.* Ed. by Mary Vereen Huguenin and Anne Montague Stoney. 21st printing: September 1976. Charleston, SC: Junior League of Charleston, Inc., 1950.

Junior League of Dallas. *The Junior League of Dallas Cook Book.* 2d ed. Dallas, TX: Junior League of Dallas, Inc., n.d.

Junior League of Houston. *The Junior League of Houston Cookbook.* Houston, TX: Junior League of Houston, Inc., 1968.

Junior League of Pasadena. *Pasadena Prefers II.* 4th ed. (revised). Pasadena, CA: Junior League of Pasadena, Inc., 1969.

KKK Cookbook. Kute Kooking Klub, Honey Grove, Texas. Cincinnati, OH: Robert Clarke Co., 1894.

Kaufman, William L. *The Hot Dog Cookbook.* Garden City, NY: Doubleday, 1966.

Kennedy, Diana. *The Cuisines of Mexico.* Foreword by Craig Claiborne. New York, Evanston, San Francisco, London: Harper & Row, 1972.

———. *Recipes from the Regional Cooks of Mexico.* New York, Hagerstown, San Francisco, London: Harper & Row, 1978.

Kephart, Horace. *Camping and Woodcraft.* New York: Macmillan Co., 1932.

Kerr Glass Manufacturing Corporation. *Home Canning Book.* Sand Springs, OK: 1950.

Kitchiner, William. *The Cook's Oracle.* Pub. under a different title in 1817. Now available, The London Library. Edinburgh: Robert Cadell, 1840.

Land, Mary. *Mary Land's Louisiana Cookery.* A reprint of the original by Cookbook Collectors Library, Favorite Recipes Press, Louisville, KY. Baton Rouge: Louisiana State University Press, 1954.

Lasswell, Mary. *Mrs. Rasmussen's Book of One-Arm Cookery with Second Helpings.* Boston: Houghton Mifflin, 1970.

Lawton, Mary. *The Queen of Cooks—And Some Kings* (The Story of Rosa Lewis). New York: Boni and Liveright, 1925.

Leaders at the Range. Centennial recipes from the files of Colorado 4-H leaders. Assembled by State 4-H Leader Officers Mrs. Peggy Case and Mrs. Evelyn Squires. Fort Collins, CO: Colorado 4-H Foundation, 1976.

Le Cookbook. Favorite recipes of French and American residents of Paris. Comp. and ed. by Elizabeth W. Sterling and the Volunteers of the American Hospital of Paris, 1974.

Linsenmeyer, Helen Walker. *From Fingers to Fingerbowls.* San Diego: Copley, 1976.

Lippincott, Henry. *The Military Bachelor Chef. A Guide for Getting Started in the Kitchen.* Palmer Lake, CO: The Filter Press, 1974.

McIlhenny Company. *The Art of Seasoning, The History of Tabasco Pepper Sauce.* Avery Island, LA: McIlhenny Co., n.d.

Marshall, Mel. *Cooking Over Coals.* New York: Winchester Press, 1971.

Merchant, Charles J. *Francisca's Mexican Cookbook.* Tucson, AZ: 1966.

Montagne, Prosper. *Larousse Gastronomique, The Encyclopedia of Food, Wine & Cookery.* Introductions by A. Escoffier and Ph. Gilbert. 7th printing. New York: Crown Publishers, Inc., 1966.

Montana Department of Fish and Game. *Savoring the Wild—Game, Fish, and Wild Plant Cookery.* Kay Ellerhoff, ed. Helena, MT: Montana Outdoors, n.d.

Morgan, Sarah. *The Saga of Texas Cookery.* Austin, TX: The Encino Press, 1973.

Moss, James A. (Captain 24th Infantry). *The Story of a Troop Mess.* Menasha, WI: The George Banta Publishing Co., 1909.

Myers, Mrs. E. G., ed. *The Capitol Cook Book.* A selection of tested recipes by The Ladies of Albert Sidney Johnson Chapter, Daughters of the Confederacy. Austin, TX: Von Boeckmann, Schutze & Co., Printers, 1899. (Houston Public Library, rare Texas books). Reprinted in Austin, TX: The Brick Row Book Shop, 1966.

Newman, Edwin. *Strictly Speaking. Will America Be the Death of English?* New York: Warner Books, 1975.

207

Ortiz, Elizabeth Lambert. *The Complete Book of Mexican Cooking*. Philadelphia, PA: Evans, 1967.

Orwell, George. *Down and Out in Paris and London*. New York: The Berkley Publishing Corp., 1961.

Pain, Alfonso C. *Western Mexican Cook Book*. Tucson, AZ: 1959.

Palmer, Lilli. *Change Lobsters—And Dance, An Autobiography*. First pub. by Droemer Knaur Verlag Schoeller & Co., Zurich, 1974, titled *Dicke Lilli—Gutes Kind*. New York: Warner Paperbacks, 1976.

The Paris Cookbook. Paris, TX: First Methodist Church, 1931.

Price, Mary and Vincent. *A Treasury of Great Recipes*. Princeton, NJ: Ampersand Press, Inc., 1965.

Ramsdell, Charles. *San Antonio*. Austin, TX: University of Texas Press, 1968.

Rawlings, Marjorie Kinnan. *Cross Creek Cookery*. New York: Scribner's, 1942.

Read, R. B. *Gastronomic Tour of Mexico*. Garden City, NY: Dolphin Books, 1972.

Rector, George. *Dining in New York with Rector. A Personal Guide to Good Eating*. New York: Prentice-Hall, Inc., 1939.

Reiger, Barbara and George. *The Zane Grey Cookbook*. Englewood Cliffs, NJ: Prentice-Hall, 1976.

Ricardo, Don. *Early California & Mexico Cookbook*. Toluca Lake, CA: Pacifica House, 1968.

Rickey, Don, Jr. *Forty Miles a Day on Beans and Hay: The Enlisted Soldier Fighting in Indian Wars*. Norman, OK: University of Oklahoma Press, 1963.

Root, Waverly, and Richard de Rochement. *Eating in America*. New York: William Morrow & Co., 1976.

Rosengarten, Frederic, Jr. *The Book of Spices*. Wynnewood, PA: Livingston Publishing Co., 1969.

Safford, Virginia. *Food of My Friends*. Minneapolis: University of Minnesota Press, 1944.

St. John, Adela Rogers. *Some Are Born Great*. New York: New American Library, Inc., 1975.

Sandoz, Mari. *These Were the Sioux*. 2nd printing. New York: Dell Yearling Book, 1972.

Sarvis, Shirley. *Simply Stews*. New York: The New American Library, Inc., 1973.

Sebastiani, Sylvia. *Mangiamo (Let's Eat!), A Collection of Family Recipes*. St. Helena, CA: Sebastiani Vineyards, 1970.

Señan, Jose, O.F.M. *The Letters of Jose Señan, O.F.M.* Translated by Paul D. Nathan. Ed. by Lesley Byrd Simpson. Printed by John Howell Books. Ventura, CA: The Ventura County Historical Society, 1962.

Smith, H. Allen. *Buskin' with H. Allen Smith.* New York: Trident Press, 1968.

———. *The Great Chili Confrontation, "A Dramatic History of the Decade's Most Impassioned Culinary Embroilment (with Recipes)."* New York: Trident Press, 1969.

———. *The Life and Legend of Gene Fowler.* New York: William Morrow, 1976.

Smith, S. Compton. *Chile Con Carne; or, The Camp and the Field.* New York and Milwaukee: Miller & Curtis, 1857.

Southwesterners Write. Selected and ed. by T. M. Pearce and A. P. Thomason. Albuquerque, NM: University of New Mexico Press, 1946.

Steelman, Abigail Doughty. *Abbie D.'s Cookbook.* East Haddam, CT: Jean B. Meyer, 1976.

Steinbeck, John. *Travels with Charley.* New York: Viking Press, 1962.

Stern, Jane and Michael. *Roadfood.* New York: Random House–David Obst, 1977.

Szathmary, Louis. *Southwestern Cookery.* New York: Promontory Press, 1974.

Tannahill, Reay. *Food in History.* New York: Stein and Day, 1973.

Tinkle, Lon. *Mr. De—Biography of Everette Lee DeGolyer.* Boston: Little, Brown, 1970.

Tolbert, Frank X. *A Bowl of Red.* Garden City, NY: Doubleday, 1966.

Trahey, Jane. *A Taste of Texas.* New York: Random House, 1949.

Trappey's Sons, Inc., B. F. *The Secret of Creole Cooking.* 11th ed. New Iberia, LA: 1971.

Trillin Calvin. *American Fried, Adventures of a Happy Eater.* Garden City, NY: Doubleday, 1974.

———. *Alice, Let's Eat, Further Adventures of a Happy Eater.* New York: Random House, 1978.

Vestal, Stanley. *Jim Bridger, Mountain Man.* Lincoln, NE: University of Nebraska Press, 1946.

Waldo, Myra. *Dictionary of International Food and Cooking Terms.* New York: The Macmillan Co., 1967.

Walker, Stanley. *Mrs. Astor's Horse.* 4th ed. New York: Frederick A. Stokes, 1935.

———. *Home to Texas.* New York: Harper & Bros., 1956.

———. *Texas.* New York: Viking Press, 1962.

Wechsberg, Joseph, and the editors of Time-Life Books. *The Cooking of Vienna's Empire.* Foods of the World. New York: Time-Life Books, 1968.

Wilder, James Austin ("Pine Tree Jim"). *Jack-Knife Cookery.* New York: Dutton, 1929.

WPA Federal Writers Project. *Texas, a Guide to the Lone Star State.* Harry Hansen, ed. New rev. ed. New York: Hastings House, 1969.

Zelayeta, Elena. *Elena's Secrets of Mexican Cooking.* Englewood Cliffs, NJ: Prentice-Hall, 1961.

————. *Elena's Fiesta Recipes.* 5th ed. Los Angeles: The Ward Ritchie Press, 1966.

Index

Achiotina, 162
Adoue, Ted, 55, 56
Air Force Association, 52–53
A. K. Swann's Chili, 118
Alamo Chile House, New York, 56
Alaska, 8, 40–42
Alcohol, 63, 64, 73–74, 90
Alice, Let's Eat (Trillin), 42
Allmond, Ruby, 9
Allspice, 27, 67
American Cafe, Georgetown, D.C., 55
American Indians, 12, 21, 65, 94
American Spice Trade Association, 148
Ancho chiles, 80, 83, 157
Anchor Brewing Company, 156
Anchorage, Alaska, 8, 40–41
Anise seed, 67
Anita's Chili Parlor, New York, 55
Annatto, 162
Annie Little John's Chili, 104
Annuum, 80
Apollo-Soyuz link-up, 8–9
Apple Con Carne, 168
Arizona, 9, 86, 95
Army chili, 12–13, 48, 99–103
Army Chili 1896, "Old," 19, 99
Army Chili TM 10–405 (for 100), 101
Army Chili TM 10–412 (for 100), 48, 102
Arnold, Sam, 13
Art's (chili parlor), Los Angeles, 45
Augustus, Bob, 16
Aztec beans, 69, 165

Baked Chili, 177
Ball Corporation, 77, 189, 190

Bar-b-que, 19
Barney's Beanery, Los Angeles, 45
Barron, Woody, 20, 111
    Texas Chili, 111
Barrymore, John, 145, 146
Basil, 67
Baskin, Bob, 53
Baxter's Chili Mix, 34, 124
Baxter's Chili Parlor, Oklahoma City, 104, 124
Bay leaf, 67
Bayer, Babs, 69
Beans, 67–69, 165
Beard, James, 55, 188
Beck, Fred, 47
Beef, 10–11, 13, 60–64, 112
Beer, 73, 90
    Lucy Maytag's Anchor Steam Beer Chili,
      156
Bell peppers, 80, 81
Bellamy, Ralph, 142
    Chili, 142
    Chili "Side," 143
Bergstrom, Walter, 119
Bernays, Anne, 164
Beverages, 90
Beverly Hills, California, 49–51
Bicentennial, 52
Bill Williamson's Chili, 148
Bishop, Mary (Grandma), 36
Bishop's (chili parlor), Chicago, 36
B. J.'s Moose Chili, 172
Black, Alexander, 18
Black, Colonel William L., 18
Blender Chili, 76–77, 186
Blue Book (Ball Corporation), 190

211

Bob Marsh's Buffalo Chili for 600, 105
Bob's Big Boy, 44
Bockelmann, J. A., 25, 26
Bogley, Rose Marie, 160–161
    Chili, 160
Bolt, Richard, 28
    Chili, 117
Bory, Edmond, 58
Bottcher, Nancy, 166
    Chili, 166
Bowl of Red, A (Tolbert), 4, 23
Braising, 75
Branin, Jeanette, 70
    Rainy Day Chili, 149
Brick chili, 12, 21, 78
Brick Chili, Classic, 98
Briscoe, Dolph, Jr. and Janie, 115
Brook Hollow Country Club, 30
Brunswick, Maine, 42–43
Brussels, Belgium, 58
Buckley, Ed, 43
Bucklin, Mrs. John, 168
Buffalo Chili for 600, 105
Buffalo meat, 11
Burka, Paul, 67
Bush, Susan and Jack, 118
Bushick, Frank, 16
Butel, Jane, 58

Cafe Serghi, Ile de Re, 58
Calf fries, 106
Caliente Chili Company, 5
California chili recipes, 139–159
Camp Chili with Jerky, Deluxe, 94
Campuks, 19
Canary Island, 16–17
Canned chili, 4, 17–18, 183, 189
    home, 77–78, 189
Canned Roast Beef Chili in a Hurry, 182
Canteen Corporation, 26
Capote, Truman, 90
Capsaicin, 82
Capsicum, 4, 9, 21, 63–65, 79. See also Chiles
Caraway, 67
Cardamon, 27, 67
Carey, Olive, 143–144
Carlos Chili, Acapulco, 56
Carne Adovada, Casados Farms, 129
Carne en Chile Colorade, 17, 20, 32, 63, 86,
    129, 131
Carne fresco, 14
Carne seco, 14, 95
Carroll Shelby's Chili, 139
Carroll Shelby's Original Texas Brand Chili
    Preparation, 7

Carter, Jimmy, 44
Casados, Peter, 84, 129
Casados Farms, 84, 129, 130
    Carne Adovada, 129
    Chile Caribe Sauce, 130
Castañeda, Pedro de, 11, 95
Catarina Ranch Chili, 115
Cathedral Mountain Chili Cook-off and Easter
    Egg Hunt with Sunrise Services, 8
Cattle drives, 19–20, 28
Cayenne, 80, 81
Celery seed, 67
Chapattis, 177
Charles Pendergrast's Texas Chili, 112
Charles Willeford's Texas Chili, 163
Charqui, 94
Chartier, Mme Frederick, 173
Chase Sons Chili (Gloria Pitzer), 144
Chasen, Dave, 49
Chasen, Maude, 50, 145
Chasen's, Beverly Hills, 49–50
Child, Julia, 164, 188
Chile, defined, 4
Chile (New Mexico State Univ.), 82
Chile (NMSU Circular 463), 131–133
Chile Caribe, 83
    Sauce (Casados Farms), 130
Chile con carne, 4, 14, 15
Chile Con Carne, U.S.O., 173
Chile molido, 83, 84, 85
Chiles (capsicum), 63–65, 157
    commercial, 85
    hotness of, 82, 83
    preparation of, 82–83
    toasting, 86
    types of, 80–81
Chiles tepines, 98
Chili:
    additions to, 69–74
    canned. See Canned chili
    defined, 4
    origins of, 9, 10–22
    trimmings with, 51, 52, 88–90
Chili and Beans with Jalapeño Dumplings, 185
Chili Appreciation Society International
    (CASI), 6, 56, 139, 140
    cook-off, 6–7, 23, 25, 68, 69, 73, 116, 121,
    139
Chili Bowl, Anchorage, 40
Chiliburger, 35
Chili Con Carne (for 60), War Dept. 1910,
    101
Chilicast (KBUC, San Antonio), 8
Chili Con Carne; or, The Camp and the Field
    (Smith), 14

Chili Factory, Santa Barbara, 32, 183
Chiliheads, 6
Chili Hotline (KILT, Houston), 8
Chili in General, Wolf Brand in Particular (West), 20
Chili John's (Burbank, Green Bay), 38–40, 137
Chili-mac, 26–27, 37
Chili Meat Sauce, 137
Chili Mendow, 167
Chili paste, 83, 125, 126
Chili Pie, 183
Chilipiquíns, 11, 80, 98, 127
Chili powder, 26, 76–77, 84–85
  basic recipe, 86
Chili queens, 14–16, 20
Chili rice, 29–30
Chili Rice, 121
Chili's (parlor), 183
Chili Salad, 184
Chili size, 47
Chili's Restaurant, 32
Chili with Peanuts, 169
Chilli Man Chilli, 25
Chilli Mix, 25
Chilomaline, 26
Chilpotle, 81
Chilympiad, 8
Chimayó, New Mexico, 84
Chocolate Chili, 69–70, 73
Chorizo sausage, 173
Chuck Wagon Cookin' (Hughes), 52, 70, 107, 126
Chuckwagon cooks, 19–20, 28
Cincinnati, Ohio, 9, 26–27
"Cincy" Chili, 135
Cinnamon, 27, 67
Civil War, 12, 16, 17, 19
Claiborne, Craig, 10, 70
Clark, Will, 31
Classic Brick Chili, 98
Cloves, 27, 67
Clyde's, Georgetown, D.C., 55
Coffee in chili, 73
Collins, Reba, 34
Cone, John, 16
Coney Island Chili Sauce (Les Fuller), 136
Congressional Record, 54
Conways, Paris, 57
Cookbook, Le, 173
Cooking of Vienna's Empire, The, 21
Cooking Over Coals (Marshall), 113–114
Cook-offs, 4, 6, 8, 69, 116, 121, 168
Cooley, J. C., 85

Cooper, Joe, 6, 7, 14, 32, 68, 71, 105, 108, 127
  Chili, 108
Corbitt, Helen, 71, 122, 123
  Low-Calorie Chili, 122
Corey, Anita Carr, 55
Coriander, 27, 67
Corn, 72
Cornbread, Jalapeño, 185
Cornett, Steve, 107
Coronado, Francisco, 11, 95
Corsicana, Texas, 20, 28
Cowboys, 19–20, 28
Cox, E. Aubrey, 52–53
Crackers, 46, 72
Cree Indians, 97
Crewdson, John M., 7
Cross-Eyed Mule, 8
Cuisinart Chili (Mark Kauffman), 188
Cumin, 16–17, 19, 26, 64, 66, 85, 86, 114
  toasted, 31
Cummings, Stuart, 73
Curbelo family, 17
Curry, 67
Curtis, Gwynne S., Jr., 12
Curtis, Victory Birdseye, 12
C. V. Wood, Jr.'s Chili, 140
Czhilispiel, 8

Dallas, Texas, 29–32
Dallas Petroleum Club, 30
Dave Mayo's Chili Parlor, Texas, 45
DeFrates, Joe, 25–26
DeFrates, Ray, 26
DeFrates, Walt (Port), 26
DeGolyer, Everett Lee, 10, 34
  Chili, 107
Delgado family, 17
Deluxe Camp Chili with Jerky, 94
Depression, Great, 3, 46
DePrida, Cecil, 144
deRochement, Louis, 10
DeVallier, Preston, 172
Deviled Beef with Chiles, 19, 20
Dew Chilli Parlors, 25
Dew Drop Inn, Paris, 57
Dixon's restaurants, 44
Dobie, J. Frank, 60, 68, 97
Dominici, Péte, 54
Driskill Hotel, Austin, 123
Dry Red Chile Sauce, 132

East Coast chili recipes, 160–166
E. DeGolyer's Chili, 107
Eirten, John, 37, 38

213

Electric Roaster Chili, 178
Ellis, Merle, 61–62, 157
  Second Best Chili, 157
Elmore, Albert, 124
El Paso, Texas, 32
El Rancho, New York, 56, 189
Emmons, "Uncle T," 43
Empress Chili, 26–27, 135
England, 59, 175
England, Judy and Gene, 84, 125
  Chili, 125
English Chili (Jenne Hatton), 175
Erwin, Jim, 121
Erwin, Tom, 30–31
  Chili Rice, 121
Evans, George W. B., 11
Everett, Donald E., 16

Farkleberry, 67
Fat, 60, 64
Fat-free chili, 61, 110, 111
Fat, low chili, 113–114
Father Tom Warren's Oso Flaco Chili, 151
Fauchon, Paris, 58
Federal Writers Project (WPA), 14
Fellows of the Red Squeezin's of the Chili
  Pod (FORSCP), 6
Fennel, 67
Festival of American Folklife, 52
Finlay, Kent, 68
Firehouse Cantina restaurants, 45, 77, 188
Food of My Friends (Safford), 167
Food processor chili, 77, 188
Ford, John, 143, 144
  Favorite Chili, 143
Fort Worth, Texas, 26
Forty Years Behind the Lid (Bolt), 117
Fowler, Gene, 145, 146
Fowler, Gordon Wick, 5, 23–24, 32, 35, 48,
  52, 56, 71, 116, 142
  Original Chili, 109
Frank Hunter's New Original Chili, 121
Freezing, 76, 78, 99
Fresh Red Chile Sauce, 132
Front Page, Paris, 57
Fryingpans West (Arnold), 13
Fuller, Les, Coney Island Chili Sauce, 136

"G" Troop Chili, 100
Garcia, Juan, 64–65
Garlic, 19, 26, 64, 65–66
Gary Nabhan's Yaqui Deer Dancer Salsa, 127
Gebhardt, William, 4–5
Gebhardt products, 4, 37, 56, 58, 120, 135
Gene England's Chili, 125

German Chili, 168
Germander, 67
Ginger, 27, 67
Glamorous Days (Bushick), 16
Gloria Pitzer's Chase Sons Chili, 144
Goat chili, 18, 25
Goat Gap Gazette, 8, 53, 67, 71
Goldwater, Barry, 54
Goodfellow Air Force Base cook-off (1977),
  168
Gordy, Frank, 44
Goulash, 21–22
Gourmet magazine, 153
Goya products, 162
Grande Tortilla Factory, Tucson, 45
Great Chili Confrontation, The (Smith), 23,
  116
Green, Ben K., 89
Green chiles, 63, 82–83
Gressett, Helen, Red Wine Chile, 154
Guadalajara, 8
Guest, C. Z., 90
Guinness Book of World Records, The, 106
Guisado de Jerky, 96–97
Gulyás, 21–22
Gustafson, Sandra A., 57, 58

Haddaway, George, 6
H. Allen Smith's Perfect Chili, 134
Hamburger Hamlet, 44
Hansen, Barbara, 69
Happy Valley Chili, 171
Hard Rock, The, Brussels, 58
Hardtack, 12
Harris, Ann Lee and Jack, 153, 154
Harris, Gertrude, 75
Harris Ranch Beans, 153
Harris Ranch Chili, 153
Hatton, Jenne, 59
  English Chili, 175
Hawaii, 8
Haynes, Leroy, 58
Haynes, Paris, 58
Heidelberg (chili parlor), Springfield, 26
Helen Corbitt Cooks for Company (Corbitt),
  123
Helen Corbitt Cooks for Looks (Corbitt), 122
Helen Corbitt's Low-Calorie Chili, 122
Helen Gressett's Red Wine Chili, 154
Higginbotham, Hattie and Rufus, 119
Highland Park Cafeteria, Dallas, 31
Hock, Conrad, Jr., 178
Hodge, Otis, 37
Hodge Chili Company, 37
Hodge's chili parlor, 37

Hoehne, Harry and Dorothy, 38–39, 137
Holloran, Frances Dolan, 37
Holmes, Bea, 115
Home-canning, 77–78
Home-Canning Book, 189
Honey Chili, 70
"Hoot 'n' Holler" chili mix, 8
Hormel Chili, 5
Horseradish, 67
Hot-Smak, 89–90
House of Representatives, 52
Houston, Sam, 17
Houston, Texas, 33
Huddleston, Sam, 32
    Chili, 114
Hudson's Bay Company, 97, 98
Hughes, Stella, 52, 70, 107, 126
    Arizona Chili, 126
Hunter, Frank and Faye, 42
    New Original Chili, 121

*If You Know Beans About Chili, You Know
    That Chili Has No Beans* (Finlay), 68
Ike's Chili Parlors, Tulsa, 34
Illinois, 24–26, 36
International Chili Society (ICS), 6, 140
    cook-off, 6, 7
International Connoisseurs of Green and
    Red Chile (ICG&RC), 6
Irish Stew theory, 20
Iron Kettle Brand Chili, 5
Ironware, 21, 75–76
Isaac, John, 38–40

Jacobs, Jody, 50, 51
Jacobs, Marvin, Chili Recipe (30 lbs.), 104
Jalapeño, 81, 88, 185
Jalapeño Dumplings with Chili and Beans, 185
James, Grace, 148
James, Jimmy, 29–30
James (Papadakis) Brick Chili, 33
James Coney Island, Houston, 33
Janouch, Joe, 36
Japonés, 80
Jazzy Snazzy Continental Chili, 51–52
Jeannette Branin's Rainy Day Chili, 149
Jefferson, B. C., 31, 70
Jenne Hatton's English Chili, 175
Jerky, 10–11, 94–95, 97
    chili, 10–12, 95–98
Jessie's Chili, 123
Jim Bridger, Mountain Man (Vestal), 97
Jo Lathwood's Chili, 147
Joe Allen (restaurant), Paris, 58
Joe Cooper's Chili, 108

Joe Jordan's Chili, 45
John Ford's Favorite Chili, 143
John Nation's Chili Piquante, 145
John Withee's Big Bean Chili, 165
Johnson, Ike, 34–35
Johnson, Lyndon B., 4, 71, 110–111
    Pedernales River Chile, 4, 110
Johnson, William Weber, 107–108
Jones, Frances Autry and B. J., 40, 172, 173
Junior League of Houston Cookbook, 178
Juniper berries, 67

Kannengieser, Richard P., 171
Kaplan, Justin, 164
Kauffman, Mark, 45, 77, 188
    Cuisinart Chili, 188
Kay, Monte, 51
Kerr Glass Manufacturing Corporation, 77,
    189, 190
Kiradjieff family, 26–27
Klug, Jerry, 36
Koritze, George, 36

Lambrinides family, 27
Lamere, Mickey, 39–40, 137
LaMotte, Clyde, 53, 54
Lang, Henry and George, 31
Lang's chili parlors, Dallas, 31, 32, 63, 70
Lasswell, Mary, 32
Lathwood, Jo, 147
    Chili, 147
Lavanderas, 13–15
Lavine, Larry, 32
LBJ Pedernales River Chili, 4, 110
Leche de cabro, 14
Lee, Robert E., 17
Les Fuller's Coney Island Chili Sauce, 136
Lewis, Sam, 8
Life and Legend of Gene Fowler, The (Smith),
    145
Linguisa, 147
Little John, Annie, Chili, 104
Lone Star Cafe, New York, 55
Longhorns, The (Dobie), 97
Los Angeles Times, 50, 51, 69, 71
Louisiane, La, Paris, 58
Low-Calorie Chili, 122
Low-fat chili, 113–114
Lucy Maytag's Anchor Steam Beer Chili, 156
Lucy Wade's Chili, 162
Lynn News, 175

McCormick's products, 166
McDonald, Richard, 107 ˚
McDonald, T. H., 29

Mace, 27, 67
Machaca, 12, 95–96
Machaca Chili, 95–96
McIlhenny, Paul C. P., 70
Magyars, 21
Mangiamo (Sebastiani), 158
Manning, Margaret and Robert, 77
  Chili, 164
Manual for Army Cooks (1896), 100
Manual for Army Cooks (1910), 101
Margaret Manning's Chili, 164
Marinko, Joe, 50
Marjoram, 13, 67
Marsh, Bob "Yeller Dog," 8, 44, 106
  Buffalo Chili for 600, 105
Marshall, Mel, 13, 113, 114
  Chili, 113
Martin, Mary, 50, 55–56
Marvin Jacob's (Restaurant Size) Chili
  Recipe (30 lbs.), 104
Masa harina, 72, 117
Maverick, Maury, 116
Maverick, Sam, 116
Maverick Chili, 116
Maytag, Fritz and Lucy, 156
  Anchor Steam Beer Chili, 156
Mel Marshall's Chili, 113
Mendow, Hiram Z., 167
Merle Ellis's Second Best Chili, 157
Mesquite blossoms and honey, 70
Mexican Chilley Supply Company, 26
Mexican Chili, 56–57
Mexican Gold Trail (Evans), 11
Mexican War, 14, 15, 48, 100
Mexico, 9, 12, 13, 32, 67, 69, 79
Microwave Chili, 76, 178
Midwestern chili recipes, 88, 134–138
Military Plaza, San Antonio, 15, 16
Miller, Bea, 51–52
Miss Brunswick Diner, 43
Mom Unser's Chili, 128
Monte Carlo, 58
Moon, Clarence, 45
Moose Chili (B.J.'s), 172
Moosemeat, 40–41
Moss, Captain James A., 100
Mother Earth's, Paris, 57
Mountain Oyster Chili, 106
Mustard, 27, 67
Muzzy, Ed, 150
  Chili Supreme, 150

Nabhan, Gary Paul, 128
  Yaqui Deer Dancer Salsa, 127
Nakagawa, Toshi, 66

Nancy Bottcher's Chili, 166
Nation, John, 146
  Chili Piquante, 145
National Culinary Salon and Competition, 48
National Homemakers Newsletter, 145
National Press Club, Washington, D.C., 53, 54
National Restaurant Association, 48
Nelson, Mrs. Richard R., 178
Nevada State championship cook-off, 8
New Mexico, 6, 9, 32, 86
New York City, chili, 6, 55–56
New York Times, The, 7, 10, 29
Night Hawk restaurants, Austin, 47
"Nobody Knows More About Chili Than I
  Do" (Smith), 23
North Slope Chili, 170
Nutmeg, 27, 67

O'Dell, Al, 168
Oil, 60
"Old" Army Chili, 19, 99
Old California Chili, 155
Olde Tyme Foods, Inc., 121
Onion, wild, 19
Oregano, 26, 64, 67, 85
Ortega products, 128
Orwell, George, 65
Oso Flaco Chili (Father Tom Warren), 151.
Oven Baked Chili, 177
Oyster crackers, 38

Pancakes with chili, 89
Papadakis, Helen and Tom, 33
Paprika, 19, 21, 81
Paris, 57–58
Paris Hilton, 57
Pasadena Junior League Apple Con Carne, 168
Pasta, 26–27, 28, 72
Pat's Chili, Tucson, 45
Peanuts, in chili, 71–72, 169
Peary, Admiral Robert E., 97
Pecos River products, 58
Pedernales River Chili, LBJ, 4, 110
Pegler, Westbrook, 46, 56
Peirano, Nick, 64–65
Peirano family, 151–152
Pemmican, 10–11, 12, 21, 97
Pemmican Chili, 11, 12, 97–98
Pendergrast, Sam, 8, 69, 112
Pendergrast's (Charles) Texas Chili, 112
Pendery, DeWitt Clinton, 26
Peperone rosso, 83, 98
Pepper, black, 19, 79, 80

"The Perfect Chili" (Smith), 134
Peters, Bernadette, 51
Philippe's, Los Angeles, 44
Phillips, Dean, 41
Phoenix Hyatt Regency Hotel, 45
Piccadilly's cafeterias, 35
Pie, Chili, 183
Pinks Chili Parlor, Los Angeles, 45
Pitzer, Gloria, 144–145
    Chase Sons Chili, 144
P. J. Clarke's, New York, 55
Plains Indians, 97
Plaza de Armas, San Antonio, 15, 16
Poff, Baxter, 33–34, 124, 125
Poff, Henry, 33–34, 104, 124, 125
Pool, Robert Sprinkle, 32, 68, 140
Pool's (Chili parlor), 32
Post, Wiley, 33–34
Pots, 21, 75–76
Pots & Pans, etc. (Harris), 75
Prairie Oysters, 106
Prescott, Jacqueline, 54
Pressure Cooker Chili, 76, 179
Ptomaine Tommy's, Los Angeles, 47
Punkie's Chili, 151

Quaker Oats Company, 5

Ralph Bellamy's Chili, 142
Ramsdell, Charles, 16
Ranch Style, Incorporated, 5
Rangoon Racquet Club, Beverly Hills, 7, 49, 50, 140
Raven, John (Bad McFad), 8
Ray's Brand Products, 26
Rebekah Prizewinning Rose Bowl Chili, 147
Red chile, 13, 83
    Sauce, Dry, 132
    Sauce, Fresh, 132
Red Skinner's North Slope Chili, 170
Red Wine Chili (Helen Gressett), 154
Rice, with chili, 29–30, 72
Richard Bolt's Chili, 117
Rick's American Cafe, Brussels, 58
Roast Beef Chili in a Hurry, Canned, 182
Rogers, Will, 33, 34, 56, 107
Roosevelt, Theodore, 99
Roosevelt Tamale Parlor, San Francisco, 45
Root, Waverley, 10, 64
Rose Marie Bogley's Chili, 160
Rosebud, Paris, 57–58
Ross, Harold, 49
Rough Riders, 99–100
Russell, Nipsey, 44

Safford, Virginia, 167
Sage, 67
Saint-Tropez, France, 58
Salad, Chili, 184
Salisbury, James, 64
Salt and Substitutions, 114
Salt-free chili, 50, 70
Sam, Frank, 42
Sam Huddleston's Chili, 114
San Antonio, Texas, 9, 15–20, 105, 106
San Antonio (Ramsdell), 16
San Antonio Express, 17
San Antonio Spice Company, 85
San Antonio, The Flavor of Its Past (Everett), 16
San Diego Union, 127
Santa Cruz Chili & Spice Company, 84, 125
Sauces:
    canned, 84
    Casados Farms Chile Caribe, 130
    Chili Meat, 137
    Dry Red Chile, 132
    Fresh Red Chile, 132
    Les Fuller's Coney Island, 136
    Yaqui Deer Dancer Salsa, 127
Sebastiani, Sylvia and August, 158
    Chili Beans with Wine, 158
Secret Restaurant Recipes Duplicated (Pitzer), 145
Serranos, 80, 88
Shanghai Jimmy's restaurants, 29–30, 121, 122
Sheehan, James, 25
Sheep and Goat Raiser, 18
Shelby, Carroll, 6, 7, 51, 52, 139, 174
    Chili, 139
Shelby Texas Chili Company, 7
Shockley, Ray, 29, 68
Short, Bobby, 55
Sib's Chili Parlor, Palm Springs, 50
Sioux Indians, 97
Six Powder Chili, 187
Skinner, Rellis (Red), 41–42, 170
    North Slope Chili, 42, 170
Skyline Chili, 26–27, 135
Slow Cooker Chili, 76, 180
Smith, H. Allen, 16, 23–24, 32, 65–66, 116, 134, 145
    Perfect Chili, 134
Smith, Jack, 71
Smith, Nelle, 65–66
Smith, Paul G., 80
Smith, S. Compton, 14–15
Smitty's, El Paso, 33
Smoke-drying, 94–95
Sol's (chili parlor), El Paso, 33

217

Son-of-a-bitch stew, 13
Sonora, Mexico, 12, 94, 95, 128
South America, 64, 67, 71
Southern California Chili, 51–52
Southern Pit Barbecue, Beverly Hills, 49
Southwestern chili recipes, 124–133
Spaghetti red, 27
Spanish, in the New World, 11, 71–72, 79, 80, 95
Spices, 27, 67
  groves, 19
  toasted, 86–87
Spitted beef, 19
Springfield, Illinois, 9, 24–26
Squeeze-In, Missouri, 43
St. Louis, Missouri, 36–38
St. Louis Fair (1904), 24, 25, 37
Stafford, Tom, 9
Stagg Chili Laredo, 183
Stella Hughes' Arizona Chili, 126
Stevens, Bob, 40
Storey, Ralph, 147
Story of a Troop Mess, The (Moss), 100
Strauss, Robert, 54
Strom, Arvid, 56, 189
Stuart, Robert E., 19
Suet, 60, 61
Sugar, 70
Super "C" Supper, 186
Sutton, Horace, 56
Swann, A. K., Chili, 118
Sweet woodruff, 67
Sylvia Sebastiani's Chili Beans with Wine, 158
Szent-Gyorgi, Dr., 64

Tabasco, 65, 80, 88
Taft, Robert, 54
Tallow (taller), 60, 61
Tamales, 14, 37
Tarkenton, Fran, 39
Taylor, Charles O., 24, 25, 37
Taylor, Ed, 24, 25
Taylor, Ed, Jr., 24
Taylor, Elizabeth, 49
Taylor, Tom, 24
Taylor, Zachary, 14, 15
Terlingua, CASI cook-off at, 6–7, 23, 25, 68, 69, 73, 116, 121, 139
Texas, 3–22, 28–33, 67, 68, 69
  chili recipes, 104–123
Texas, a Guide to the Lone Star State, 14
Texas Cattle Feeders Association, 107
Texas Chili Parlor, Austin, 32
Texas Cooking Under Six Flags, Holy Cross Episcopal Church Guild, 104

"Texas Gulasch," 4, 168
Texas Monthly, 67
Texas Prison Chili, 117
Texas Rangers, 9
Tex-Mex Cookbook, The (Huddleston), 115
"That Bowl of Fire Called Chili" (Tolbert), 4
Thickeners, 72
Thyme, 67
Toasted spice, 86–87
Tobin, William Gerard, 17–18, 25
Tobin Canning Company of San Antonio, 17–18
Tolbert, Frank X., 4, 24, 31
Tolbert's Texas Chili Parlor and Museum of Chili Culture, Dallas, 31
Tolbert's Chili Parlor and Saloon, Dallas, 31
Tom Erwin's Chili Rice, 121
Tomato, 71
Tommy's, Los Angeles, 35–36
Tony Velasquez's Chili, 130
Tortillas, 14
Tower, John, 54
Trail drives, 19–20, 28
Trillin, Calvin, 42–43
Tropico, ICS cook-off at, 7, 25
Truman, Harry, 44
Tumeric, 27, 67
23 Dayvilles, 58

Unser's (Mom) Chili, 128
U.S. Army cooking, 12–13, 48, 99–103
U.S.O. Chili Con Carne, 173
USSR, 8

Valdez Chili, 172
Vance House, San Antonio, 17
Varsity restaurants, 44
Velasquez, Tony J., 130
  Chili, 130
Venison, 11, 61, 110, 111, 115
Vestal, Stanley, 97
Vietnam War, 48
Vinegar, 70, 88

W (magazine), 58, 160, 164
Wade, Lucy and Floyd, 162
  Chili, 162
Wagon trains, 12
Waldron, Martin, 29
Wallace, Ed, 46
Walter's Chili, 119
Ward, Beverly, 41, 171
Warren, Father Tom, 156
  Oso Flaco Chili, 151

Washington, D.C., 52–55
Wasna, 97
Wechsberg, Joseph, 21–22, 169
Weinstock, Matt, 5
Wendy's restaurants, 44
West, Doyle L., 20, 21, 28
West Germany, 8
Western, Le, Paris, 57
White House, 4
Wick Fowler's Original Chili, 109
Wick Fowler's 2-Alarm Chili Mix, 5, 6, 56,
    109, 142, 164
Willeford, Charles, 163
    Texas Chili, 163
Williams, C. L., 178
Williams Chili Seasoning, 178
Williamson, Bill, Chili, 148
Wilson, Mary Jane Higginbotham, 119
Wimberly, Hal John, 8, 67
Wine, 73, 90
    Helen Gressett's Red Wine Chili, 154
    Sylvia Sebastiani's Chili Beans with, 158
Wine and Food Society of London, 51

With or Without Beans (Cooper), 6, 7, 14,
    23, 68
Withee, John (Bean Man), 43, 68–69, 165,
    166
    Big Bean Chili, 165
Wolf Brand Chili, 5, 20, 28, 29, 68
Wood, C. V., Jr., 6, 7, 50, 73, 140
    Chili, 140
Woody Barron's Texas Chili, 111
World War I, 66, 101
World War II, 3, 40, 42, 48, 101
Worsham, Harriet Long, 119
Wright, Jim, 70

Yaqui Deer Dancer Salsa, 127
Yates, Edmund, 31
Yeller Dog's (chili saloon), Leon Springs, 8,
    44
Yellow chiles, 88

Zodiac Room, Neiman-Marcus, Dallas, 71,
    122
Zwaaf, Manny, 50